Soups Stews and Mash

Soups Stews and Mash

C O N T E

Pea and ham soup, page 40

Chicken and orange casserole, page 172

Zarzuela, page 184

French onion soup, page 67

Osso buco with gremolata and milanese risotto, page 136

Veal with sweet vegetables, page 145

Mini wholemeal loaves, page 230

Swede and orange mash, page 213

All recipes are double-tested by our team of home economists. When we test our recipes, we rate them for ease of preparation. The following cookery ratings are on the recipes in this book, making them easy to use and understand.

A single Cooking with Confidence symbol indicates a recipe that is simple and generally quick to make —perfect for beginners.

Two symbols indicate the need for just a little more care and a little more time.

Three symbols indicate special dishes that need more investment in time, care and patience—but the results are worth it.

IMPORTANT

Those who might be at risk from the effects of salmonella food poisoning (the elderly, pregnant women, young children and those suffering from immune deficiency diseases) should consult their GP with any concerns about eating raw eggs.

Soup & Stew Secrets

There are no secret tricks to making wonderful soups and stews... no fancy
techniques or difficult finishes... just a kitchen filled with delicious aromas and a tender, flavoursome
meal that will satisfy the whole family from one pot.

Soups and stews are versatile, varied and above all delicious. Fish and fowl, meat and pulses, vegetables and even fruit can all be prepared in these ways. Once you have mastered the basics you will quickly realise that most soups or stews, from the humblest to the most exotic, are put together along similar lines. The differences lie in the ingredients and embellishments. We are all envious of those confident casual cooks who can just throw a few ingredients into the pot and produce a richly fragrant sauce packed with tender meat and flavoursome vegetables. But once you have gained confidence with the techniques you will find it easy to adapt them for your own variations. For example, many soups are blended in a food processor, (always let the soup cool a little first, so that you won't splash yourself with scalding liquid), but you may like to vary the textures by leaving some of the soup unpuréed.

Always pick the best ingredients. Your soup or stew is only as good as the sum of its parts. Use fresh bright-coloured meat and pick fresh firm vegetables that are in season

CHEAP EATS

You may be using the freshest ingredients you can find but they certainly don't need to be the most expensive. One of the great advantages of soups and stews is that they are generally better made with the more economical cuts of meat. Unlike expensive cuts, which are usually cooked quickly, the cheaper cuts of meat are best when slowly simmered in liquid as the process tenderises the meat. You can tell when the meat is cooked because the pieces will break up easily with a fork. Beef cuts such as blade, chuck, round or topside steak are ideal and generally have more flavour than fillet or rump. Some of the lamb cuts which we rarely use are ideal for

COATING AND BROWNING MEAT

By coating the meat in seasoned flour and then browning it on all sides in oil or butter you will give it a crisp brown coating and delicious taste. The flour also helps to thicken the liquid—usually once you have coated the meat in flour you won't need to use another thickener. (If you find at the end of cooking you still need to thicken the soup or stew a little more it is always better to reduce the liquid by fast simmering for a while, uncovered, rather than adding more flour.)

Don't coat the meat until you are ready to start cooking or the moisture in the meat will absorb the flour. It will no longer be a coating and could change the whole texture of the dish. If the flour *is* absorbed for some reason, re-coat the meat just before use and shake off any excess.

To coat meat in flour you can lay the flour on greasproof paper, sprinkle with a little seasoning and then turn the meat in the flour with your fingers or a pair of tongs. A cleverer and less messy method is to put the seasoned flour in a bag, add the meat cubes in batches, shake and then pick out the meat. Shake off any excess flour.

Browning the meat also seals in the juices and gives a good rich colour to the stew. Meat is browned quickly over fairly high heat and turned often to prevent sticking and to brown all sides. Oil is often used rather than butter, as butter burns at a lower temperature. However, a combination of the two means the oil prevents the butter burning and the butter adds flavour to the coating. It may be necessary to brown the meat in batches if there is a lot of it—too much meat crowded into the pan will merely stew in its own juices and become tough.

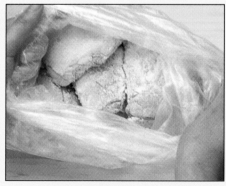

An easy way to coat meat with flour is to put them both in a bag and shake.

Brown meat quickly on all sides, over high heat, to seal in the juices.

producing tasty stews—neck chops and lamb shanks are perfect and easy on the budget. Trim away any excess fat and sinew—these will toughen during cooking and can cause the meat to shrink. Cut the meat into even-sized pieces that will cook at the same rate.

About 2–3 cm cubes is probably best, any smaller and the meat will fall into shreds while cooking and not look as appetising. Any chicken pieces are suitable for stews, but take care they are simmered gently, not boiled, or the meat will toughen.

SIMMERING

Generally, when making soups or stews the ingredients are browned, liquid is added and the food is brought to the boil. The heat is then reduced and the pan covered and left to simmer slowly until the ingredients are tender. Fish soups and stews are different in that the sauce is often prepared first and the fish added later to ensure it is not overcooked, tough or dry. Fast-cooking vegetables, such as snow peas, broccoli or mushrooms, are also usually added towards the end of cooking to prevent them becoming too soft.

Soups and stews should never be boiled for long periods, or the meat will become tough and stringy and lose its flavour and any vegetables will break up. A lazy simmer is best—tiny bubbles will appear at a slower pace on the surface of the food.

By the time a stew is cooked there is quite likely to be a thin layer of fat on the surface which you can easily skim off with a spoon or some paper towels to make the dish healthier. This is even easier if you are refrigerating the dish overnight—the fat will set and can be lifted off.

A dish is boiling when large bubbles appear in quick succession.

Soups and stews are best cooked at a lazy simmer.

PANS

When choosing a pan for making soups and stews, buy one that can be taken straight from the freezer to the stove or oven. A pan with a heavy base ensures an even distribution of heat which is important when dishes are simmering in liquid for a long time. A tight-fitting lid is essential to keep in moisture. The size of the dish is important. If it's too small the liquid might overflow, too large and the food will dry out because the liquid will reduce too quickly. The food should come approximately three-quarters of the way up the dish for the best result.

SEASONING

When making both soups and stews it is best to add seasoning at the end of the cooking process. Often the liquid has been reduced during simmering which makes the flavours more concentrated. Chilled soups should be tasted after chilling and may need more seasoning than hot soups. Some dishes thicken if left to stand and may need to have water added to bring them back to the right consistency—don't forget to taste for seasoning.

Don't sprinkle salt directly onto raw meat before cooking as it draws out the moisture and can make the meat tough and dry.

STORING AND FREEZING

For busy cooks, a great advantage of soups and stews is that both methods lend themselves to cooking in batches and storing. Fish soups and stews and the delicate oriental soups should be eaten immediately: their textures and flavours disintegrate on reheating. But most meat dishes, especially those which are highly spiced, such as curries, positively benefit from being refrigerated for a day or two before serving. This lets the flavours mature and also gives you the opportunity to easily lift off any fat which may have formed on the surface of the dish.

Many stews and some soups can be successfully frozen for 1 to 3 months. Don't add cream before freezing as it can curdle. Add it when you reheat to serve.

The food should be frozen as soon as it has cooled—and it should be cooled as quickly as possible to prevent bacteria forming. Skim any fat from the surface before freezing. The easiest way to freeze a soup or stew is to put a plastic bag inside a jug or bowl, spoon the food into it, tie loosely and then put the jug or bowl in the freezer. When the food has frozen, remove the bag from the container, squeeze out as much air as possible and seal securely. Label and date it before returning it to the freezer. If you are cooking in bulk it may be sensible to divide it into portions that can be thawed singly.

It is always best to thaw food completely before reheating but if you are in a hurry it is possible to reheat straight from the freezer. Remove from the bag or container and heat slowly in a pan or microwave for about 20 minutes depending on the amount.

Line a jug or bowl with a plastic bag and spoon in the soup or stew.

Seal the bag and label with the date, then freeze and remove the jug.

Stock

Soup is a dish whose sum is definitely greater than its parts. And one of its most important parts is stock. A good stock makes the difference between an ordinary and a spectacular soup, giving full-bodied flavours and a sound base for the other ingredients. If you are looking at these recipes and thinking the cooking times seeming very long and it all looks like too much trouble, think again. It doesn't take long to chop up the ingredients and then you can leave your stock to simmer lazily while you get on with other things.

BEEF STOCK

Preparation time: 20 minutes
  + refrigeration
Total cooking time: 4 hours 50 minutes
Makes about 7 cups (1.75 litres)

2 kg (4 lb) beef bones
2 unpeeled carrots, chopped
2 unpeeled onions, quartered
2 tablespoons tomato paste
2 sticks celery, leaves included, chopped
1 bouquet garni
12 black peppercorns

1 Preheat the oven to hot 210°C (415°F/Gas 6–7). Put the bones in a baking dish and bake for 30 minutes, turning occasionally. Add the carrot and onion and cook for a further 20 minutes. Allow to cool.

2 Put the bones, carrot and onion in a large, heavy-based pan. Drain the excess fat from the baking dish and pour 1 cup (250 ml/8 fl oz) of water into the dish. Stir to dissolve any pan juices; add the liquid to the pan.

3 Add the tomato paste, celery and 10 cups (2.5 litres) water. Bring to the boil, skimming the surface as required and add the bouquet garni and peppercorns. Reduce the heat to low and simmer gently for 4 hours. Skim the froth from the surface regularly.

4 Ladle the stock in batches into a fine sieve sitting over a bowl. Gently press the solids with a ladle to extract all the liquid. Discard the bones and vegetables and set aside to cool. Refrigerate until cold and spoon off any fat that has set on the top. At this stage you can reduce the stock to concentrate its flavour (dilute before using) and store in the refrigerator for up to 2 days or in the freezer for up to 6 months.

CHICKEN STOCK

Preparation time: 20 minutes
  + refrigeration
Total cooking time: 3 hours 10 minutes
Makes about 10 cups (2.5 litres)

2 kg (4 lb) chicken bones
2 unpeeled onions, quartered
2 unpeeled carrots, chopped
2 sticks celery, leaves included, chopped
1 bouquet garni
12 black peppercorns

1 Put the chicken bones, onion, carrot, celery and 14 cups (3.5 litres) of water in a large, heavy-based pan. Bring slowly to the boil. Skim the surface as required and add the bouquet garni and peppercorns. Reduce the heat to low and simmer gently for 3 hours. Skim the froth from the surface regularly.

2 Ladle the stock in batches into a fine sieve sitting over a bowl. Gently press the solids with a ladle to extract all the liquid. Let the stock cool, then refrigerate until cold and spoon off any fat that has set on the top. At this stage you can reduce the stock to concentrate its flavour (dilute before using) and store in the refrigerator for up to 2 days or in the freezer for up to 6 months.

FISH STOCK

Preparation time: 20 minutes
+ refrigeration
Total cooking time: 30 minutes
Makes about 7 cups (1.75 litres)

2 kg (4 lb) chopped fish bones,
    heads and tails
1 stick celery, leaves included,
    roughly chopped
1 onion, chopped
1 unpeeled carrot, chopped
1 leek, sliced
1 bouquet garni
12 black peppercorns

1 Place the fish bones, celery, onion, carrot, leek and 8 cups (2 litres) of water in a large, heavy-based pan. Bring slowly to the boil. Skim the surface as required and add the bouquet garni and peppercorns. Reduce the heat to low and simmer very gently for 20 minutes. Skim the froth from the surface regularly.
2 Ladle the stock in batches into a sieve lined with damp muslin sitting over a bowl. To keep a clear fish stock, do not press the solids, but simply allow the stock to strain undisturbed. Allow to cool, then store in the refrigerator for up to 2 days or in the freezer for up to 6 months.

VEGETABLE STOCK

Preparation time: 20 minutes
+ refrigeration
Total cooking time: 1½ hours
Makes about 10 cups (2.5 litres)

1 tablespoon oil
1 onion, chopped
2 leeks, chopped
4 carrots, chopped
2 parsnips, chopped
4 sticks celery, leaves included,
    chopped
2 bay leaves
1 bouquet garni
4 unpeeled cloves garlic
    (see Note)
8 black peppercorns

1 Heat the oil in a large, heavy-based pan and add the onion, leek, carrot, parsnip and celery. Cover and cook for 5 minutes without colouring. Add 12 cups (3 litres) of water. Bring to the boil. Skim the surface if required. and add the bay leaves, bouquet garni, garlic and peppercorns. Reduce the heat to low and simmer for 1 hour. Skim the froth from the surface of the stock regularly.
2 Ladle the stock in batches into a fine sieve sitting over a bowl. Gently press the solids to extract all the liquid.

3 Allow the stock to cool, then refrigerate until cold and spoon off any fat that has set on the top. At this stage you can reduce the stock to concentrate its flavour (dilute before using) and store in the refrigerator for up to 2 days or in the freezer for up to 6 months.
Note: Like a bouquet garni, unpeeled garlic added to a stock adds a subtle flavour and will not cloud the soup.

FREEZING STOCKS

Freezing your stock is useful if you want to prepare ahead. Simply pour the stock into a measuring jug lined with a plastic bag so you can measure how much stock you have and freeze it in convenient portions. Remove the bag from the jug, label the bag, seal securely and freeze.

Alternatively, pour the stock into ice cube trays and freeze. This is useful for fairly concentrated stocks.

BOUQUET GARNI

To make a bouquet garni, wrap the green part of a leek loosely around a bay leaf, sprig of thyme, some celery leaves and a few stalks of parsley, then tie with string. Leave enough string for easy removal.

Meat &Poultry Soups

CHICKEN CURRY LAKSA

Preparation time: 30 minutes
Total cooking time: 25 minutes
Serves 4

1 large onion, roughly chopped
5 cm (2 inch) piece fresh ginger, chopped
8 cm (3 inch) galangal, chopped
1 stem lemon grass, white part only, chopped
2 cloves garlic
1 fresh red chilli, chopped
2 teaspoons vegetable oil
2 tablespoons mild curry paste
500 g (1 lb) chicken breast fillets, cubed
1/2 litre chicken stock
60 g (2 oz) rice vermicelli
50 g (1 3/4 oz) dried egg noodles
400 ml (13 fl oz) light coconut milk
10 snow peas, halved
3 spring onions, finely chopped
1 cup (90 g/3 oz) bean sprouts
15 g (1/2 oz) coriander leaves

1 Process the onion, ginger, galangal, lemon grass, garlic and chilli in a food processor until finely chopped. Add the oil and process until paste-like. Spoon into a wok, add the curry paste and stir over low heat for 1–2 minutes, until aromatic. Take care not to burn.
2 Increase the heat to medium, add the chicken and stir for 2 minutes, or until well coated. Stir in the chicken stock. Bring slowly to the boil, then simmer for 10 minutes, or until the chicken is cooked through.
3 Cut the vermicelli into shorter lengths. Cook the vermicelli and egg noodles separately in boiling water for 5 minutes each. Rinse in cold water.
4 Add the light coconut milk and snow peas to the chicken and heat through. To serve, divide the vermicelli and noodles among four bowls. Pour the hot laksa over the top and garnish with the spring onion, bean sprouts and coriander leaves.

NUTRITION PER SERVE
Protein 30 g; Fat 8 g; Carbohydrate 4.5 g; Dietary Fibre 3 g; Cholesterol 65 mg; 945 kJ (225 cal)

Stir the curry paste into the onion mixture, over low heat, until aromatic.

Just before serving, stir the coconut milk into the chicken and heat through.

CHICKPEA, CHORIZO AND PORK RIB SOUP

Preparation time: 20 minutes
+ overnight soaking
Total cooking time: 40 minutes
Serves 6–8

180 g (6 oz) dried chickpeas
300 g (10 oz) smoked bacon
    ribs
2 tablespoons olive oil
1 onion, finely chopped
1 clove garlic, crushed
2 tomatoes, peeled, seeded and
    finely chopped
1 potato, cubed

1 carrot, sliced
200 g (6¹/2 oz) pumpkin,
    chopped
150 g (5 oz) chorizo or
    pepperoni sausage, sliced
¹/4 teaspoon dried oregano
6 cups (1.5 litres) chicken stock

1 Place the chickpeas in a bowl and cover with cold water. Leave to soak overnight, then drain.
2 Blanch the bacon ribs in boiling water for 30 seconds, then plunge into iced water. Drain and slice into pieces.
3 Heat the oil in a large, heavy-based pan and cook the onion over medium heat for 3–4 minutes, stirring continuously. Add the garlic and

tomato and cook for a further 5 minutes.
4 Add the chickpeas, ribs, potato, carrot, pumpkin, chorizo, dried oregano and stock. Bring to the boil, then reduce the heat and simmer, covered, for 30 minutes, or until the chickpeas are tender. Season to taste.

NUTRITION PER SERVE (8)
Protein 15 g; Fat 15 g; Carbohydrate 15 g; Dietary Fibre 4 g; Cholesterol 30 mg; 1110 kJ (240 cal)

COOK'S FILE

Note: If bacon ribs are unavailable, use 150 g (5 oz) smoked bacon instead.
Serving suggestion: Serve with Roasted red capsicum buns.

Halve the peeled tomatoes and scoop out the seeds using a teaspoon.

Use chorizo, pepperoni or another type of spicy sausage.

Drain the blanched ribs, then cut into smaller sections.

MULLIGATAWNY SOUP

Preparation time: 20 minutes
Total cooking time: 1 hour 15 minutes
Serves 4

30 g butter
375 g chicken thigh cutlets, skin and fat removed
1 large onion, finely chopped
1 green apple, peeled, cored and finely chopped
1 tablespoon curry paste
2 tablespoons plain flour

3 cups chicken stock
1/4 cup basmati rice
1 tablespoon chutney
1 tablespoon lemon juice
1/4 cup cream
salt and black pepper

1 Heat the butter in a large heavy-based pan and brown the chicken for 5 minutes; remove and set aside. Add the onion, apple and curry paste to the pan. Cook for 5 minutes, until the onion is soft. Stir in the flour; cook for 2 minutes then add half the stock. Stir until the mixture boils and thickens.

2 Return the chicken to the pan with the remaining stock. Stir until boiling, reduce the heat, cover and simmer for 1 hour. Add the rice for the last 15 minutes of cooking.

3 Remove the chicken with tongs; bone and dice the meat finely and return to the pan. Add the chutney, lemon juice, cream and seasoning to taste. If you prefer a thinner soup add up to a cup of water.

NUTRITION PER SERVE
Protein 25 g; Fat 16 g; Carbohydrate 25 g; Dietary Fibre 2 g; Cholesterol 28 mg; 1396 kJ (333 cal)

Once the mixture has thickened, return the browned chicken thighs to the pan.

Add the basmati rice during the last 15 minutes of cooking.

Add the chutney, lemon juice and cream at the end of cooking.

HOT BEEF BORSCHT

Preparation time: 30 minutes
Total cooking time: 2 hours 50 minutes
Serves 4–6

500 g (1 lb) gravy beef, cut into
    large pieces
500 g (1 lb) fresh beetroot
1 onion, finely chopped
1 carrot, cut into short strips
1 parsnip, cut into short strips
1 cup (75 g/2½ oz) finely
    shredded cabbage
sour cream and chopped chives,
    to serve

1 Put the beef in a large, heavy-based pan with 4 cups (1 litre) of water and bring slowly to the boil. Reduce the heat, cover and simmer for 1 hour. Skim the surface as required.

2 Cut the stems from the beetroot, wash well and place in a large, heavy-based pan with 4 cups (1 litre) of water. Bring to the boil, reduce the heat and simmer for 40 minutes, or until tender. Drain, reserving 1 cup (250 ml/8 fl oz) of the liquid. Cool, then peel and grate the beetroot.

3 Remove the meat from the stock, cool and dice. Skim any fat from the surface of the stock. Return the meat to the stock and add the onion, carrot, parsnip, beetroot and reserved liquid. Bring to the boil, reduce the heat, cover and simmer for 45 minutes.

4 Add the cabbage, stir and simmer for a further 15 minutes. Season to taste. Serve topped with the sour cream and chives.

NUTRITION PER SERVE (6)
Protein 20 g; Fat 10 g; Carbohydrate 10 g; Dietary Fibre 5 g; Cholesterol 80 mg; 940 kJ (225 cal)

To avoid stains, wear rubber gloves to grate the beetroot.

Allow the meat to cool, then cut into dice using a sharp knife.

Pour the reserved beetroot liquid into the soup and bring to the boil.

SCOTCH BROTH

Preparation time: 40 minutes
  + 1 hour soaking
  + overnight refrigeration
Total cooking time: 4 hours
Serves 8

1 kg (2 lb) lamb shanks, cut in
    half through the bone
    (ask your butcher to do this)
3 onions, chopped
3 turnips, chopped
2 carrots, chopped
1 tablespoon black peppercorns
1/2 cup (110 g/3 1/2 oz) pearl
    barley

1 carrot, diced, extra
2 onions, finely chopped, extra
1 leek, chopped
1 stick celery, diced
2 turnips, diced, extra
chopped flat-leaf parsley

1 To make the stock, put the lamb shanks, onion, turnip, carrot, peppercorns and 8 cups (2 litres) of water in a large pan. Bring to the boil, reduce the heat and simmer, covered, for 3 hours. Skim the surface as required.
2 Remove the shanks and any meat that has fallen off the bones and cool slightly. Remove the meat from the bones and finely chop, then cover and refrigerate. Strain the stock, discarding

the vegetables. Cool the stock and refrigerate overnight, or until the fat has set on top and can be spooned off. Cover the barley with water and soak for 1 hour.
3 Put the stock in a large pan and gently reheat. Add the drained barley, extra carrot, onion, leek, celery and turnip. Bring to the boil, reduce the heat and simmer for 30 minutes, or until the barley and vegetables are just cooked. Return the meat to the pan and simmer for 5 minutes. Season well and serve with the parsley.

NUTRITION PER SERVE
Protein 35 g; Fat 3 g; Carbohydrate 20 g; Dietary Fibre 6 g; Cholesterol 80 mg; 970 kJ (230 cal)

Use a skimmer or slotted spoon to skim the surface of the stock.

Place the barley in a bowl and cover with plenty of cold water.

The vegetables for the soup should be evenly and finely diced.

SPICY LAMB SOUP

Preparation time: 40 minutes
Total cooking time: 1 hour 30 minutes
Serves 4–6

2 large onions, roughly chopped
3 red chillies, seeded, chopped
   (or 2 teaspoons dried chilli)
3–4 cloves garlic, peeled
2 cm piece ginger, chopped
1 teaspoon ground black pepper
6 cm piece lemon grass root,
   white only, finely chopped
1/2 teaspoon ground cardamom
2 teaspoons ground cumin

1/2 teaspoon ground cinnamon
1 teaspoon ground turmeric
2 tablespoons peanut oil
1.5 kg lamb neck chops
2–3 tablespoons vindaloo paste
2 1/3 cups coconut cream
1/4 cup soft brown sugar
2–3 tablespoons lime juice
4 kaffir lime leaves

1 Put the onion, chilli, garlic, ginger, pepper, lemon grass, cardamom, cumin, cinnamon and turmeric in a food processor. Process to a paste. Heat half the oil in a large pan and brown the chops in batches. Remove and drain on paper towels.

2 Add the remaining oil to the pan and cook the spice and vindaloo pastes for 2–3 minutes. Add the chops and 7 cups water, cover and bring to the boil. Reduce the heat and simmer, covered, for 1 hour. Remove the chops from the pan and stir in the coconut cream. Remove the meat from the bones, shred and return to the pan.

3 Add the sugar, lime juice and leaves. Simmer, uncovered, over low heat for 20–25 minutes, until slightly thickened. Garnish with coriander.

NUTRITION PER SERVE (6)
Protein 55 g; Fat 38 g; Carbohydrate 17 g; Dietary Fibre 3 g; Cholesterol 166 mg; 2602 kJ (622 cal)

Wear disposable gloves when working with chillies to avoid smarting and burns.

Process the onions with the chilli, garlic and spices to make a paste.

Trim away any excess fat from the chops before cooking.

CHICKEN NOODLE SOUP

Preparation time: 15 minutes
+ 1 hour refrigeration
Total cooking time: 1 hour 20 minutes
Serves 4–6

1.25 kg (2½ lb) chicken wings
2 sticks celery, chopped
1 carrot, chopped
1 onion, chopped
1 bay leaf
1 sprig thyme
4 parsley stalks
45 g (1½ oz) dried fine egg
    noodles, gently crushed

250 g (8 oz) chicken breast
    fillets, finely chopped
2 tablespoons chopped parsley
chopped chives, to serve

1 To make the chicken stock, rinse the chicken wings and place in a large pan with the celery, carrot, onion, bay leaf, thyme, parsley stalks, 1 teaspoon salt and 8 cups (2 litres) of water. Bring to the boil slowly, skimming the surface as required. Simmer, covered, for 1 hour. Allow to cool slightly, then strain and discard the chicken and vegetables.
2 Cool the stock further, then cover and refrigerate for at least 1 hour, or

until fat forms on the surface and can be spooned off.
3 Place the stock in a large pan and bring to the boil. Add the noodles, return to the boil and simmer for 8 minutes, or until tender. Add the chopped chicken and parsley and simmer for a further 4–5 minutes. Serve topped with the chives.

NUTRITION PER SERVE (6)
Protein 45 g; Fat 8 g; Carbohydrate 8 g; Dietary Fibre 2 g; Cholesterol 135 mg; 1205 kJ (290 cal)

COOK'S FILE

Serving suggestion: This soup is delicious with Onion buns.

Using a skimmer or slotted spoon, skim the surface of the stock as required.

Using a spoon, remove the fat that forms on the surface of the chilled stock.

Add the crushed noodles, then simmer for 8 minutes, or until tender.

AVGOLEMONO
(Greek Egg and Lemon Soup)

Preparation time: 20 minutes
Total cooking time: 10 minutes
Serves 4–6

6 cups chicken stock
3/4 cup white,
    long-grain rice
2 eggs, separated
1/2 cup lemon juice

1 Bring the stock to the boil in a large heavy-based pan. Add the rice and allow to simmer for 8–10 minutes until tender.
2 Beat the egg whites in a large dry mixing bowl until soft peaks form. Add the yolks and beat until they are combined.
3 Gradually pour in the lemon juice and then about 1–2 cups of the rice and stock soup, beating continuously. Gradually fold this into the pan of rice soup and serve immediately.

NUTRITION PER SERVE (6)
Protein 4 g; Fat 2 g; Carbohydrate 20 g; Dietary Fibre 0.5 g; Cholesterol 60 mg; 500 kJ (120 cal)

COOK'S FILE

Hint: Assemble all the ingredients and utensils beforehand, work quickly and serve this soup immediately—it does not reheat well.
Variation: Egg and lemon soup can also be made with fish stock instead of the chicken stock.

Beat the egg whites in a large dry mixing bowl until soft peaks form.

Beat continuously while you pour in the lemon juice and stock.

To keep the soup light and fluffy, use a large metal spoon to fold gently.

PORK BALL AND VEGETABLE SOUP

Preparation time: 45 minutes
Total cooking time: 10 minutes
Serves 6–8

90 g (3 oz) stale white bread,
   crusts removed
500 g (1 lb) pork mince
2 teaspoons chopped coriander
   roots and stems
3 teaspoons chopped coriander
   leaves
1/2 teaspoon five-spice powder
1 teaspoon grated ginger
1 egg white
3 cups (270 g/9 oz) bean sprouts

2 teaspoons sesame oil
9 cups (2.25 litres) chicken
   stock
1 small red chilli, chopped
2 carrots, cut into strips
2 sticks celery, cut into strips
6 spring onions, cut into strips
1½ tablespoons lime juice
coriander leaves, to serve

1 Line a baking tin with baking paper. Cover the bread with cold water, then squeeze out the liquid. Mix with the mince, coriander, five-spice powder, ginger, egg white and 1/4 teaspoon each of salt and pepper.
2 Roll 1/2 tablespoons of the mixture into balls and lay in the tin. Divide the bean sprouts among bowls. Mix the

sesame oil and stock in a large pan, bring to the boil and add the balls in batches. Return to the boil and, when they float, divide among the bowls.
3 Add the chilli, carrot, celery and spring onion to the stock, bring to the boil and simmer for 1 minute. Remove from the heat, season to taste and add the lime juice. Ladle into bowls and top with a few coriander leaves.

NUTRITION PER SERVE (8)
Protein 4 g; Fat 8 g; Carbohydrate 10 g; Dietary Fibre 2 g; Cholesterol 2 mg; 575 kJ (160 cal)

COOK'S FILE

Note: Five-spice is a mixture of Szechwan pepper, star anise, fennel, cloves and cinnamon.

Coarsely chop the roots and stems from the coriander and then chop finely.

Cut the vegetables into short lengths, then cut into fine (julienne) strips.

Soak the bread in water, then squeeze out the liquid.

SPICY CHICKEN BROTH WITH CORIANDER PASTA

Preparation time: 40 minutes
Total cooking time: 50 minutes
Serves 4

350 g chicken thighs or wings,
 skin removed
2 carrots, finely chopped
2 sticks celery, finely chopped
2 small leeks, finely chopped
3 egg whites
6 cups chicken stock
Tabasco sauce

Coriander Pasta
1/2 cup plain flour
1 egg
1/2 teaspoon sesame oil
small bunch coriander leaves

1 Put the chicken pieces, carrots, celery and leeks in a large heavy-based pan. Push the chicken to one side and add the egg whites to the vegetables. Using a wire whisk, beat for a minute or so until frothy (take care not to use a pan that can be scratched by the whisk).

2 Warm the stock in another pan, then add gradually to the first pan, whisking continuously to froth the egg whites. Continue whisking while slowly bringing to the boil. Make a hole in the froth on top with a spoon and leave to simmer, uncovered, for 30 minutes without stirring.

3 Line a large strainer with a damp tea towel or double thickness of muslin and strain the broth into a clean bowl (discard the chicken and vegetables). Season with salt, pepper and Tabasco to taste. Set aside.

4 To make the Coriander Pasta: sift the flour into a bowl and make a well in the centre. Whisk the egg and oil together and pour into the well. Mix together to make a soft pasta dough and knead on a lightly floured surface for 2 minutes, until smooth.

5 Divide the pasta dough into four even portions. Roll one portion out very thinly and cover with a layer of evenly spaced coriander leaves. Roll out another portion of pasta and lay this on top of the leaves, then gently roll the layers together. Repeat with the remaining pasta and coriander.

6 Cut out squares of pasta around the leaves. The pasta may then be left to sit and dry out if it is not needed immediately. When you are ready to serve, heat the chicken broth gently in a saucepan. As the broth simmers, add the pasta and cook for 1 minute. Serve immediately.

NUTRITION PER SERVE
Protein 25 g; Fat 4 g; Carbohydrate 18 g; Dietary Fibre 4 g; Cholesterol 90 mg; 915 kJ (220 cal)

COOK'S FILE

Hint: Beg, borrow or steal a pasta machine for making this fine, delicate pasta. A rolling pin will suffice if necessary but try to roll the pasta as thinly as possible.

Note: The egg whites added to the vegetable and chicken stock pot make the broth very clear rather than leaving it with the normal cloudy appearance of chicken stock. This is called clarifying the stock. When you strain the broth through muslin or a tea towel, don't press the solids to extract the extra liquid or the broth will become cloudy. It is necessary to make a hole in the froth on top to prevent the stock boiling over.

Use a wire whisk to beat the egg white and vegetables.

Use a metal spoon to make a hole in the froth on top of the soup.

Strain the broth through a damp tea towel or double thickness of muslin.

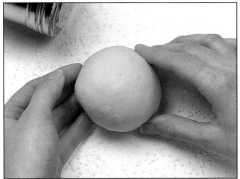

Knead the dough on a lightly floured surface until it is smooth.

Lay a second layer of thin pasta over the coriander leaves.

Cut out neat squares of pasta around each coriander leaf.

WON TON SOUP

Preparation time: 45 minutes
Total cooking time: 20 minutes
Serves 4–6

4 dried Chinese mushrooms
4 spring onions, very finely
    sliced, to garnish
125 g pork and veal mince
60 g raw prawn meat,
    finely chopped
salt, to taste
3 teaspoons soy sauce
1 teaspoon sesame oil
1 spring onion, finely chopped
2 teaspoons grated ginger
1 tablespoon finely chopped
    water chestnuts
24 won ton wrappers
5 cups chicken stock

1 Place the mushrooms in a small bowl, cover with hot water and leave to soak for 30 minutes. Meanwhile, to prepare the garnish, put the very fine strips of spring onion in a bowl of icy cold water (this makes the strips curl).
2 Squeeze the mushrooms dry with your hands. Remove the stems and chop the caps finely. Mix together the mushrooms, mince, prawn meat, salt, soy sauce, sesame oil, spring onion, ginger and water chestnuts.
3 Working with only one won ton wrapper at a time (cover the other wrappers with a damp tea towel), place a level teaspoon of the filling in the centre of each wrapper. Moisten the edges of the wrapper with a little water and bring the sides up to form a pouch. Set aside on a plate dusted with flour while making the rest.
4 Cook the won tons in batches in a large pan of rapidly boiling water for 4–5 minutes; remove and drain. Bring the stock to the boil in another pan. Put the won tons in small bowls, garnish with the curls of spring onion and pour in the hot stock.

NUTRITION PER SERVE (6)
Protein 12 g; Fat 1 g; Carbohydrate 25 g; Dietary Fibre 3 g; Cholesterol 30 mg; 650 kJ (155 cal)

COOK'S FILE

Note: Won ton wrappers are available from Asian food stores and can be frozen very successfully.

Slice the spring onions very finely and leave in iced water to make them curl.

Gently squeeze the excess liquid from the rehydrated mushrooms.

Moisten the edges of the wrapper and bring the sides up to make a pouch.

Cook the won tons in batches in a large pan of rapidly boiling water.

Add the spices to the pan with the onion and stir to thoroughly combine.

Add the stock to the mixture of spices and vegetables.

Saffron threads are expensive but will add a subtle flavour and golden colour.

Do not stir in the couscous until you are ready to serve the soup.

CHICKEN AND COUSCOUS SOUP

Preparation time: 25 minutes
Total cooking time: 30 minutes
Serves 6

1 tablespoon olive oil
1 onion, sliced
1/2 teaspoon ground cumin
1/2 teaspoon paprika
1 teaspoon grated ginger
1 clove garlic, crushed
2 sticks celery, sliced
2 small carrots, sliced
2 zucchini, sliced
4 1/2 cups chicken stock
2 chicken breast fillets, sliced
pinch of saffron threads, optional
1/2 cup instant couscous
2 tablespoons chopped parsley

1 Heat the oil in a large heavy-based pan. Add the onion and cook over medium heat for 10 minutes until very soft, stirring occasionally. Add the cumin, paprika, ginger and garlic and cook, stirring, for 1 minute further.
2 Add the celery, carrot and zucchini and stir to coat with spices. Stir in the stock. Bring to the boil, then reduce the heat and simmer, partially covered for about 15 minutes, or until the vegetables are tender.
3 Add the chicken and saffron threads (if you are using them) to the pan and cook for about 5 minutes, until the chicken is just tender; do not overcook. Stir in the couscous and chopped parsley and serve.

NUTRITION PER SERVE
Protein 24 g; Fat 6 g; Carbohydrate 53 g;
Dietary Fibre 5 g; Cholesterol 37 mg;
1482 kJ (350 cal)

COOK'S FILE

Hint: Add the couscous to the soup just before serving: it absorbs liquid quickly and becomes very thick.

GOULASH SOUP

Preparation time: 15 minutes
Total cooking time: 1 hour 15 minutes
Serves 4–6

650 g blade steak
2 tablespoons oil
1 large leek, sliced
2 cloves garlic, crushed
1 teaspoon paprika
1 teaspoon caraway seeds

400 g can crushed tomatoes
4 cups beef stock
2 potatoes, peeled and diced
sour cream, to serve

1 Cut the meat into small cubes. Heat the oil in a large pan, brown the meat in batches and set aside.
2 Add the leek to the pan and cook for 5 minutes until soft. Add the garlic and paprika and cook for 1 minute. Add the caraway seeds, crushed tomatoes, stock and meat. Bring to the boil,

reduce the heat and simmer, partially covered, for 30 minutes.
3 Add the potatoes and simmer for a further 30 minutes, until very tender. Serve with a dollop of sour cream.

NUTRITION PER SERVE (6)
Protein 25 g; Fat 17 g; Carbohydrate 9 g; Dietary Fibre 2 g; Cholesterol 75 mg; 1220 kJ (290 cal)

COOK'S FILE

Storage time: The soup will keep for up to 2 days in the refrigerator.

Trim the blade steak of any fat and sinew when you cut it into small cubes.

Brown the meat in small batches so that it fries rather than stews.

Add the caraway seeds, tomatoes, stock and meat to the pan.

JUNGLE SOUP

Preparation time: 10 minutes
Total cooking time: 35 minutes
Serves 4

2 teaspoons oil
1 medium onion, finely sliced
225 g butternut pumpkin,
   peeled and diced
225 g fresh pineapple or mango,
   chopped

1 clove garlic, crushed
1 dried red chilli, finely chopped
2 teaspoons grated ginger
4 cups chicken stock
2 tablespoons lime juice
350 g chicken breast, skinned,
   cut diagonally into thin strips

1 Heat the oil in a large heavy-based pan and cook the onion for 5 minutes, or until golden brown. Add the pumpkin and cook for 5 minutes, or until just browned. Add the pineapple or mango, garlic, chilli and ginger and toss the contents of the pan together.

2 Add the stock and lime juice, bring to the boil and then reduce the heat to simmer for 20 minutes, or until the pumpkin is nearly tender.

3 Add the chicken and simmer for 5 minutes, or until the chicken is cooked. Serve immediately.

NUTRITION PER SERVE
Protein 22 g; Fat 4 g; Carbohydrate 10 g; Dietary Fibre 2.5 g; Cholesterol 45 mg; 700 kJ (170 cal)

Peel and chop the pineapple or mango into bite-sized pieces.

Add the pumpkin to the onion in the pan and cook until browned.

Use two wooden spoons to toss together the contents of the pan.

MOROCCAN CHICKPEA SOUP

Preparation time: 35 minutes
+ overnight soaking
Total cooking time: 1 hour 10 minutes
Serves 4

250 g (8 oz) dried chickpeas
2 tablespoons olive oil
1 onion, finely sliced
2 teaspoons ground cumin
2 teaspoons sweet paprika
1 teaspoon ground ginger
1 teaspoon ground cinnamon
1/4 teaspoon allspice

250 g (8 oz) boneless lamb leg
  steaks, cut into strips
500 g (1 lb) tomatoes, finely
  chopped
8 cups (2 litres) vegetable stock
  or water
2 teaspoons grated lemon rind
1/2 cup (110 g/31/2 oz) short-
  grain rice
1/4 cup (7 g/1/4 oz) chopped
  parsley
2 tablespoons chopped
  coriander

1 Soak the chickpeas in cold water overnight. Drain. Heat the oil in a large pan over low heat and add the onion and spices. Cook for 15 minutes, covered, stirring occasionally.

2 Add the chickpeas, lamb, tomato and stock. Bring to the boil, reduce the heat and simmer for 35 minutes. Skim the surface as required. Add the lemon rind and rice and cook for 12 minutes, or until the rice is tender. Add the herbs and season to taste.

NUTRITION PER SERVE
Protein 30 g; Fat 15 g; Carbohydrate 45 g; Dietary Fibre 10 g; Cholesterol 40 mg; 1760 kJ (420 cal)

COOK'S FILE

Note: Short-grain rice is plump and sticks together when cooked.

Soak the chickpeas in plenty of cold water and leave overnight. Drain well.

Use a sharp knife to cut the lamb leg steaks into strips.

Add the onion, cumin, paprika, ginger, cinnamon and allspice to the pan.

CREAMY SPINACH AND CHICKEN SOUP

Preparation time: 40 minutes
Total cooking time: 55 minutes
Serves 6

1 tablespoon oil
1 kg (2 lb) chicken pieces
1 carrot, chopped
2 celery sticks, chopped
1 onion, chopped
6 black peppercorns
2 cloves garlic, chopped
1 bouquet garni

800 g (1 lb 10 oz) white sweet
  potato, chopped
2 bunches (about 500 g/1 lb)
  English spinach
½ cup (125 ml/4 fl oz) cream

1 Heat the oil in a large pan, add the chicken in batches and brown well. Drain on paper towels. Pour off the excess fat, leaving 1 tablespoon in the pan. Return the chicken to the pan with the carrot, celery, onion, peppercorns, garlic, bouquet garni and 6 cups (1.5 litres) of water. Bring to the boil, reduce the heat and simmer for 40 minutes. Strain, returning the

stock to the pan. Pull the chicken meat from the bones, shred and set aside.
2 Add the sweet potato to the stock in the pan. Bring to the boil, reduce the heat and simmer until tender. Add the spinach leaves and cook until wilted. Process in batches in a food processor until finely chopped.
3 Return to the pan, add the chicken and stir in the cream. Season to taste. Reheat gently before serving but do not allow the soup to boil.

NUTRITION PER SERVE
Protein 40 g; Fat 15 g; Carbohydrate 25 g;
Dietary Fibre 4 g; Cholesterol 110 mg;
1720 kJ (410 cal)

To make a bouquet garni, tie parsley, thyme and a bay leaf with string.

Brown the chicken in batches then drain on paper towels.

Add the spinach leaves to the soup and cook, stirring, until just wilted.

CABBAGE AND HAM SOUP WITH CHEESE DUMPLINGS

Preparation time: 40 minutes
Total cooking time: 1 hour 10 minutes
Serves 6

1/4 cup (60 ml/2 fl oz) olive oil
350 g (11 oz) piece of Kasseler
 or double-smoked ham,
 chopped into cubes
2 teaspoons soft brown sugar
2 onions, thinly sliced
2 leeks, thinly sliced
3 cloves garlic, finely chopped
1 tablespoon plain flour
2 cups (500 ml/16 fl oz) chicken
 stock
250 g (8 oz) bacon bones
3 potatoes, chopped
1/2 savoy cabbage, finely
 shredded
1 tablespoon white wine vinegar

Cheese dumplings
30g (1 oz) cold butter, cut into
 small pieces
2 cups (250 g/8 oz) self-raising
 flour
60 g (2 oz) finely grated
 Cheddar
2 teaspoons finely chopped
 thyme
2 teaspoons finely grated lemon
 rind, optional

1 Heat 1 tablespoon of the oil in a large pan and add the ham and sugar. Sauté over high heat, stirring continuously, for 5 minutes, or until just golden. Remove with a slotted spoon and drain on paper towels. Take care not to overcook or the ham will become dry.

2 Add the remaining oil, onion, leek and garlic and cook for 15 minutes over low heat, stirring regularly. Add the flour and cook for 1 minute, stirring. Remove from the heat and gradually add the stock, bacon bones and 6 cups (1.5 litres) of water. Return to the heat and cook, stirring, until the mixture comes to the boil and thickens slightly. Reduce the heat and simmer for 30 minutes, skimming the surface as required.

3 Remove the bacon bones, cut off the meat and discard the bones. Shred the meat into small pieces. Return to the pan with the potato and simmer for 10 minutes, or until the potato is tender. Add the ham, cabbage and vinegar and season with pepper, cover and cook over very low heat for 5–10 minutes while preparing the dumplings.

4 To make the dumplings, rub the butter into the flour until crumbly. Mix in the Cheddar, thyme and about 1/2 cup (125 ml/4 fl oz) of water, or enough to bind the mixture together. Roll 2 level teaspoons of the mixture into balls. Place into the soup and simmer, covered, for 8 minutes, or until the dumplings are plump. Season to taste and scatter with the lemon rind. Serve immediately.

NUTRITION PER SERVE
Protein 20 g; Fat 20 g; Carbohydrate 47 g; Dietary Fibre 6 g; Cholesterol 53 mg; 1947 kJ (467 cal)

COOK'S FILE

Note: Kasseler ham is cured and smoked ham—a traditional German speciality.
Hint: Avoid crusty-looking bacon bones as they are extremely salty. Taste before adding any extra salt to this recipe.

Using a sharp knife, cut the ham into slices and then into cubes.

Remove the ham with a slotted spoon and drain on paper towels.

Add the water, stock and bacon bones to the pan.

Add the peeled chopped potato to the pan and simmer until tender.

With a flat-bladed knife, mix in the cheese and thyme, then add the water.

The dumplings are ready when they are plump and float to the surface.

COCK-A-LEEKIE

Preparation time: 10 minutes
+ 2 hours refrigeration
Total cooking time: 1 hour 40 minutes
Serves 4–6

1.5 kg (3 lb) chicken
250 g (8 oz) chicken giblets
(optional), (see Note)
1 onion, sliced
8 cups (2 litres) chicken stock
4 leeks, thinly sliced
1/4 teaspoon ground coriander
pinch of nutmeg
1 bouquet garni

12 pitted prunes
pinch of cayenne pepper
3 sprigs thyme
thyme sprigs, extra, to serve

1 To make the chicken stock, put the chicken in a large pan and add the giblets (if using), onion and stock. Bring to the boil, skimming the surface as required. Add the leek, coriander, nutmeg and bouquet garni. Reduce the heat, cover and simmer for 1 1/4 hours.

2 Remove the chicken and bouquet garni and lift out the giblets with a slotted spoon. Cool the stock, then refrigerate for 2 hours. Spoon off the fat from the surface and discard. Remove the meat from the bones and shred. Discard the skin and carcass.

3 Return the meat to the soup with the prunes, cayenne pepper and thyme. Simmer for 20 minutes. Season to taste and garnish with the extra thyme sprigs, if you want.

NUTRITION PER SERVE (6)
Protein 60 g; Fat 6 g; Carbohydrate 7 g;
Dietary Fibre 1 g; Cholesterol 125 mg;
1310 kJ (315 cal)

COOK'S FILE

Note: The chicken giblets are optional for this recipe but they will give the soup great flavour.

Trim the ends from the leeks and slice thinly, including some green parts.

Add the chicken stock to the pan with the chicken, giblets (if using) and onion.

Add the prunes and thyme sprigs to the soup and stir to combine.

Halve the tomatoes and scoop out the seeds with a teaspoon.

Brown the shanks in 2 batches, remove with tongs and drain on paper towels.

Stir the paprikas and flour into the onion mixture until it just begins to colour.

Spoon off the fat that forms on the surface of the soup.

RUSTIC HOTPOT

Preparation time: 40 minutes
+ 1 hour refrigeration
Total cooking time: 2 hours
Serves 4

2 tablespoons olive oil
8 lamb shanks
2 onions, sliced
4 cloves garlic, finely chopped
3 bay leaves, torn in half
1–2 teaspoons hot paprika
2 teaspoons sweet paprika
1 tablespoon plain flour
3 tablespoons tomato paste
6 cups (1.5 litres) vegetable
   stock
4 potatoes, chopped
4 carrots, sliced
3 sticks celery, thickly sliced
3 tomatoes, seeded and chopped

1 To make the lamb stock, heat 1 tablespoon of the oil in a large, heavy-based pan over medium heat. Brown the shanks well in two batches and drain on paper towels.

2 Add the remaining tablespoon of oil to the pan and cook the onion, garlic and bay leaves over low heat for 10 minutes, stirring regularly. Add the paprikas and flour and cook, stirring continuously, for 2 minutes. Gradually add the combined tomato paste and stock. Bring to the boil, stirring continuously, and return the shanks to the pan. Reduce the heat to low and simmer, covered, for 1½ hours, stirring occasionally.

3 Remove the bay leaves and discard. Remove the shanks, allow to cool slightly and then cut the meat from the bone. Discard the bones. Cut the meat into pieces and refrigerate. Refrigerate the stock for about 1 hour, or until fat forms on the surface and can be spooned off.

4 Return the meat to the soup along with the potato, carrot and celery and bring to the boil. Reduce the heat and simmer for 15 minutes. Season and add the chopped tomato to serve.

NUTRITION PER SERVE
Protein 70 g; Fat 15 g; Carbohydrate 30 g; Dietary Fibre 8 g; Cholesterol 170 mg; 2200 kJ (525 cal)

BEEF CONSOMME

Preparation time: 30 minutes
+ overnight refrigeration
Total cooking time: 5 hours
Serves 4–6

1 kg (2 lb) gravy beef, cut into
    small pieces
500 g (1 lb) beef bones
    including marrow, cut into
    small pieces (ask your
    butcher to do this)
1 leek, cut into small pieces
2 onions, quartered
2 carrots, chopped
2 sticks celery, chopped
6 black peppercorns
6 whole cloves
3 sprigs thyme
3 sprigs parsley
3 bay leaves
1 egg shell, crumbled
1 egg white, lightly beaten
2 tablespoons chopped parsley

1 Preheat the oven to moderate 180°C (350°F/Gas 4). Place the gravy beef and beef bones in a single layer in a baking dish. Bake for 45 minutes, or until lightly browned, turning once.
2 Put the meat, bones, vegetables, peppercorns, cloves, herbs, bay leaves and 1 teaspoon of salt in a large pan. Add 3 litres of water and slowly bring to the boil. Reduce the heat to low, cover and simmer for 4 hours. Set aside to cool slightly. Remove the larger pieces of meat and discard. Ladle the liquid through a muslin-lined sieve into a bowl. Discard the remaining meat and vegetables.
3 Cover the liquid and refrigerate for several hours, or overnight. Spoon off the fat from the surface. Return to a clean pan with the egg shell and the lightly beaten egg white.
4 Slowly heat the stock to simmering and simmer for 10 minutes. A frothy scum will form on the surface. Remove from the heat and leave for 10 minutes. Skim the surface and ladle the stock through a muslin-lined sieve. Reheat, season if needed, and serve with the chopped parsley.

NUTRITION PER SERVE (6)
Protein 35 g; Fat 5 g; Carbohydrate 4 g;
Dietary Fibre 2 g; Cholesterol 110 mg;
858 kJ (205 cal)

Lay the gravy beef and bones in a single layer in a large baking dish.

Carefully ladle the stock into the muslin-lined sieve placed over a bowl.

Gently stir in the egg shell and egg white with a balloon whisk or wooden spoon.

A froth will form on the surface as the stock gently simmers.

ROASTED LEEK, GARLIC AND BACON SOUP

Preparation time: 25 minutes
Total cooking time: 1 hour 30 minutes
Serves 4–6

1 tablespoon olive oil
20 g (³/4 oz) butter
2 rashers bacon, chopped
3 leeks, chopped
2 cloves garlic, chopped
1 stick celery, coarsely chopped
2 zucchini, coarsely chopped
2 bay leaves
6 cups (1.5 litres) chicken or
   vegetable stock
¹/3 cup (80 ml/2³/4 fl oz) cream

¹/4 cup (15 g/¹/2 oz) finely
   chopped parsley
2 rashers bacon, extra, to serve

1 Preheat the oven to warm 160°C (315°F/Gas 2–3). Heat the oil and butter in a large roasting tin. Add the bacon rashers and stir over medium heat for 1–2 minutes. Add the leek, garlic, celery, zucchini and bay leaves and cook, stirring, for 2–3 minutes, without allowing to brown.

2 Transfer the roasting tin to the oven and roast the vegetables and bacon for 40 minutes, turning a couple of times. Cover with foil if starting to brown. Transfer to a large pan, pour on the stock and bring to the boil. Lower the heat and simmer for 30 minutes. Cool slightly, strain and return the liquid to the pan. Remove the bay leaves.

3 Put the vegetables and bacon in a food processor with a ladleful of the cooking liquid and process until smooth, adding more liquid if necessary. Return the purée to the pan with the liquid and add some pepper, the cream and parsley. Reheat gently.

4 To make the bacon garnish, trim off the rind and excess fat from the bacon and grill until crisp. Drain on paper towels, then crumble with your fingers and serve on top of the soup.

NUTRITION PER SERVE (6)
Protein 7 g; Fat 15 g; Carbohydrate 2 g; Dietary Fibre 1 g; Cholesterol 45 mg; 640 kJ (150 cal)

Turn the vegetables during cooking and cover with foil to prevent browning.

Process the vegetables and bacon until smooth. Add more liquid if necessary.

Grill the bacon until it is very crisp, then crumble to make a garnish.

CHICKEN AND VEGETABLE SOUP

Preparation time: 1 hour + refrigeration
Total cooking time: 1 hour 25 minutes
Serves 6–8

1.5 kg (2½ lb) chicken
2 carrots, roughly chopped
2 sticks celery, roughly chopped
1 onion, quartered
4 parsley sprigs
2 bay leaves
4 black peppercorns
50 g (1¾ oz) butter
2 tablespoons plain flour
2 potatoes, chopped
250 g (8 oz) butternut pumpkin,
    chopped into bite-sized pieces
2 carrots, extra, cut into
    matchsticks
1 leek, cut into matchsticks
3 sticks celery, extra, cut into
    matchsticks
100 g (3½ oz) green beans, cut
    into short lengths or baby
    green beans, halved
200 g (6½ oz) broccoli, cut into
    small florets
100 g (3½ oz) sugar snap peas,
    trimmed
50 g (1¾ oz) English spinach
    leaves, shredded
½ cup (125 ml/4 fl oz) cream
¼ cup (15 g/½ oz) chopped
    parsley

1 To make the chicken stock, place the chicken in a large pan with the carrot, celery, onion, parsley, bay leaves, 2 teaspoons of salt and the peppercorns. Add 3 litres of water. Bring to the boil, reduce the heat and simmer for 1 hour, skimming the surface as required. Allow to cool for at least 30 minutes. Strain and reserve the liquid.

2 Remove the chicken and allow to cool enough to handle. Discard the skin, then cut or pull the flesh from the bones and shred into small pieces. Set the chicken meat aside.

3 Heat the butter in a large pan over medium heat and, when foaming, add the flour. Cook, stirring, for 1 minute. Remove from the heat and gradually stir in the stock. Return to the heat and bring to the boil, stirring continuously. Add the potato, pumpkin and extra carrot and simmer for 7 minutes. Add the leek, extra celery and beans and simmer for a further 5 minutes. Finally, add the broccoli and sugar snap peas and cook for a further 3 minutes.

4 Just before serving, add the chicken meat, spinach, cream and chopped parsley. Reheat gently but do not allow the soup to boil. Keep stirring until the spinach has wilted. Season to taste with plenty of salt and freshly ground black pepper. Serve immediately.

NUTRITION PER SERVE (8)
Protein 50 g; Fat 15 g; Carbohydrate 15 g; Dietary Fibre 6 g; Cholesterol 130 mg; 1700 kJ (400 cal)

COOK'S FILE

Hint: Do not overcook the vegetables, they should be tender yet crispy.
Note: The chicken stock (up to the end of Step 1) can be made 1 day ahead and kept, covered, in the refrigerator. This can, in fact, be beneficial—before reheating the stock, spoon off the fat which will have formed on the surface.
Serving suggestion: This soup is delicious served with Fougasse, as shown here.

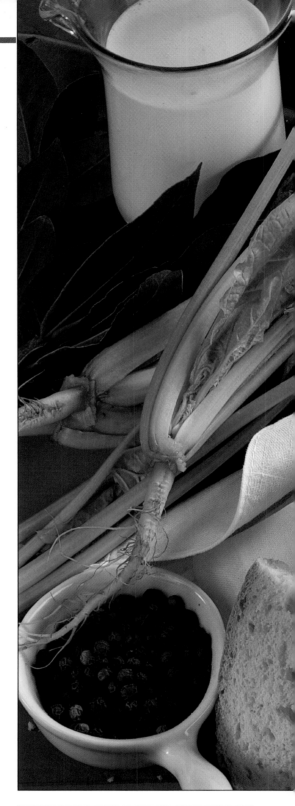

Cut the extra celery into short lengths, then into matchsticks.

Using a knife, trim the tops from the peas, pulling down to remove the string.

Add the parsley sprigs and bay leaves to the pan.

Remove the skin from the chicken, then shred the meat.

Add the potato, pumpkin and extra carrot to the boiling soup.

Pour in the cream and stir until the spinach has wilted. Reheat gently.

THAI-STYLE CHICKEN AND BABY CORN SOUP

Preparation time: 30 minutes
Total cooking time: 15 minutes
Serves 4

150 g (5 oz) whole baby corn
   cobs
1 tablespoon oil
2 stalks lemon grass, white part
   only, very finely sliced
2 tablespoons finely grated
   ginger
6 spring onions, chopped
1 red chilli, finely chopped
4 cups (1 litre) chicken stock

1½ cups (375 ml/12 fl oz)
   coconut milk
250 g (8 oz) chicken breast
   fillets, thinly sliced
130 g (4¼ oz) creamed corn
1 tablespoon soy sauce
2 tablespoons finely chopped
   chives, to serve
1 red chilli, thinly sliced,
   to serve

1 Cut the baby corn in half or quarters lengthways, depending on their size. Set aside.

2 Heat the oil in a pan over medium heat and cook the lemon grass, ginger, spring onion and chilli for 1 minute, stirring continuously. Add the stock and coconut milk and bring to the boil—do not cover or the coconut milk will curdle.

3 Stir in the corn, chicken and creamed corn and simmer for 8 minutes, or until the corn and chicken are just tender. Add the soy sauce, season well and serve garnished with the chives and chilli.

NUTRITION PER SERVE
Protein 20 g; Fat 25 g; Carbohydrate 15 g; Dietary Fibre 3 g; Cholesterol 30 mg; 1520 kJ (360 cal)

COOK'S FILE

Note: Canned baby corn can be substituted for fresh corn. Add during the last 2 minutes of cooking.

Grate the peeled ginger on the fine side of the grater.

Cut the baby corn lengthways into halves or quarters.

Add the corn, chicken and creamed corn to the pan.

OSSO BUCO, BARLEY AND VEGETABLE SOUP

Preparation time: 25 minutes
Total cooking time: 50 minutes
Serves 6

500 g (1 lb) veal shanks with
    bones (osso buco), cut into
    5 cm (2 inch) pieces
    (ask your butcher to do this)
2 tablespoons olive oil
1 onion, diced
1–2 garlic cloves, crushed
425 g (14 oz) can chopped
    tomatoes
1 tablespoon tomato paste
1/2 teaspoon dried oregano
6 cups (1.5 litres) beef stock,
300 g (10 oz) potatoes, cubed
300 g (10 oz) pumpkin, cubed
3/4 cup (165 g/51/2 oz) pearl
    barley
200 g (61/2 oz) zucchini, sliced

1 Trim the meat from the bones and cut into cubes. Scrape out the marrow from the bones, if you want to use it, and discard the bones. Heat the oil in a heavy-based pan and brown the meat and marrow, in batches if necessary, until rich brown. Remove and drain on paper towels. Set the fried marrow aside, to garnish.

2 Add the onion to the pan and cook for 4–5 minutes over low heat; then add the garlic and cook for 1 minute longer. Add the meat, tomato, tomato paste, oregano, stock, potato and pumpkin.

3 Wash the barley in a sieve until the water runs clean, then drain and add to the soup. Bring to the boil, reduce the heat to low and simmer, covered, for 20 minutes. Add the zucchini and cook, covered, for 10 minutes, or until the barley is cooked. Serve garnished with the fried marrow.

NUTRITION PER SERVE
Protein 25 g; Fat 10 g; Carbohydrate 30 g;
Dietary Fibre 6 g; Cholesterol 70 mg;
1310 kJ (315 cal)

COOK'S FILE

Note: Osso buco (or *ossobuco*) is the Italian word for marrowbone. Osso buco is a traditional Italian stew made with the knuckle of veal, usually served in a tomato sauce.

Trim the meat from the bones and cut into cubes.

Add the meat, tomato, tomato paste, oregano, stock, potato and pumpkin.

Wash the barley in a sieve under running water until the water runs clear.

Add the zucchini to the boiling soup and cook for 10 minutes.

COUNTRY LENTIL, BACON AND GARLIC SOUP

Preparation time: 35 minutes
Total cooking time: 1 hour 5 minutes
Serves 4–6

1/4 cup (60 ml/2 fl oz) olive oil
3 onions, finely chopped
6 cloves garlic, thinly sliced
150 g (5 oz) speck or bacon, finely chopped
3 carrots, finely chopped
2 parsnips, finely chopped
3 sticks celery, sliced
200 g (6 1/2 oz) red lentils, rinsed
4 cups (1 litre) vegetable stock
1/4 cup (60 g/2 oz) tomato paste
1/4 cup (65 g/2 1/4 oz) risoni (rice-shaped pasta)
4 spring onions, finely chopped
1/4 cup (15 g/1/2 oz) chopped parsley
2 teaspoons finely grated lemon rind
100 g (3 1/2 oz) grated Parmesan, to serve

1 Heat the oil in a large pan. Add the onion, garlic and speck and cook, stirring occasionally, over low–medium heat for 15 minutes, or until a deep golden brown.

2 Add the carrot, parsnip and celery, stir well, cover and cook for 5 minutes, or until softened. Stir in the lentils, stock, tomato paste and 4 cups (1 litre) of water. Bring to the boil, reduce the heat and simmer, uncovered, for 30 minutes, or until the lentils are tender; skim the surface as required.

3 Stir in the risoni and 2 cups (500 ml/16 fl oz) of water. Return to the boil and simmer for 10 minutes.

4 Add the spring onion, parsley and lemon rind and season to taste with salt and pepper. Serve topped with the grated Parmesan.

NUTRITION PER SERVE (6)
Protein 25 g; Fat 20 g; Carbohydrate 30 g; Dietary Fibre 10 g; Cholesterol 30 mg; 1590 kJ (380 cal)

COOK'S FILE

Serving suggestion: This soup is delicious served with Parmesan and prosciutto loaf.

Using a sharp knife, slice the garlic and finely chop the speck.

Add the well-drained lentils to the pan and stir well to combine.

LEMON CHICKEN SOUP

Preparation time: 10 minutes
Total cooking time: 10 minutes
Serves 4

2 chicken breast fillets
1 lemon
4 cups (1 litre) chicken stock
2 sprigs lemon thyme, plus
     extra, to garnish (see Note)

1 Trim any excess fat from the chicken. Using a vegetable peeler, cut 2 strips of rind from the lemon and remove the pith. Place the stock, rind and thyme in a shallow pan and slowly bring almost to the boil. Reduce to simmering point, add the chicken and cook, covered, for 7 minutes, or until the meat is tender.
2 Remove the chicken from the pan, transfer to a plate and cover with foil.
3 Strain the stock through a sieve lined with 2 layers of damp muslin into a clean pan. Finely shred the chicken and return to the stock. Reheat gently and season to taste with salt and freshly ground black pepper. Serve immediately, garnished with the extra sprigs of thyme.

NUTRITION PER SERVE
Protein 25 g; Fat 3 g; Carbohydrate 0 g; Dietary Fibre 0 g; Cholesterol 55 mg; 535 kJ (130 cal)

COOK'S FILE

Note: You can use ordinary thyme if lemon thyme is not available.
Hint: If you don't have time to make your own stock, poultry shops or butchers sometimes sell their own. These may have more flavour and contain less salt than commercially-made stock cubes.

Using a small knife, remove the white pith from the lemon rind.

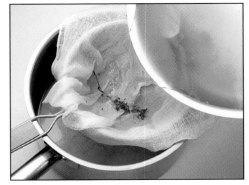

Pour the stock through a sieve lined with damp muslin into a clean pan.

Finely shred the chicken into thin pieces and return to the soup.

PEA AND HAM SOUP

Preparation time: 20 minutes
Total cooking time: 2 hours 45 minutes
Serves 6–8

1 tablespoon oil
2 onions, diced
2 carrots, diced
2 sticks celery, diced
1 parsnip, diced
1½ cups (330 g/10½ oz) green
    split peas
1 teaspoon black peppercorns
2 teaspoons dried thyme
    leaves

1 ham hock (850 g/1 lb 12 oz),
    cut into smaller pieces
    (ask your butcher to do this)

1 Heat the oil in a large pan and add the onion, carrot, celery and parsnip. Cook over low heat for 10 minutes, or until the vegetables have softened and the onion is translucent.

2 Add the split peas, peppercorns, thyme, the pieces of ham hock and 8 cups (2 litres) of water. Slowly bring to the boil, reduce the heat to low and simmer, covered, for 2½ hours, or until most of the meat has fallen off the bones and the vegetables and split peas are very soft. Stir occasionally.

3 Remove the bones from the pan, pulling off any of the meat that hasn't fallen away. Chop any large pieces and return to the pan. Season well with salt and pepper, if necessary.

NUTRITION PER SERVE (8)
Protein 20 g; Fat 10 g; Carbohydrate 7 g; Dietary Fibre 3 g; Cholesterol 55 mg; 845 kJ (200 cal)

COOK'S FILE

Serving suggestion: This soup goes very well with Caramelised onion braids, as shown
Note: Ham hocks can be quite salty, so check the amount of salt on the ham; if it is crusted it is too mature.

Using a sharp knife, dice the onions, carrots, celery and parsnip.

Add the pieces of ham hock to the softened vegetables in the pan.

Using a sharp knife, trim off any meat that hasn't fallen away from the bones.

RICH OXTAIL SOUP

Preparation time: 35 minutes
+ 2 hours refrigeration
Total cooking time: 2 hours 25 minutes
Serves 4

2 oxtails, cut into pieces
   (ask your butcher to do this)
2 tablespoons olive oil
3 onions, chopped
4 cloves garlic, finely chopped
1 tablespoon plain flour
4 cups (1 litre) rich beef
   stock
2 bay leaves, torn in half
2 tablespoons tomato paste

2 teaspoons Worcestershire
   sauce
4 potatoes, chopped
2 parsnips, chopped
2 carrots, chopped
3 tomatoes, chopped
2 tablespoons chopped parsley

1 Cut the excess fat from the oxtail. Heat the oil in a heavy-based pan over medium heat. Add the oxtail, onion and garlic and cook for 8 minutes, turning regularly, or until well browned. Add the flour and cook for 1 minute, stirring. Mix in 2 cups (500 ml/16 fl oz) of the stock and bring to the boil, stirring continuously. Remove from the heat and refrigerate for 2 hours, or until the fat can be spooned off the surface.

2 Add the remaining stock, 4 cups (1 litre) of water, the bay leaves, 1/2 teaspoon each of salt and pepper, tomato paste and Worcestershire sauce. Bring to the boil, reduce the heat to low and simmer, covered, for 2 hours, stirring occasionally.

3 Add the potato, parsnip and carrot and simmer for 10 minutes, or until tender. Remove the bay leaves and discard. Serve with the chopped tomato and parsley.

NUTRITION PER SERVE
Protein 8 g; Fat 16 g; Carbohydrate 40 g; Dietary Fibre 10 g; Cholesterol 10 mg; 1620 kJ (390 cal)

Using a sharp knife, trim away the excess fat from the oxtail.

Sprinkle the flour over the browned oxtail and cook, stirring, for 1 minute.

Add the parsnip, carrot and potato and simmer for 10 minutes.

Crostini & Croutons

Crostini (crisp thin slices of baked bread) and croutons (irresistibly crunchy cubes of browned bread) make wonderful accompaniments to any soup, whether it's a broth, creamy soup or chowder.

ROASTED GARLIC CROSTINI

Preheat the oven to moderate 180°C (350°F/Gas 4). Wrap 2 garlic bulbs separately in foil. Bake for 1 hour, or until the garlic feels very soft to touch. Cool. Cut 1 long bread stick diagonally into twenty 2 cm (3/4 inch) thick slices. Lay in a single layer on a large baking tray and brush with 3 tablespoons olive oil. Bake for 10 minutes, or until crisp and golden. Remove any that brown too quickly. Cut the tops off the garlic and squeeze out the flesh. Spread the garlic paste on the bread, sprinkle with a few thyme leaves, salt and freshly ground black pepper. Drizzle on a little extra olive oil, if you want. Serves 4.

NUTRITION PER SERVE
Protein 8 g; Fat 10 g; Carbohydrate 40 g; Dietary Fibre 0 g; Cholesterol 0 mg; 1200 kJ (290 cal)
Note: The garlic becomes very sweet when roasted. Roast an extra garlic bulb if you want more paste.

HERBED CROSTINI FINGERS

Preheat the oven to moderate 180°C (350°F/Gas 4). Combine 80 g (2¾ oz) of softened butter with 1 tablespoon each of chopped dill, flat-leaf parsley and basil. Mix until well combined. Stir through 3 tablespoons finely grated Parmesan. Cut 1 long bread stick into diagonal slices, 2 cm (3/4 inch) thick. Spread with the herbed butter. Cut each slice in half lengthways. Place the bread fingers on a baking tray and bake for 10–12 minutes, or until the butter has melted and the edges are crispy. Serves 4.

NUTRITION PER SERVE
Protein 9 g; Fat 20 g; Carbohydrate 36 g; Dietary Fibre 2 g; Cholesterol 60 mg; 1530 kJ (365 cal)

CRISPY CROSTINI

Preheat the oven to moderate 180°C (350°F/Gas 4). Cut half a day old crusty Italian loaf of bread (Ciabatta) into wafer-thin slices. Place the slices in a single layer on a baking tray and brush lightly on one side with a little olive oil. Cook for 8–10 minutes, or until lightly golden. Watch carefully as it is very easy for them to overbrown. Allow to cool. Serves 4.

NUTRITION PER SERVE
Protein 4 g; Fat 15 g; Carbohydrate 25 g; Dietary Fibre 1 g; Cholesterol 0 mg; 1050 kJ (250 cal)

ARTICHOKE AND GARLIC CROSTINI

Preheat the oven to moderate 180°C (350°F/Gas 4). Finely chop ¼ cup (55 g/2 oz) marinated artichoke hearts and 3 teaspoons capers. Mix with 50 g (1¾ oz) softened butter and 2 crushed cloves garlic. Spread the mixture onto 8 thick slices of crusty Italian bread. Cut each slice in half diagonally. Lay on a baking tray and bake for 10–12 minutes, or until the edges are crispy. Serves 4.

NUTRITION PER SERVE
Protein 4 g; Fat 10 g; Carbohydrate 20 g; Dietary Fibre 1 g; Cholesterol 30 mg; 790 kJ (190

GARLIC AND HERB CROUTONS

Preheat the oven to moderate 180°C (350°F/Gas 4). Cut two 2 cm (3/4 inch) thick slices from a loaf. Remove the crusts and cut each bread slice into 16 cubes. In a bowl, mix together 3 tablespoons olive oil, 2 crushed cloves garlic, 1 tablespoon chopped oregano, 2 teaspoons chopped thyme, 1 teaspoon chopped rosemary and a pinch of chilli flakes. Add the bread cubes to the herbed oil and toss until all the oil has been absorbed. Lay the bread cubes in a single layer on a baking tray and bake in the oven for 10–12 minutes, or until the croutons are golden brown. Turn once during baking. Serves 4.

NUTRITION PER SERVE
Protein 1 g; Fat 15 g; Carbohydrate 7 g; Dietary Fibre 1 g; Cholesterol 0 mg; 690 kJ (165 cal)

Note: Croutons are best made with day-old bread, which holds together better than fresh bread.

PARMESAN TRIANGLE CROUTONS

Preheat the oven to moderate 180°C (350°F/Gas 4). Lightly grease a baking tray. Remove the crusts from 4 slices of bread and cut the slices in half diagonally. Cut each triangle in half and then in half again so that you end up with 8 small triangles. Combine 1/3 cup (80 ml/2 3/4 fl oz) olive oil with 1/3 cup (50 g/1 3/4 oz) finely grated Parmesan. Add the triangles and toss in the mixture. When you add the Parmesan to the oil most of the oil will be absorbed, but you should have enough to coat the triangles. Place the triangles on a lightly greased baking tray. Bake for 10–15 minutes, or until golden. Turn once during baking. Some triangles may be ready before others; if this is the case, remove the golden ones and continue to cook the rest. Serves 4.

NUTRITION PER SERVE
Protein 6 g; Fat 25 g; Carbohydrate 15 g; Dietary Fibre 1 g; Cholesterol 10 mg; 1200 kJ (290 cal)

SPICY CROUTONS

Preheat the oven to moderate 180°C (350°F/Gas 4). Remove the crusts from 4 slices of bread and cut the slices into cubes or, using a small round cutter, cut into circles. Combine 1/4 cup (60 ml/2 fl oz) olive oil, 1 teaspoon each of ground cumin and coriander, 1/2 teaspoon ground cinnamon and a pinch each of ground nutmeg and cloves. Add the bread to the oil and toss until all the oil has been absorbed. Lay the bread in a single layer on a baking tray and bake for 10–15 minutes, or until crisp and golden. Serves 4.

NUTRITION PER SERVE
Protein 1 g; Fat 15 g; Carbohydrate 7 g; Dietary Fibre 0 g; Cholesterol 0 mg; 685 kJ (165 cal)

SUN-DRIED TOMATO AND OLIVE LAVASH BITES

Preheat the oven to moderately hot 190°C (375°F/Gas 5). Soften 40 g (1 1/4 oz) butter and place in a small bowl. Add 2 tablespoons finely chopped sun-dried tomato, 1 tablespoon finely chopped olives, 2 crushed cloves garlic and 2 tablespoons shredded basil. Mix well. Spread the mixture over 1 slice of lavash bread. Cut the lavash into strips then into small triangles. Bake for 5–10 minutes. Watch carefully as they can overbrown quickly. Serves 4.

NUTRITION PER SERVE
Protein 3 g; Fat 8 g; Carbohydrate 12 g; Dietary Fibre 0 g; Cholesterol 25 mg; 590 kJ (140 cal)

Seafood Soups

BOUILLABAISSE

Preparation time: 40 minutes
Total cooking time: 1 hour 20 minutes
Serves 4–6

4–6 tomatoes
500 g (1 lb) raw king prawns
1 raw lobster tail
1–2 fish heads
1 cup (250 ml/8 fl oz) red wine
3 onions, finely chopped
6 cloves garlic, crushed
3 bay leaves
1/4 cup (60 ml/2 fl oz) olive oil
1 leek, finely sliced
1/4 cup (60 g/2 oz) tomato paste
small piece of orange rind
500 g (1 lb) white fish fillet,
    cut into small pieces
12 mussels, firmly closed,
    beards removed
200 g (6 1/2 oz) scallops with
    corals
1/2 cup (30 g/1 oz) chopped fresh
    parsley
1/4 cup (15 g/1/2 oz) shredded
    basil leaves

1 Score a cross in the base of each tomato. Cover with boiling water for 1 minute, plunge in cold water, drain and peel away the skins.

2 To make the fish stock, peel and devein the prawns and set the shells, heads and tails aside. Shell the lobster tail, keeping the shell and chopping the meat. Put the lobster and prawn trimmings in a large pan. Add the wine, 1 onion, 2 cloves garlic, 1 bay leaf and 2 cups (500 ml/16 fl oz) of water. Bring to the boil, reduce the heat and simmer for 20 minutes. Strain through a fine sieve.

3 Heat the oil in a large, heavy-based pan. Add the leek and remaining onion and garlic. Cover and simmer, stirring occasionally, over low heat for 20 minutes, or until browned. Add the tomato, remaining bay leaves, tomato paste and orange rind and stir well. Simmer, uncovered, for 10 minutes. Add the reserved fish stock, bring to the boil, reduce the heat and simmer for 10 minutes, stirring occasionally.

4 Add the prawns, lobster, fish pieces, mussels and scallops. Simmer, covered, for 4–5 minutes. Discard any unopened mussels, the rind and bay leaves. Add the herbs and season well. Shown here with Rouille (page 62).

NUTRITION PER SERVE (6)
Protein 45 g; Fat 30 g; Carbohydrate 15 g; Dietary Fibre 6 g; Cholesterol 185 mg; 2165 kJ (520 cal)

Cut on either side of the soft underside of the lobster tail, and lift up.

Strain the fish stock through a fine sieve and discard the trimmings.

PRAWN WON TON SOUP

Preparation time: 50 minutes
+ 30 minutes soaking
Total cooking time: 40 minutes
Serves 4

2 dried Chinese mushrooms
15 raw prawns
100 g (3½ oz) pork mince
2 spring onions, chopped
1 teaspoon grated ginger
2 tablespoons canned water
    chestnuts, chopped
2 teaspoons chopped lemon
    grass, white part only
1 clove garlic, finely chopped

3 tablespoons soy sauce
225 g (7 oz) won ton
    wrappers
coriander leaves
6 cups (1.5 litres) beef stock
3 baby carrots, cut into slices,
    diagonally
3 spring onions, cut diagonally

1 Soak the mushrooms in hot water for 30 minutes. Peel and devein the prawns, then cut in half lengthways. Drain the mushrooms, remove the stems and chop the caps.

2 Mix the chopped mushroom with the pork, spring onion, ginger, water chestnut, lemon grass, garlic and 1 tablespoon of the soy sauce. Work with 1 won ton wrapper at a time, keeping the rest covered. Put 2–3 coriander leaves, half a prawn and a heaped teaspoon of the pork mixture in the centre of a wrapper. Brush the edges with water and lay another wrapper on top. Press to seal. Repeat with the remaining wrappers.

3 Bring the stock, remaining soy sauce, carrot and spring onion to the boil. Bring another large pan of water to the boil and cook the won tons in batches for 4–5 minutes; drain. Pour the hot soup over the won tons.

NUTRITION PER SERVE
Protein 20 g; Fat 4 g; Carbohydrate 50 g; Dietary Fibre 5 g; Cholesterol 90 mg; 1290 kJ (310 cal)

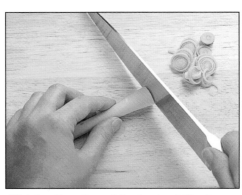

Thinly slice the white part of the lemon grass, then chop finely.

Remove the stems from the soaked mushrooms and finely chop the caps.

Lightly brush the edges with a little water, then lay another wrapper on top.

SMOKED HADDOCK CHOWDER

Preparation time: 20 minutes
Total cooking time: 35 minutes
Serves 4–6

500 g (1 lb) smoked haddock
1 potato, diced
1 stick celery, diced
1 onion, finely chopped
50 g (1¾ oz) butter
1 rasher bacon, rind removed
   and finely chopped
2 tablespoons plain flour
½ teaspoon dried mustard
½ teaspoon Worcestershire
   sauce
1 cup (250 ml/8 fl oz) milk
½ cup (15 g/½ oz) chopped
   parsley
¼ cup (60 ml/2 fl oz) cream
   (optional)

1 To make the fish stock, put the fish in a frying pan, cover with water and bring to the boil. Reduce the heat and simmer for 8 minutes, or until the fish flakes easily. Drain, reserving the fish stock, then peel, bone and flake the fish. Set aside.

2 Put the potato, celery and onion in a medium pan and pour over enough reserved fish stock to cover the vegetables. Bring to the boil, reduce the heat and simmer for 8 minutes, or until the vegetables are tender. Set aside.

3 Melt the butter in a large pan, add the bacon and cook, stirring, for 3 minutes. Add the flour, mustard and Worcestershire sauce and stir until combined. Cook for 1 minute. Remove from the heat and gradually pour in the milk, stirring continuously, until smooth. Return to the heat and stir for 5 minutes, until the mixture comes to the boil and has thickened. Stir in the vegetables and remaining stock, then add the parsley and fish. Simmer over low heat for 5 minutes, or until heated through. Taste for seasoning and serve with some cream, if you want.

NUTRITION PER SERVE (6)
Protein 20 g; Fat 10 g; Carbohydrate 8 g; Dietary Fibre 1 g; Cholesterol 90 mg; 970 kJ (230 cal)

COOK'S FILE

Note: Chowder is a thick, hearty soup, made with seafood, fish, vegetables or chicken.

Simmer the haddock in a frying pan until it flakes easily when lifted with a fork.

Lay the fish on paper towels to drain well, then flake into small pieces.

Gradually add the milk, stirring continuously with a wooden spoon.

MANHATTAN-STYLE SEAFOOD CHOWDER

Preparation time: 30 minutes
Total cooking time: 30 minutes
Serves 4–6

60 g (2 oz) butter
3 rashers bacon, chopped
2 onions, chopped
2 cloves garlic, finely chopped
2 sticks celery, sliced
3 potatoes, diced
5 cups (1.25 litres) fish or
   chicken stock
3 teaspoons chopped thyme

1 tablespoon tomato paste
425 g (14 oz) can chopped
   tomatoes
375 g (12 oz) boneless white
   fish fillets, cut into chunks
12 large raw prawns, peeled,
   deveined and halved
310 g (10 oz) can baby clams,
   undrained
2 tablespoons chopped parsley
grated orange rind, to garnish

1 Melt the butter in a large pan and cook the bacon, onion, garlic and celery over low heat, stirring occasionally, for 5 minutes, or until soft but not brown. Add the potato,

stock and thyme and bring to the boil.
2 Reduce the heat and simmer, covered, for 15 minutes. Stir in the tomato paste and tomato and return to the boil. Add the fish pieces, prawns and clams and simmer for 3 minutes.
3 Season to taste and stir in the parsley. Serve garnished with grated orange rind, if you want.

NUTRITION PER SERVE (6)
Protein 35 g; Fat 10 g; Carbohydrate 15 g;
Dietary Fibre 3 g; Cholesterol 200 mg;
1270 kJ (300 cal)

COOK'S FILE

Note: Prawns are not in a traditional chowder but are an excellent addition.

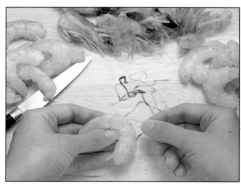

Devein the prawns by gently making a slit down the back and removing the vein.

Cook the bacon and vegetables over low heat until softened.

Add the potato, stock and chopped thyme and bring to the boil.

SAFFRON FISH SOUP

Preparation time: 20 minutes
Total cooking time: 30 minutes
Serves 4

1 kg (2 lb) white fish bones
    (heads and trimmings),
    chopped
2 cups (500 ml/16 fl oz) dry
    white wine
1 onion, chopped
1 carrot, chopped
1 stick celery, chopped
1 bay leaf
6 black peppercorns
³/₄ teaspoon saffron threads
50 g (1³/₄ oz) butter
¹/₄ cup (30 g/1 oz) plain flour
12 scallops, trimmed
250 g (8 oz) boneless white fish
    fillets, cut into cubes
1 cup (250 ml/8 fl oz) cream

1 To make the saffron fish stock, place the fish bones, 3 cups (750 ml/ 24 fl oz) of water, the wine, onion, carrot, celery, bay leaf and peppercorns in a large pan. Bring to the boil slowly, skimming the surface as required. Simmer, covered, for 20 minutes. Strain and discard the fish and vegetables. Take 4 cups (1 litre) of the hot stock and stir in the saffron threads. (If you have any stock leftover at this stage, you can simply freeze it for use in another recipe.)

2 Melt the butter in a large pan and stir in the flour. Cook, stirring continuously, over low heat for 3 minutes but do not allow the mixture to colour. Remove from the heat and gradually pour in the reserved fish stock. Return to the heat and stir continuously until the mixture boils and thickens slightly. Add the scallops and fish cubes, bring back to the boil and simmer for 1–2 minutes.

3 Stir in the cream and reheat gently, but do not allow the soup to boil. Season to taste with salt and freshly ground white pepper. Garnish with sprigs of chervil, if you want.

NUTRITION PER SERVE
Protein 25 g; Fat 40 g; Carbohydrate 10 g; Dietary Fibre 1 g; Cholesterol 190 mg; 2425 kJ (580 cal)

Using a sharp knife, remove the dark vein from the scallops.

Add the bay leaf and peppercorns to the pan.

Combine the reserved hot fish stock and saffron threads in a jug or bowl.

Add the scallops and fish cubes to the soup and simmer for 1–2 minutes.

TOM YAM GOONG

Preparation time: 25 minutes
Total cooking time: 45 minutes
Serves 4–6

500 g (1 lb) raw prawns
1 tablespoon oil
2 tablespoons Thai red curry
  paste
2 tablespoons tamarind purée
2 teaspoons turmeric
1 teaspoon chopped red chillies
4 kaffir lime leaves, shredded
2 tablespoons fish sauce
2 tablespoons lime juice

2 teaspoons soft brown sugar
coriander leaves, to serve

1 Peel and devein the prawns, leaving the tails intact. Heat the oil in a large pan and cook the prawn shells and heads for 10 minutes over medium-high heat, tossing frequently, until the heads are deep orange.

2 Add 1 cup (250 ml/8 fl oz) water and the curry paste. Boil for 5 minutes, or until reduced slightly. Add another 8 cups (2 litres) of water and simmer for 20 minutes. Strain, discarding the shells and heads, and return the stock to the pan.

3 Add the tamarind, turmeric, chilli and kaffir lime leaves; bring to the boil and cook for 2 minutes. Add the prawns and cook for 5 minutes, or until pink. Mix in the fish sauce, lime juice and sugar. Serve sprinkled with coriander leaves.

NUTRITION PER SERVE (6)
Protein 17 g; Fat 6 g; Carbohydrate 2 g;
Dietary Fibre 0 g; Cholesterol 125 mg;
560 kJ (135 cal)

COOK'S FILE

Hint: If you can't find tamarind purée, soak one quarter of a block of tamarind in warm water for 10 minutes, work the mixture with your fingertips and remove the stones.

Add the red curry paste and a cup of water to the pan.

Add the tamarind, turmeric, chilli and kaffir lime leaves.

Add the prawns to the boiling soup mixture and cook until pink.

LOBSTER BISQUE

Preparation time: 60 minutes
Total cooking time: 1 hour
Serves 4

400 g (13 oz) raw lobster tail
100 g (3½ oz) butter, softened
7 spring onions, chopped
1 onion, chopped
1 carrot, chopped
4 cups (1 litre) fish stock
4 sprigs parsley
1 bay leaf
4 peppercorns
⅓ cup (40 g/1¼ oz) plain flour
1¾ cups (440 ml/14 fl oz)
    tomato purée
1 tablespoon sherry, optional
½ cup (125 ml/4 fl oz) cream
pinch of nutmeg
2 teaspoons chopped fresh
    tarragon

1 Cut the lobster tail in half lengthways.
2 Melt half the butter in a pan, add the spring onion and onion and cook for 5 minutes, or until soft but not coloured. Add the carrot and cook for 2 minutes. Add the lobster halves, fish stock, parsley, bay leaf, peppercorns and 2½ cups (600 ml/20 fl oz) of water. Bring to the boil, reduce the heat and simmer for 20 minutes, skimming the surface as required.
3 Remove the lobster from the stock, cool slightly and take the meat from the shells. Crush the shells and return to the pan. Continue simmering for a further 40 minutes. Strain the stock, then strain again through a sieve lined with 2 layers of damp muslin.
4 Cut some thin slices from the lobster to use as a garnish and set

aside. In a blender, blend the remaining lobster flesh with a little of the strained stock until smooth. Mix the flour and remaining butter to a paste. Add the puréed lobster to the pan along with the flour paste, tomato purée, sherry, cream, nutmeg and salt and pepper, to taste. Mix well.
5 Add the tarragon and remaining stock and cook, stirring continuously,

over high heat until the soup boils and thickens. Reduce the heat and simmer gently for 5 minutes. Season to taste and serve garnished with the reserved lobster and some sprigs of tarragon, if you want.

NUTRITION PER SERVE
Protein 30 g; Fat 35 g; Carbohydrate 20 g; Dietary Fibre 4 g; Cholesterol 220 mg; 2080 kJ (500 cal)

Lift the meat out of the lobster shells and lightly crush the shells with a mallet.

Add the puréed lobster, flour paste, tomato purée, sherry, cream and nutmeg.

Add the chopped tarragon and remaining stock to the pan.

SEAFOOD LAKSA

Preparation time: 45 minutes
Total cooking time: 40–45 minutes
Serves 4–6

1 kg (2 lb) raw prawns
1/2 cup (125 ml/4 fl oz) oil
2–6 red chillies, seeded
1 onion, roughly chopped
3 cloves garlic, halved
2 cm (3/4 inch) piece of ginger
    or galangal, quartered
1 teaspoon ground turmeric
1 tablespoon ground coriander
3 stalks lemon grass, white part
    only, chopped
1–2 teaspoons shrimp paste
21/2 cups (600 ml/20 fl oz)
    coconut cream
2 teaspoons grated palm sugar
4 kaffir lime leaves
200 g (61/2 oz) packet fish
    balls
190 g (61/2 oz) packet fried
    bean curd pieces
250 g (8 oz) thin fresh egg
    noodles
250 g (8 oz) bean sprouts
1/3 cup (20 g/1 oz) chopped
    mint, to serve
1/4 cup (7 g/1/4 oz) coriander
    leaves, to serve

1 Peel and devein the prawns, and set the shells, heads and tails aside. Set the prawns aside separately.
2 To make the prawn stock, heat 2 tablespoons of the oil in a large, heavy-based pan and add the prawn shells, heads and tails. Stir until the heads are bright orange, then add 4 cups (1 litre) of water. Bring to the boil, reduce the heat and simmer for 15 minutes. Strain the stock through a fine sieve, discarding the shells. Wipe the pan clean.
3 Put the chillies, onion, garlic, ginger (or galangal), turmeric, coriander, lemon grass and 1/4 cup (60 ml/2 fl oz) of the prawn stock in a food processor and process until finely chopped.
4 Heat the remaining oil in the clean pan and add the chilli mixture and shrimp paste. Stir over low heat for 3 minutes, or until fragrant. Pour in the remaining stock and simmer for 10 minutes. Then add the coconut cream, palm sugar, kaffir lime leaves and 2 teaspoons of salt. Simmer for a further 5 minutes.
5 Add the prawns and simmer for 2 minutes, until they are just pink. Remove and set aside. Add the fish balls and bean curd and simmer gently until just heated through.
6 Bring a pan of water to the boil and cook the noodles for 2 minutes, then drain and place in a bowl. Lay the bean sprouts and prawns on the noodles and pour the soup over the top. Sprinkle with the chopped mint and coriander leaves, to serve.

NUTRITION PER SERVE (6)
Protein 50 g; Fat 50 g; Carbohydrate 40 g; Dietary Fibre 8 g; Cholesterol 270 mg; 3340 kJ (800 cal)

COOK'S FILE

Hint: For a really fiery soup, garnish with extra sliced red chilli.
Note: Laksa originated in Singapore and can also be made using fresh or dried rice noodles. Shredded cucumber can be added with the bean sprouts.
Variation: Laksa can be made without the fish balls or bean curd. Instead, use a combination of seafood or replace the seafood with bite-sized pieces of chicken or pork.

Wearing rubber gloves, halve the chillies lengthways and remove the seeds.

Stir-fry the prawn shells, heads and tails until they turn bright orange.

Put the chillies, onion, garlic, lemon grass, spices and stock in a food processor.

Add the shrimp paste to the pan and stir in with a wooden spoon.

Add the coconut cream, palm sugar, salt and kaffir lime leaves and simmer.

Stir the fish balls into the simmering soup, then the bean curd.

SNOW PEA AND PRAWN SOUP

Preparation time: 10 minutes
Total cooking time: 25 minutes
Serves 4

350 g (11 oz) snow peas, topped
    and tailed
45 g (1½ oz) butter
1 leek, chopped
1 clove garlic, crushed
2 teaspoons grated fresh ginger
1½ tablespoons plain flour
4 cups (1 litre) chicken or fish
    stock
12 raw prawns, peeled,
    deveined and chopped
coriander leaves, to serve

1 Roughly chop the snow peas. Melt the butter in a large saucepan and add the leek, garlic and ginger. Cook over moderate heat until the leek is soft but not brown. Stir in the flour and cook for 1 minute.

2 Remove the pan from the heat and gradually stir in the stock. Return to the heat and bring to the boil, stirring continuously, until the mixture thickens slightly. Reduce the heat, cover the pan and simmer for 5 minutes. Add the snow peas and simmer for 5 minutes.

3 Purée the soup in batches in a blender or food processor, until smooth. Return to a clean pan, bring to the boil and add the prawns. Simmer for 2 minutes, or until the prawns turn pink and are cooked through.

4 Season to taste with salt and freshly ground black pepper. Serve immediately, sprinkled with fresh coriander leaves.

NUTRITION PER SERVE
Protein 17 g; Fat 10 g; Carbohydrate 8 g;
Dietary Fibre 5 g; Cholesterol 110 mg;
780 kJ (185 cal)

COOK'S FILE

Hint: If you have one, it is best to purée this soup in a blender rather than a food processor. A food processor will give the soup a slightly granular and inferior texture.

Serving suggestion: This soup is delicious served with Ricotta and dill buns, as shown.

Starting from the tail end, pull the string from the snow peas and trim the tops.

Remove the heads, then peel away the shell from the body and tail of the prawn.

NEW ENGLAND CLAM CHOWDER

Preparation time: 25 minutes
Total cooking time: 45 minutes
Serves 4

30 g (1 oz) butter
2 rashers bacon, finely chopped
1 large onion, finely chopped
4 potatoes, cut into 1 cm
   (1/2 inch) cubes
2 cups (500 ml/16 fl oz) fish
   stock
1 bay leaf
1/2 cup (125 ml/4 fl oz) milk

4 x 105 g (31/2 oz) cans baby
   clams, drained and chopped
1/4 cup (15 g/1/2 oz) finely
   chopped parsley
1 cup (250 ml/8 fl oz) cream

1 Heat the butter in a large pan. Cook the bacon and onion for 2–3 minutes, or until softened. Add the potato and stir. Cook for a further 2–3 minutes and gradually pour on the stock. Add the bay leaf.
2 Bring to the boil, reduce the heat and simmer, covered, for 20 minutes, or until the potato is cooked. Simmer for a further 10 minutes, or until the soup is reduced and slightly thickened. Remove the bay leaf and discard.
3 Add the milk, chopped clams, parsley and cream. Stir to reheat, but do not allow the soup to boil. Season to taste with salt and freshly ground black pepper.

NUTRITION PER SERVE
Protein 20 g; Fat 40 g; Carbohydrate 20 g; Dietary Fibre 3 g; Cholesterol 250 mg; 2090 kJ (500 cal)

COOK'S FILE

Note: New England clam chowder is one of the many types to come from the north-east of America—it is, of course, named after the state.

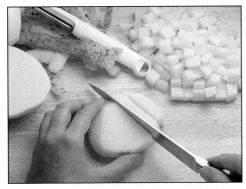

Peel and cut the potatoes into strips then small cubes.

Remove the bay leaf with a pair of tongs or a spoon.

Add the milk, clams and parsley and pour in the cream.

SAFFRON AND MUSSEL SOUP

Preparation time: 15 minutes
Total cooking time: 35 minutes
Serves 4

500 g (1 lb) mussels
1 stick celery, chopped
1 carrot, chopped
1 onion, chopped
3 black peppercorns
3–4 parsley stalks
100 g (3¹/2 oz) butter, softened
10 spring onions, finely chopped
²/3 cup (40 g/1¹/4 oz) finely
    chopped parsley
2 cloves garlic, crushed

3/4 cup (185 ml/6 fl oz) dry
    white wine
¹/3 cup (40 g/1¹/4 oz) plain flour
1 cup (250 ml/8 fl oz) cream
pinch of saffron threads

1 To make the mussel stock, scrub the mussels, remove their beards and discard any open mussels. Place the mussels, celery, carrot, onion, peppercorns and parsley stalks in a pan with 6 cups (1.5 litres) of water and bring to the boil. Reduce the heat to low and simmer, covered, for 6 minutes.

2 Discard any unopened mussels. Strain the stock through a sieve lined with 2 layers of damp muslin. Rinse out the pan and reserve the mussels.

Return the stock to the pan and simmer for 15 minutes. Set aside.

3 Melt half the butter in a pan, add the spring onion and cook over moderate heat for 3–4 minutes, or until softened. Add the parsley, garlic and wine and season well with salt and freshly ground black pepper.

4 Mix the flour and remaining butter to a paste. Add the reserved stock to the pan and stir in the flour paste, cream and saffron threads, stir until the soup boils and thickens slightly. Simmer for 2–3 minutes. Add the mussels and stir gently until reheated.

NUTRITION PER SERVE
Protein 25 g; Fat 55 g; Carbohydrate 15 g; Dietary Fibre 4 g; Cholesterol 290 mg; 2870 kJ (690 cal)

Discard any unopened mussels with a pair of tongs.

Strain the stock through a sieve lined with damp muslin over a bowl.

Saffron is expensive, but only a pinch is needed to give the colour and flavour.

Using a fine strainer, drain the liquid from the crab meat.

Using a sharp knife, peel the ginger, cut into strips, then chop finely.

Fold over the wrapper to enclose the filling and press firmly.

Cut the spring onions into lengths, then into thin strips.

LARGE CRAB DUMPLING SOUP

Preparation time: 25 minutes
Total cooking time: 20 minutes
Serves 4

170 g (5½ oz) can crab meat, drained
2 tablespoons finely chopped spring onions
2 cloves garlic, finely chopped
2 teaspoons sesame oil
3 teaspoons chopped ginger
12 small gowgee or won ton wrappers
2 spring onions, extra
5 cups (1.25 litres) chicken stock
1 tablespoon soy sauce
1 tablespoon mirin (see Note)
1 teaspoon sugar

1 To make the crab filling, mix the crab with the spring onion, 1 clove of garlic, 1 teaspoon of sesame oil and 1 teaspoon of the ginger.

2 Place 2 teaspoons of filling on one half of each wrapper. Moisten the edge with some water and fold over to form a crescent. Press the edges together firmly. Lay the dumplings on a lightly floured surface.

3 Cut the extra spring onions into thin strips and set aside. Heat the remaining sesame oil in a pan, add the remaining garlic and ginger and cook over medium heat for 3–4 minutes, or until the garlic is lightly golden. Add the stock, soy sauce, mirin and sugar. Bring to the boil, add the spring onion strips and simmer for 2–3 minutes.

4 Bring a large pan of water to the boil, add 3–4 dumplings at a time and cook for 5 minutes, or until just cooked. Place in bowls, ladle the stock over the dumplings and serve.

NUTRITION PER SERVE
Protein 30 g; Fat 20 g; Carbohydrate 35 g; Dietary Fibre 5 g; Cholesterol 50 mg; 1800 kJ (430 cal)

COOK'S FILE

Note: Mirin is a Japanese sweetened rice wine which is used frequently in cooking.

MEDITERRANEAN FISH SOUP

Preparation time: 25 minutes
Total cooking time: 25 minutes
Serves 6–8

1 kg white fish fillets
1/4 cup olive oil
2 large onions, chopped
1–2 cloves garlic, crushed
4 large tomatoes, peeled, seeded and chopped
2 tablespoons tomato paste
1/2 cup chopped small gherkins
1 tablespoon chopped capers

1 tablespoon pitted and chopped green olives
1 tablespoon pitted and chopped black olives
3 cups fish stock
1 cup white wine
bay leaf
salt and freshly black pepper
1/4 cup chopped fresh basil
1 cup chopped fresh parsley

1 Remove the skin and bones from the fish and chop into bite-sized pieces. Heat the oil in a large heavy-based pan and cook the onion and garlic for 8 minutes until soft.
2 Stir in the tomato and paste. Cook,

stirring, for 2–3 minutes, or until the tomato is soft. Stir in the gherkins and half the capers and olives.
3 Add the fish, stock and white wine. Add the bay leaf and season. Bring slowly to the boil, reduce the heat and simmer for 10–12 minutes, or until the fish is just cooked. Stir in the basil and parsley. Add the remaining capers and olives and serve.

NUTRITION PER SERVE (8)
Protein 20 g; Fat 11 g; Carbohydrate 7 g; Dietary Fibre 2.5 g; Cholesterol 88 mg; 1101 kJ (263 cal)

COOK'S FILE

Note: Unsuitable to freeze.

Peel the tomatoes by soaking in boiling water. Remove the seeds with a spoon.

Use salt to help you keep a firm grasp on the fish while removing the skin.

Add the fish to the pan and pour in the stock and white wine.

FRESH CLAM CHOWDER

Preparation time: 35 minutes
Total cooking time: 40 minutes
Serves 4

1½ kg fresh clams in shell
    (vongole)
1 tablespoon oil
3 rashers bacon, chopped
1 onion, chopped
1 clove garlic, crushed
4 potatoes, peeled and cubed
1¼ cups fish stock
2 cups milk
½ cup cream
¼ cup chopped fresh parsley

1 Sort through the clams and discard any which are already open. Put the remainder in a large heavy-based pan with 1 cup water and simmer, covered, over low heat for 5 minutes, or until the shells open (discard any clams which do not open during cooking). Strain the liquid and reserve. Remove the clam meat from the shells, discarding the shells.

2 Heat the oil in the clean pan and then add the bacon, onion and garlic. Cook, stirring, until the onion is soft and the bacon golden. Add the potato and stir to combine.

3 Measure the reserved clam liquid and add enough water to make it up to 1¼ cups. Add this to the pan with the stock and milk. Bring to the boil and then reduce the heat, cover and simmer for 20 minutes, or until the potato is tender.

4 Uncover and leave to simmer for a further 10 minutes, or until reduced and slightly thickened. Add the cream, clam meat, salt and pepper to taste and parsley. Heat through gently before serving but do not allow to boil or the flavour will be impaired.

NUTRITION PER SERVE
Protein 5 g; Fat 12 g; Carbohydrate 17 g; Dietary Fibre 3 g; Cholesterol 20 mg; 825 kJ (197 cal)

COOK'S FILE

Variation: Fresh clams, often available at fish markets, give the best flavour but you can use canned. Don't use the brine from the can—drain them before using and make up the liquid with fresh fish stock.

Use your fingers to remove the clam meat from the shells.

Add the potato cubes to the cooked bacon, onion and garlic.

Simmer the chowder for 20 minutes, or until the potato is tender.

Add the cream, clam meat and parsley and then heat through gently.

NORWEGIAN FISH SOUP

Preparation time: 20 minutes
Total cooking time: 25 minutes
Serve 4–6

30 g butter
2 carrots, diced
1 parsnip, peeled and diced
1 medium leek, white part only,
   sliced
1 teaspoon celery seeds
500 g skinned and boneless
   white fish fillets
2 cups milk
3/4 cup white wine
2 teaspoons cornflour
1 tablespoon milk, extra
2 egg yolks
1/2 cup sour cream
1/2 cup chopped fresh parsley

1 Heat the butter in a large heavy-based pan, add the vegetables and celery seeds and stir over medium heat for 3 minutes, without allowing the vegetables to brown. Chop the fish into bite-sized pieces and add to the vegetables in the pan.

2 Stir in the milk and white wine and bring to the boil, reduce the heat and simmer for 15 minutes. Remove from the heat.

3 Blend the cornflour and extra milk and mix together with the egg yolks and sour cream. Add to the pan, reduce the heat and stir continuously for 3–5 minutes until the soup thickens a little, but doesn't boil. Stir in the parsley and season to taste with salt and pepper.

NUTRITION PER SERVE (6)
Protein 20 g; Fat 16g; Carbohydrate 10 g; Dietary Fibre 3 g; Cholesterol 155 mg; 1201 kJ (285 cal)

COOK'S FILE

Storage time: The soup is best served immediately, but will keep, covered and refrigerated for up to a day. It is unsuitable to freeze.

Variations: Replace the wine and/or some of the milk with fish stock. Use cream instead of sour cream. For a less chunky soup, finely chop the vegetables in a food processor.

Stir the vegetables and celery seeds over medium heat.

Stir in the milk and white wine and bring to the boil.

Mix the blended cornflour and milk with the egg yolks and sour cream.

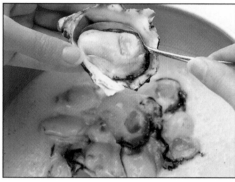

Use a sharp knife to chop the two bulbs of fennel.

Remove the oysters from the shells with a small spoon, avoiding any grit.

FENNEL AND OYSTER SOUP WITH SESAME PITTAS

Preparation time: 25 minutes
Total cooking time: 40 minutes
Serves 4–6

40 g butter
1 medium onion, chopped
2 fennel bulbs (about 600 g), chopped
2 cups fish stock
1/2 cup dry white wine
1/2 cup water
1/2 cup cream
1/2 teaspoon nutmeg
24 oysters, opened
1 teaspoon lemon juice
salt and white pepper
2 tablespoons chopped parsley, to serve

Sesame Pittas
2 small pitta breads
60 g butter, melted
2 teaspoons sesame seeds

1 Melt the butter in a large heavy-based pan and cook the onion over medium heat for 5 minutes, until soft but not browned. Add the fennel and cook, covered, for a further 5 minutes. Add the stock, wine and water, bring to the boil, reduce the heat to simmer, partially covered, for 30 minutes, until the fennel is very soft.

2 Allow to cool before processing in batches until smooth. Return to the pan and reheat gently. Stir in the cream, nutmeg and oysters (and any liquid in the shells).

3 Simmer until the oysters just begin to curl at the edges (about 2 minutes). Do not overcook or the oysters will be tough. Stir in the lemon juice and add salt and pepper to taste. Garnish with chopped parsley.

4 To make Sesame Pittas: preheat the oven to moderately hot 200°C. Split the breads in half and brush both sides with melted butter; put them on a baking tray and sprinkle with sesame seeds. Bake for about 10 minutes, until golden and crisp, and serve immediately.

The oysters are cooked when they just begin to curl at the edges.

Spread the pitta breads with butter and sprinkle with sesame seeds.

NUTRITION PER SERVE (6)
Protein 7 g; Fat 25 g; Carbohydrate 18 g; Dietary Fibre 4 g; Cholesterol 85 mg; 1325 kJ (317 cal)

Stir-ins

Quick and easy to make, these vegetarian stir-ins are a fabulous way to dress up your soups. Serve them on the table for diners to help themselves, or add a generous dollop to each bowl when you're dishing up. Either way, they turn a simple bowl of soup into something quite special.

SPICED CARROT PUREE

Melt 50 g (1³/₄ oz) butter in a medium pan. Peel and finely chop 500 g (1 lb) carrots and add to the butter, stirring until they are well coated. Add 1 teaspoon each ground cumin and coriander, ¹/₂ teaspoon ground cinnamon and a pinch each of ground cloves and nutmeg. Cook over medium heat for 3–4 minutes. Cover and cook for a further 10 minutes. Remove the lid, add ¹/₂ cup (125 ml/4 fl oz) vegetable stock and simmer for 15 minutes. Place the carrots and the liquid into a blender and blend until smooth. Season to taste with salt and freshly cracked pepper. Shown here with Lentil and spinach soup, but also delicious with French onion or most meat soups. Serves 6.

NUTRITION PER SERVE
Protein 1 g; Fat 7 g; Carbohydrate 5 g; Dietary Fibre 2 g; Cholesterol 20 mg; 350 kJ (80 cal)

ROUILLE

Cut 1 large red capsicum in half and remove the seeds and white membrane. Place skin-side-up under a preheated hot grill. Cook for 5 minutes, or until the skin has charred and blackened. Place in a plastic bag and allow to cool, then peel away the skin. Roughly chop and place in a food processor. Cut 1 potato into cubes. Cook until tender and, while still warm, place in the food processor with 2 chopped cloves garlic and 1 egg yolk. Process until smooth. With the motor running, gradually pour in ¹/₂ cup (125 ml/4 fl oz) olive oil in a thin stream, until you have a thick mixture. Shown here with Bouillabaisse, but also good with most fish soups. Serves 6.

NUTRITION PER SERVE
Protein 2 g; Fat 2 g; Carbohydrate 4 g; Dietary Fibre 1 g; Cholesterol 30 mg; 900 kJ (205 cal)

From left to right: Spiced carrot purée; Rouille; Aïoli; Rocket and sun-dried tomato pesto; Coriander pesto; Yoghurt and herb stir-in

AIOLI

Crush 6–8 cloves garlic and place in a food processor. Add 2 egg yolks and a pinch of salt and process until well combined. With the motor running, very slowly add 1 cup (250 ml/8 fl oz) olive oil, in a thin stream. Shown here with Spicy tomato and chickpea soup. Serves 6.

NUTRITION PER SERVE
Protein 1 g; Fat 10 g; Carbohydrate 0 g; Dietary Fibre 1 g; Cholesterol 30 mg; 405 kJ (100 cal)

ROCKET AND SUN-DRIED TOMATO PESTO

Add 2 cups (70 g/2¼ oz) finely shredded rocket leaves to a food processor. Add 2 crushed cloves garlic and ½ cup (50 g/1¾ oz) finely grated Parmesan. Finely chop ¼ cup (35 g/1¼ oz) sun-dried tomatoes and add to the rocket. Process until finely chopped. Add ¼ cup (60 ml/2 fl oz) olive oil and process again until well combined. Shown here with Roasted tomato soup, but good with most vegetable soups. Serves 6.

NUTRITION PER SERVE
Protein 3 g; Fat 10 g; Carbohydrate 0 g; Dietary Fibre 0 g; Cholesterol 8 mg; 515 kJ (120 cal)

CORIANDER PESTO

Place 2 cups (100 g/3½ oz) chopped coriander leaves and stems into a food processor. Finely chop 3 cloves garlic and add to the processor along with ½ cup (50 g/1¾ oz) grated Parmesan and a pinch of salt. Process until finely chopped. With the motor running, gradually add ¼ cup (60 ml/2 fl oz) olive oil, processing until all the ingredients are combined. Shown here with Spring vegetable soup, and good with vegetable broths. Serves 6.

NUTRITION PER SERVE
Protein 3 g; Fat 10 g; Carbohydrate 0 g; Dietary Fibre 0 g; Cholesterol 8 mg; 510 kJ (122 cal)

YOGHURT AND HERB STIR-IN

Combine ¾ cup (185 g/6 oz) thick natural yoghurt with 2 cloves crushed garlic, 3 tablespoons finely chopped mint and 2 tablespoons finely chopped coriander. Stir through 1 tablespoon lemon juice and season well. Add a generous spoonful to Borscht, Mulligatawny or Pumpkin soup as shown here. Serves 6.

NUTRITION PER SERVE
Protein 2 g; Fat 1 g; Carbohydrate 2 g; Dietary Fibre 0 g; Cholesterol 5 mg; 100 kJ (25 cal)

Vegetable Soups

PIE-CRUST MUSHROOM SOUP

Preparation time: 25 minutes
Total cooking time: 35 minutes
Serves 4

60 g butter
1 small onion, finely chopped
1 clove garlic, crushed
400 g field mushrooms, chopped
¼ cup plain flour
3 cups chicken stock
2 tablespoons fresh thyme leaves
2 tablespoons sherry
1 cup cream
1 sheet frozen puff pastry, thawed
1 egg, lightly beaten

1 Preheat the oven to 200°C. Melt the butter in a large pan and cook the onion and garlic until soft. Add the mushrooms and cook until soft. Add the flour and stir for 1 minute.
2 Add the stock and thyme and bring to the boil. Cover and simmer for 10 minutes. Process in batches. Return to the pan, stir in the sherry and cream and pour into ovenproof bowls.
3 Cut rounds of pastry slightly larger than the bowls and cover each bowl with pastry. Seal the edges and brush lightly with the beaten egg. Bake for 15 minutes, until golden and puffed.

NUTRITION PER SERVE
Protein 15 g; Fat 50 g; Carbohydrate 25 g; Dietary Fibre 4 g; Cholesterol 180 mg; 2517 kJ (600 cal)

Sprinkle the flour over the mushrooms in the pan.

Process the soup in batches, then return to the pan and add the sherry and cream.

Use a lid or cutter to cut pastry rounds a little larger than the bowls.

Seal the edges of the pastry and brush lightly with beaten egg.

CREAM OF TOMATO SOUP

Preparation time: 25 minutes
Total cooking time: 30 minutes
Serves 4

1.25 kg (2½ lb) fresh ripe
    tomatoes
1 tablespoon oil
1 onion, chopped
1 clove garlic, chopped
1½ cups (375 ml/12 fl oz)
    chicken stock
2 tablespoons tomato paste
1 teaspoon sugar
1 cup (250 ml/8 fl oz) cream

1 Score a cross in the base of each tomato. Cover with boiling water for 1 minute, plunge in iced water, drain and peel away the skins. Scoop out the seeds and discard, then roughly chop the flesh.

2 Heat the oil in a large pan and cook the onion for 3 minutes, or until soft. Add the garlic and cook for 1 minute longer. Add the tomato and cook for 5 minutes, stirring occasionally, until very soft. Stir in the stock, bring to the boil, reduce the heat and simmer for 10 minutes.

3 Cool slightly, then transfer to a food processor. Process in batches until smooth, and return to the pan. Add the tomato paste and sugar and

bring to the boil, stirring continuously. Reduce the heat and stir in the cream but do not allow the soup to boil. Season to taste before serving. Serve with an extra spoonful of cream and chopped parsley, if you want.

NUTRITION PER SERVE
Protein 5 g; Fat 30 g; Carbohydrate 10 g; Dietary Fibre 5 g; Cholesterol 85 mg; 1480 kJ (350 cal)

COOK'S FILE

Hint: It is best to use plump, ripe tomatoes for this recipe.
Note: If you are not using home-made stock, remember to taste the soup before seasoning. Shop-bought stock can be very salty.

Plunge the tomatoes into iced water, then peel away the skin.

Cook, stirring with a wooden spoon, until the tomato is very soft.

Add the tomato paste and sugar and bring to the boil, stirring until smooth.

FRENCH ONION SOUP

Preparation time: 15 minutes
Total cooking time: 1 hour 30 minutes
Serves 4–6

1 tablespoon olive oil
30 g (1 oz) butter
1 kg (2 lb) onions, thinly sliced
1½ tablespoons soft brown
  sugar
4 tablespoons plain flour
6 cups (1.5 litres) rich beef
  stock
½ cup (125 ml/4 fl oz) brandy
¼ cup (60 ml/2 fl oz) olive oil,
  extra
2 cloves garlic, crushed
1 French bread stick
1 cup (100 g/3½ oz) grated
  Parmesan

1 Heat the oil and butter in a large, heavy-based pan. Add the onion and stir over low heat for 1 minute. Cover and cook for a further 20 minutes, stirring occasionally. Add the sugar and ½ teaspoon of salt and increase the heat. Cook for 30 minutes, stirring frequently, or until the onion is golden brown.

2 Gradually add the flour. Cook for 3 minutes over medium heat, stirring. Remove from the heat and gradually add the combined stock and brandy.

3 Over medium heat, bring to the boil, stirring constantly, until slightly thickened. Partially cover the saucepan, lower the heat and simmer gently for 30 minutes, stirring occasionally. Season to taste.

4 Mix the extra oil and garlic. Cut the bread stick into thick slices and toast both sides under a preheated grill, until lightly browned. Brush on the oil and sprinkle with the Parmesan. Grill until melted and serve on the soup.

NUTRITION PER SERVE (6)
Protein 15 g; Fat 25 g; Carbohydrate 30 g; Dietary Fibre 4 g; Cholesterol 30 mg; 1800 kJ (430 cal)

COOK'S FILE

Note: Although it is more expensive, you can use Reggiano Parmesan for this recipe; it has an excellent creamy taste and rich, grainy texture. It is available from delicatessens.

Cook the onion, stirring frequently, until it is a rich golden brown.

Stirring with a wooden spoon, gradually add the combined stock and brandy.

Using a pastry brush, coat one side of the toast with the oil mixture.

VEGETABLE AND WATERCRESS SOUP

Preparation time: 40 minutes
Total cooking time: 1 hour
Serves 4

1 kg (2 lb) chicken bones
8 cm (3 inch) piece of ginger,
 roughly chopped
several celery leaves
2 carrots, roughly chopped
6 spring onions, roughly
 chopped
2 carrots, extra
2 sticks celery
2 leeks
200 g (6½ oz) whole baby corn
1 head broccoli
50 g (1¾ oz) baby beans or
 whole beans cut into short
 lengths
100 g (3½ oz) sugar snap peas
2–3 tablespoons soy sauce
1–2 tablespoons sesame oil
2 cups (60 g/2 oz) watercress
 sprigs, to serve

1 To make the chicken stock, place the chicken bones, ginger, celery leaves, chopped carrot, spring onion and a teaspoon of salt in a large pan. Cover with 8 cups (2 litres) of water and bring to the boil. Reduce the heat to low and simmer for 45 minutes, skimming the surface as required.
2 Cut the extra carrots and celery into matchsticks and the leeks into strips. Cut the corn in half lengthways and trim the broccoli into florets.
3 Strain the stock and discard the bones and vegetables. Strain again through a very fine sieve and bring the stock to a simmer. Add the carrot, corn and baby beans and cook for 3 minutes. Add the celery, leek, broccoli and sugar snap peas and cook for a further 3–4 minutes. Do not overcook the vegetables: they should be tender but crisp.
4 Add the soy sauce and sesame oil and season to taste with salt and pepper. Add the watercress and serve immediately with some extra sesame oil and soy sauce, if you want.

NUTRITION PER SERVE
Protein 9 g; Fat 6 g; Carbohydrate 25 g; Dietary Fibre 10 g; Cholesterol 0 mg; 800 kJ (200 cal)

Trim the coarse stems from the watercress.

Cut the carrots and celery into matchsticks, and the leeks into strips.

Using a sharp knife, cut the broccoli into small florets.

Strain the stock a second time through a fine sieve.

ROAST PUMPKIN SOUP

Preparation time: 10 minutes
Total cooking time: 1 hour 45 minutes
Serves 6

2 tablespoons olive oil
1 clove garlic, crushed
1½ teaspoons dried oregano
250 g (8 oz) Roma tomatoes,
    halved lengthways
850 g (1 lb 12 oz) butternut
    pumpkin, unpeeled, chopped
250 g (8 oz) carrots, quartered
180 g (6 oz) onions, quartered

200 g (6½ oz) sweet potato,
    chopped
1 tablespoon chopped oregano
6 cups (1.5 litres) chicken or
    vegetable stock
flaked toasted almonds and
    oregano sprigs, to garnish

1 Preheat the oven to moderately hot 190°C (375°F/Gas 5). Mix the oil, garlic, oregano and ½ teaspoon of salt. Put the tomatoes, cut-side-up, in a roasting tin with the pumpkin, carrot, onion and sweet potato. Brush with the oil mixture and bake for 1½ hours. Cool. Scrape the flesh from the

pumpkin and put in a large pan with the vegetables, oregano and stock.
2 Bring to the boil, reduce the heat and simmer for 10 minutes. Cool and purée in a blender or food processor. Reheat and season to taste. Garnish with the almonds and oregano sprigs.

NUTRITION PER SERVE
Protein 6 g; Fat 10 g; Carbohydrate 20 g; Dietary Fibre 6 g; Cholesterol 0 mg; 880 kJ (210 cal)

COOK'S FILE

Serving suggestion: This soup is delicious with a savoury bread such as the Cheese and herb pull-apart loaf.

Brush the vegetables with the oil mixture, leaving the tomatoes cut-side-up.

Scrape the flesh from the pumpkin using a teaspoon.

Purée the soup in batches in a blender or food processor.

GAZPACHO

Preparation time: 40 minutes
+ 3 hours refrigeration
Total cooking time: Nil
Serves 4–6

750 g (1½ lb) ripe tomatoes
1 Lebanese cucumber, chopped
1 green capsicum, chopped
2–3 cloves garlic, crushed
1–2 tablespoons finely
    chopped black olives
    (optional)
⅓ cup (80 ml/2¾ fl oz) red or
    white wine vinegar
¼ cup (60 ml/2 fl oz) olive oil
1 tablespoon tomato paste

Accompaniments
1 onion, finely chopped
1 red capsicum, finely chopped
2 spring onions, finely chopped
1 Lebanese cucumber, finely
    chopped
2 hard-boiled eggs, chopped
chopped mint or parsley
Garlic and herb croutons
    (see page 43)

1 Score a cross in the base of each tomato. Cover with boiling water for 1 minute, plunge into cold water, drain and peel away the skins. Chop the flesh so finely that it is almost a purée.

2 Mix together the tomato, cucumber, capsicum, garlic, olives, vinegar, oil, and tomato paste, and season to taste. Cover and refrigerate for 2–3 hours.

3 Use 2–3 cups (750 ml/24 fl oz) of chilled water to thin the soup to your taste. Serve chilled, with the chopped onion, capsicum, spring onion, cucumber, boiled egg, herbs and croutons served separately for diners to add to their own bowls.

NUTRITION PER SERVE (6)
Protein 5 g; Fat 2 g; Carbohydrate 7 g; Dietary Fibre 4 g; Cholesterol 70 mg; 310 kJ (75 cal)

Halve the cucumber lengthways, cut into strips and chop finely.

Put the tomatoes in a heatproof bowl and cover with boiling water.

Using a sharp knife, chop the tomato flesh very finely to a purée.

LENTIL AND SPINACH SOUP

Preparation time: 25 minutes
Total cooking time: 1 hour
Serves 8

½ cup (95 g/3 oz) brown lentils
2 tablespoons vegetable oil
1 leek, chopped
1 onion, chopped
1 stick celery, chopped
600 g (1¼ lb) potatoes, chopped
4 cups (1 litre) chicken or
    vegetable stock
250 g (8 oz) English spinach

1 Put the lentils in a pan. Cover with water and bring to the boil, reduce the heat and simmer for 20 minutes, or until tender; drain.

2 Heat the oil in a large pan. Cook the leek, onion and celery for 5 minutes, or until softened. Add the potato and cook, stirring frequently, for 10 minutes. Add the stock and bring to the boil. Reduce the heat and simmer, covered, for 20 minutes, or until the potato is tender.

3 Remove the stalks from the spinach, wash the leaves well, add to the soup and cook for 1–2 minutes. Purée in a food processor, return to the pan, add the lentils and reheat.

NUTRITION PER SERVE
Protein 5 g; Fat 5 g; Carbohydrate 15 g; Dietary Fibre 4 g; Cholesterol 0 mg; 505 kJ (120 cal)

Place the lentils in a pan and cover with plenty of cold water.

Cook the leek, onion and celery until soft, then add the chopped potato.

Add the cooked and drained lentils to the puréed soup in the pan.

Gazpacho (top)
with Lentil and spinach soup

WATERCRESS AND POTATO SOUP

Preparation time: 30 minutes
Total cooking time: 50 minutes
Serves 6–8

30 g (1 oz) butter
2 onions, chopped
1–2 cloves garlic, chopped
1 kg (2 lb) potatoes, chopped
    into chunks
8 cups (2 litres) chicken or
    vegetable stock
250 g (8 oz) watercress,
    trimmed
1/3 cup (80 ml/2³/4 fl oz) cream

Parmesan croutons
2 slices bread, crusts removed
1 tablespoon olive oil
1 tablespoon grated Parmesan

1 Heat the butter in a large pan. Cook the onion and garlic for 2–3 minutes, or until softened. Add the potato and stir for 1–2 minutes. Add the stock and bring to the boil. Reduce the heat and simmer for 30 minutes, or until the potato is cooked. Strain, reserving the cooking liquid.

2 Transfer the potato mixture to a food processor, pour on about half the cooking liquid and process until smooth. Return to the pan.

3 In a food processor, process the watercress and 2 cups (500 ml/16 fl oz) of the cooking liquid until smooth. Pour the watercress mixture, cream and any remaining cooking liquid into the pan and combine. Stir over low heat for 3 minutes, or until warmed through, but do not allow the soup to boil. Season to taste.

4 To make the croutons, preheat the oven to moderate 180°C (350°F/Gas 4). Cut the bread into cubes and mix with the oil and grated Parmesan. Bake for 10 minutes, or until golden. Serve the croutons on top of the soup.

NUTRITION PER SERVE (8)
Protein 6 g; Fat 10 g; Carbohydrate 20 g; Dietary Fibre 4 g; Cholesterol 25 mg; 880 kJ (210 cal)

Pour in half the cooking liquid over the potato mixture.

Process the watercress and liquid until smooth and pour into the pan.

Quickly mix the bread cubes in the oil and Parmesan until well coated.

SPRING VEGETABLE SOUP

Preparation time: 30 minutes
  + overnight soaking
Total cooking time: 1 hour 15 minutes
Serves 8

1/2 cup (105 g/3 1/2 oz) pinto
  beans
2 teaspoons olive oil
2 onions, finely chopped
2 cloves garlic, finely chopped
10 cups (2.5 litres) vegetable
  stock
2 sticks celery, finely chopped
2 carrots
2 potatoes
150 g (5 oz) green beans
2 zucchini
100 g (3 1/2 oz) shelled peas
  (see Hint)
2 tablespoons chopped flat-leaf
  parsley

1 Soak the pinto beans in plenty of cold water overnight. Drain.
2 Heat the oil in a large pan, add the onion and cook over low heat until soft and translucent. Add the garlic and cook for 1 minute further. Add the pinto beans, stock and celery and bring to the boil. Reduce the heat to low and simmer, covered, for 45 minutes, or until the beans are almost cooked.
3 Finely chop the carrots, potatoes, green beans and zucchini and add to the pan. Simmer gently for 15 minutes, or until the vegetables are almost cooked. Stir in the peas and simmer for a further 10 minutes.
4 Season well and stir through the chopped parsley.

NUTRITION PER SERVE
Protein 5 g; Fat 2 g; Carbohydrate 10 g; Dietary Fibre 5 g; Cholesterol 0 mg; 235 kJ (60 cal)

COOK'S FILE

Note: If pinto beans are hard to find, you can easily substitute them with borlotti beans or the smaller haricot beans.
Hint: If you can't find fresh peas, use frozen peas. Thaw and add during the last 5 minutes of cooking.
Serving suggestion: Shown here with Sunflower bread.

Add the drained pinto beans to the pan and stir in with a wooden spoon.

Chop all the vegetables into small, even-sized dice.

ROASTED TOMATO SOUP

Preparation time: 20 minutes
Total cooking time: 1 hour 10 minutes
Serves 4

1 kg (2 lb) ripe Roma (egg or
    plum) tomatoes
5 cloves garlic, unpeeled
5 tablespoons olive oil
1 teaspoon dried basil
3 tablespoons olive oil, extra
1 onion, finely chopped
1 red chilli, finely chopped
2 tablespoons balsamic vinegar
2 teaspoons soft brown sugar

1 tablespoon plain flour
4 cups (1 litre) vegetable stock
1/4 cup (7 g/1/4 oz) chopped flat-
    leaf parsley, to serve

1 Preheat the oven to moderately hot
200°C (400°F/Gas 6). Halve the
tomatoes and lay cut-side-up in a
baking tray with the garlic. Add the
oil, some seasoning and the basil.
Roast for 30 minutes. Take the garlic
out after 20 minutes if it is drying out.
2 Heat the extra oil in a heavy-based
pan. Add the onion and chilli and
cook, covered, for 10 minutes over
medium heat, stirring frequently.
3 Chop the tomatoes and squeeze the

garlic pulp from their skins. Add to
the pan along with the vinegar and
sugar. Cook, stirring, for 1 minute. Stir
in the flour and cook for 30 seconds.
4 Remove from the heat and add the
stock. Return to the heat and bring to
the boil, stirring occasionally. Simmer
for 5 minutes. Season to taste and add
the parsley.

NUTRITION PER SERVE
Protein 4 g; Fat 40 g; Carbohydrate 10 g;
Dietary Fibre 5 g; Cholesterol 0 mg;
1670 kJ (400 cal)

COOK'S FILE

Serving suggestion: Serve with
Rosemary bread trios.

*Sprinkle the dried basil over the halved
tomatoes and unpeeled garlic cloves.*

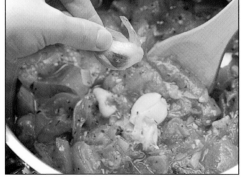

*Squeeze the garlic pulp from their skins
and add to the pan.*

*Add the chopped flat-leaf parsley to the
soup just before serving.*

MEXICAN BEAN CHOWDER

Preparation time: 20 minutes
+ overnight soaking
Total cooking time: 1 hour 10 minutes
Serves 6

¾ cup (155 g/5 oz) dried red
    kidney beans
¾ cup (165 g/5½ oz) dried
    Mexican black beans
1 tablespoon oil
1 onion, chopped
2 cloves garlic, crushed
½–1 teaspoon chilli powder
1 tablespoon ground cumin
2 teaspoons ground coriander
2 x 400 g (13 oz) cans chopped
    tomatoes
3 cups (750 ml/24 fl oz)
    vegetable stock
1 red capsicum, chopped
1 green capsicum, chopped
440 g (14 oz) can corn kernels
2 tablespoons tomato paste
grated Cheddar, to serve
sour cream, to serve

1 Soak the kidney beans and black beans in separate bowls in plenty of cold water overnight. Drain. Place in a large pan, cover with water and bring to the boil. Reduce the heat and simmer for 45 minutes, or until tender. Drain.
2 Heat the oil in a large pan, add the onion and cook over medium heat until soft. Add the garlic, chilli powder, cumin and coriander and cook for 1 minute. Stir in the tomato, stock, capsicum, corn and tomato paste. Cook, covered, for 25–30 minutes. Add the beans during the last 10 minutes of cooking. Stir occasionally.
3 Serve topped with the grated Cheddar and a spoonful of sour cream.

NUTRITION PER SERVE
Protein 20 g; Fat 7 g; Carbohydrate 40 g; Dietary Fibre 20 g; Cholesterol 3 mg; 1250 kJ (300 cal)

COOK'S FILE

Note: Mexican black beans are also known as black turtle beans and are available at good delicatessens. Do not confuse them with Chinese black beans.

Soak the red kidney beans and black beans in separate bowls overnight.

Add the tomato, stock, capsicum, corn and tomato paste.

PARSNIP AND MUSTARD SOUP

Preparation time: 25 minutes
Total cooking time: 30 minutes
Serves 4–6

30 g (1 oz) butter
1 onion, chopped
750 g (1½ lb) parsnips, chopped
4 cups (1 litre) chicken or
  vegetable stock
½ cup (125 ml/4 fl oz) milk
½ cup (125 ml/4 fl oz) cream
2–3 tablespoons wholegrain
  mustard
2 tablespoons chopped flat-leaf
  parsley, to serve

1 Melt the butter in a large pan, add the onion and cook over moderate heat, stirring occasionally, until soft but not brown.
2 Add the parsnip and stock and bring to the boil. Simmer, covered, for 25 minutes, or until the parsnip is tender. Set aside to cool slightly.
3 Blend the soup in batches, in a blender or food processor. Return to the pan, add the milk and cream and reheat gently, but do not allow the soup to boil. Stir in the wholegrain mustard and season to taste with salt and freshly ground black pepper. Serve topped with the chopped parsley.

NUTRITION PER SERVE (6)
Protein 4 g; Fat 15 g; Carbohydrate 15 g; Dietary Fibre 4 g; Cholesterol 45 mg; 850 kJ (200 cal)

COOK'S FILE

Serving suggestion: This soup is delicious with Pumpkin damper, as shown here.

Cut the peeled parsnips into strips, then chop into small pieces.

Add the parsnip and chicken stock to the pan.

Using a wooden spoon, stir in the wholegrain mustard.

GRILLED CAPSICUM SOUP WITH HERB OMELETTE

Preparation time: 20 minutes
Total cooking time: 50 minutes
Serves 4–6

1 yellow or green capsicum, quartered
4 red capsicums, quartered
1 tablespoon olive oil
1 red onion, chopped
1 clove garlic, crushed
1 potato, diced
2/3 cup (170 ml/5 1/2 fl oz) tomato juice
1 tablespoon balsamic vinegar

Herb omelette
3 eggs, lightly beaten
1 tablespoon milk
2 tablespoons chopped parsley
2 teaspoons oil
3 spring onions, finely chopped

1 Grill the capsicums skin-side-up under a hot grill until blackened. Place in a plastic bag and cool. Peel away the skin and dice the yellow and one of the red capsicums. Set aside the remaining red capsicum.

2 Heat the oil and cook the onion, stirring, over medium heat until transparent. Add the garlic and potato and cook, stirring, for 1 minute. Add the tomato juice and 3 cups (750 ml) water, bring to the boil, reduce the heat and cover. Simmer for 25 minutes, or until the potato is tender.

3 Blend the soup until smooth, in batches, with the reserved red capsicum. Return to the pan and add the diced capsicum, vinegar and seasoning. Reheat gently to serve.

4 To make the herb omelette, whisk the eggs, milk and parsley and season. Heat the oil in a frying pan. Add the spring onion and cook until just soft. Pour in the egg mixture and cook over moderate heat until set. Cool on a wire rack and cut into diamonds. Serve on top of the soup.

NUTRITION PER SERVE (6)
Protein 8 g; Fat 8 g; Carbohydrate 10 g; Dietary Fibre 3 g; Cholesterol 90 mg; 620 kJ (150 cal)

Dice the yellow capsicum and one of the red ones.

Add the reserved red capsicum to the blender or food processor.

It is best to use a non-stick frying pan, if you have one.

SPICY TOMATO AND CHICKPEA SOUP

Preparation time: 20 minutes
+ overnight soaking
Total cooking time: 1 hour 25 minutes
Serves 4

1 cup (220 g/7 oz) dried
    chickpeas
1 tablespoon oil
1 onion, finely chopped
2 cloves garlic, crushed
1/2–1 teaspoon chopped chilli
425 g (14 oz) can chopped
    tomatoes
2 cups (500 ml/8 fl oz)
    vegetable stock
2 teaspoons balsamic vinegar

1 Soak the chickpeas overnight in cold water. Drain. Cook the chickpeas in a large pan of boiling water for 1 hour, or until tender. Drain well.

2 Heat the oil in a large pan, add the onion and cook for 5 minutes, or until very soft and lightly golden. Add the garlic and chilli and cook for 1 minute, then add the tomato and stock.

3 Take 1 cup (250 ml/8 fl oz) of the soup mixture and transfer the rest to a food processor. Process until smooth, and return to the pan with the reserved soup mixture and chickpeas. Bring to the boil and simmer for 15 minutes. Stir in the vinegar and season to taste.

NUTRITION PER SERVE
Protein 10 g; Fat 8 g; Carbohydrate 25 g;
Dietary Fibre 8 g; Cholesterol 0 mg;
895 kJ (215 cal)

COOK'S FILE

Variation: If you prefer a smooth soup, process the whole amount.

Cook the chickpeas in plenty of boiling water for 1 hour, or until tender.

Add the chopped garlic and chilli (to your taste) to the onion in the pan.

Pour the reserved soup mixture back into the pan.

VICHYSSOISE

Preparation time: 10 minutes
Total cooking time: 45 minutes
Serves 4–6

80 g (2³/4 oz) butter
4 leeks, white part only, thinly
 sliced
1 white onion, thinly sliced
500 g (1 lb) potatoes, chopped
¹/4 teaspoon ground coriander
pinch of ground nutmeg
1 bay leaf
1 stick celery, quartered

3¹/2 cups (875 ml/28 fl oz)
 chicken or vegetable stock
2 teaspoons lemon juice
¹/2 cup (125 ml/4 fl oz) cream
fresh chives, snipped, to garnish

1 Melt the butter in a large pan, add the leek and onion and fry gently, stirring occasionally, for 8–10 minutes, or until the vegetables are soft but not brown.
2 Add the potato, coriander, nutmeg, bay leaf, celery, stock and lemon juice. Bring to the boil, cover and simmer for 30 minutes, or until the vegetables are tender. Remove from the heat and

allow to cool slightly. Remove the bay leaf and celery and discard.
3 Transfer to a food processor and process until smooth. Return to the pan. Whisk in the cream, then reheat gently without boiling. Serve either hot or chilled, garnished with the snipped chives.

NUTRITION PER SERVE (6)
Protein 9 g; Fat 20 g; Carbohydrate 20 g; Dietary Fibre 8 g; Cholesterol 90 mg; 1300 kJ (310 cal)

COOK'S FILE

Serving suggestion: Delicious garnished with crumbled fried bacon.

Add the chopped potato to the vegetables in the pan.

Allow the soup to cool a little before puréeing in batches until smooth.

Whisk in the cream and then reheat the soup without boiling.

ROASTED VEGETABLE SOUP

Preparation time: 30 minutes
Total cooking time: 1 hour 35 minutes
Serves 6

2 carrots, cut into large pieces
1 parsnip, cut into large pieces
500 g (1 lb) unpeeled pumpkin,
    cut into large pieces
350 g (11 oz) unpeeled sweet
    potato, cut into large pieces
1 red capsicum, cut into large
    pieces

2 onions, halved
4 cloves garlic, unpeeled
3 cups (750 ml/24 fl oz)
    vegetable stock
sour cream and thyme, to serve

1 Preheat the oven to moderate 180°C (350°F/Gas 4). Put the vegetables in a large greased baking dish and brush lightly with some olive oil.
2 Bake for 1 hour, turning often. Remove the capsicum. Bake for 30 minutes longer; cool the vegetables slightly. Remove the skin from the capsicum; place in a food processor with the carrot, parsnip and onion.

3 Scrape the pumpkin and sweet potato flesh into the processor and squeeze in the garlic pulp. Add half the stock and purée until smooth. Place in a pan with the remaining stock and heat through. Season and serve with sour cream and thyme.

NUTRITION PER SERVE
Protein 3 g; Fat 5 g; Carbohydrate 20 g; Dietary Fibre 4 g; Cholesterol 4 mg; 540 kJ (130 cal)

COOK'S FILE

Serving suggestion: For a main course soup, serve with the Savoury scroll, as shown here.

Cut the carrots, parsnip, pumpkin and sweet potato into large pieces.

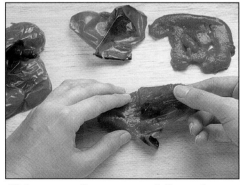

Using your fingers, carefully peel away the blackened capsicum skin.

Using a teaspoon, scrape the flesh from the sweet potato and pumpkin.

CREAM OF BROCCOLI SOUP

Preparation time: 15 minutes
Total cooking time: 25 minutes
Serves 4–6

750 g (1¹/₂ lb) broccoli
2¹/₂ cups (600 ml/20 fl oz)
   chicken stock
pinch of nutmeg
1 cup (250 ml/8 fl oz) cream

1 Cut the broccoli stems and florets into chunks. Place in a large pan with 1 cup (250 ml/8 fl oz) of the stock, cover and bring to the boil. Reduce the heat to low and simmer, covered, for 10 minutes, or until the broccoli is tender. Stir occasionally.
2 Transfer half the mixture to a food processor and process until finely chopped. Add a little of the remaining stock and blend to a purée. Return to a pan.
3 Transfer the remaining broccoli mixture and stock to the food processor and process until finely chopped. Return all the puréed soup to the pan, add the nutmeg and cream and stir over moderate heat until heated through, but do not allow the soup to boil. Before serving, season to taste with salt and freshly ground black pepper.

NUTRITION PER SERVE (6)
Protein 7 g; Fat 20 g; Carbohydrate 2 g; Dietary Fibre 5 g; Cholesterol 60 mg; 825 kJ (200 cal)

COOK'S FILE

Serving suggestion: Try with Zucchini and olive bread.
Variation: Use vegetable stock for a vegetarian meal.

Using a sharp knife, cut the broccoli stems and florets into chunks.

Process the broccoli mixture until finely chopped, then add a little stock.

Add a pinch of nutmeg and pour on the cream, stirring until heated through.

MINESTRONE PRIMAVERA

Preparation time: 15 minutes
Total cooking time: 40 minutes
Serves 4–6

1/4 cup (60 ml/2 fl oz) olive oil
45 g (1 1/2 oz) pancetta, finely
   chopped
2 onions, chopped
2 cloves garlic, thinly sliced
2 small sticks celery, sliced
8 cups (2 litres) chicken or
   vegetable stock
1/3 cup (50 g/1 3/4 oz) macaroni

2 zucchini, chopped
2 cups (150 g/5 oz) shredded
   savoy cabbage
1 1/2 cups (185 g/6 oz) green
   beans, chopped
1 cup (155 g/5 oz) frozen peas
1 cup (40 g/1 1/4 oz) shredded
   English spinach leaves
1/4 cup (15 g/1/2 oz) chopped
   basil
grated Parmesan, to serve

1 Put the oil, pancetta, onion, garlic and celery in a large pan and stir occasionally over low heat for 8 minutes, or until the vegetables are soft but not brown. Add the stock and bring to the boil. Simmer, covered, for 10 minutes.

2 Add the macaroni and boil for 12 minutes, or until almost tender. Stir in the zucchini, cabbage, beans and peas and simmer for 5 minutes. Add the spinach and basil and simmer for 2 minutes. Season to taste and serve with the grated Parmesan.

NUTRITION PER SERVE (6)
Protein 7 g; Fat 20 g; Carbohydrate 15 g; Dietary Fibre 6 g; Cholesterol 40 mg; 1030 kJ (250 cal)

COOK'S FILE

Serving suggestion: Delicious served with Savoury scroll.

Using a sharp knife, cut the pancetta into strips then chop finely.

Chop the zucchini and finely shred the savoy cabbage.

Add the shredded spinach and basil to the soup.

CREAM OF ASPARAGUS SOUP

Preparation time: 20 minutes
Total cooking time: 55 minutes
Serves 4–6

1 kg (2 lb) asparagus spears
30 g (1 oz) butter
1 onion, finely chopped
1 litre (4 cups) chicken or
    vegetable stock
1/4 cup (7 g/1/4 oz) basil leaves,
    chopped
1 teaspoon celery salt
1 cup (250 ml/8 fl oz) cream

1 Break off the woody ends from the asparagus and trim off the tips. Blanch the tips in boiling water for 1–2 minutes, refresh in cold water and set aside. Chop the remaining asparagus spears into large pieces.
2 Melt the butter in a large pan and cook the onion for 3–4 minutes over medium-low heat, or until soft and golden. Add the asparagus spears and cook for 1–2 minutes, stirring continuously.
3 Add the chicken stock, basil and celery salt. Bring to the boil, reduce the heat and simmer gently, covered, for 30 minutes.
4 Check that the asparagus is well cooked and soft. If not, simmer for a further 10 minutes. Set aside and allow to cool slightly.
5 Pour into a processor and process in batches until smooth. Then sieve into a clean pan. Return to the heat, pour in the cream and gently reheat. Do not allow the soup to boil. Season to taste with salt and white pepper.
6 Serve immediately, with the asparagus tips placed on top of the soup.

NUTRITION PER SERVE (6)
Protein 6 g; Fat 26 g; Carbohydrate 5 g; Dietary Fibre 3 g; Cholesterol 80 mg; 1130 kJ (270 cal)

COOK'S FILE

Hint: If you are not using home-made stock, always taste before adding seasoning to your soup—shop-bought stock can be very salty.
Serving suggestion: For an elegant first course, serve with warm White dinner rolls.

Break off the woody ends from the asparagus spears.

Test whether the asparagus is well cooked by piercing it with a fork.

CUBAN BLACK BEAN SOUP

Preparation time: 20 minutes
+ overnight soaking
Total cooking time: 1 hour 40 minutes
Serves 6

2 cups (440 g/14 oz) dried black
   beans (see Note)
2 tablespoons oil
1 onion, sliced
2 teaspoons ground cumin
1 teaspoon ground coriander
1/2 teaspoon chilli powder
2 cloves garlic, crushed
300 g (10 oz) bacon bones
2 tablespoons red wine vinegar

1 tablespoon soft brown sugar
3 spring onions, chopped
1 tablespoon chopped parsley
2 hard-boiled eggs, chopped

1 Soak the black beans in plenty of cold water overnight. Drain.
2 Heat the oil in a large, heavy-based pan and cook the onion over medium heat for 5 minutes, or until softened. Add the cumin, coriander, chilli powder and garlic to the pan and cook for 1 minute.
3 Add the bacon bones and 5 cups (1.2 litres) of water, stirring well. Add the beans and bring to the boil; reduce the heat and simmer, partially covered, for 1–1 1/2 hours, or until the beans are very soft.

4 Using a pair of tongs, remove the bacon bones from the pan and discard. Stir in the vinegar and sugar and season to taste. If you want a thicker soup, mash the beans slightly with a potato masher. Garnish with the spring onion, parsley and hard-boiled egg.

NUTRITION PER SERVE
Protein 20 g; Fat 9 g; Carbohydrate 30 g; Dietary Fibre 15 g; Cholesterol 70 mg; 1195 kJ (285 cal)

COOK'S FILE

Note: Black beans are also known as black turtle beans or Mexican black beans and are available at good delicatessens. They are not to be confused with Chinese black beans.

Add all the spices and crush the garlic into the pan.

The beans should be soft when crushed with a fork.

Remove the bacon bones from the pan with a pair of tongs.

BARLEY SOUP WITH GOLDEN PARSNIPS

Preparation time: 30 minutes
 + overnight soaking
Total cooking time: 2 hours 20 minutes
Serves 6

200 g (6¹/2 oz) pearl barley
1 tablespoon oil
2 onions, chopped
2 cloves garlic, finely chopped
2 carrots, chopped
2 potatoes, chopped
2 sticks celery, chopped
2 bay leaves, torn in half
8 cups (2 litres) chicken or
   vegetable stock

¹/2 cup (125 ml/4 fl oz) milk
40 g (1¹/4 oz) butter
3 parsnips, cubed
1 teaspoon soft brown sugar
chopped parsley, to serve

1 Soak the barley in water overnight. Drain. Place in a saucepan with 8 cups (2 litres) of water. Bring to the boil, reduce the heat and simmer, partially covered, for 1 hour 15 minutes, or until tender. Drain.

2 Heat the oil in a large saucepan, add the chopped onion, garlic, carrot, potato and celery and cook for 3 minutes. Stir well and cook, covered, for 15 minutes over low heat, stirring occasionally.

3 Add the barley, bay leaves, chicken stock, milk and 2 teaspoons of salt and 1 teaspoon of pepper. Bring to the boil, then reduce the heat and simmer the soup, partially covered, for 35 minutes. If it is too thick, add cold water (about 1 cup/250 ml/8 fl oz), a little at a time, until the soup reaches your preferred consistency.

4 While the soup is simmering, melt the butter in a frying pan, add the parsnip and toss in the butter. Sprinkle with the sugar and cook until golden brown and tender. Serve the parsnip on top of the soup and sprinkle with the parsley.

NUTRITION PER SERVE
Protein 7 g; Fat 10 g; Carbohydrate 40 g; Dietary Fibre 8 g; Cholesterol 20 mg; 1190 kJ (285 cal)

Using a sharp knife, chop the potatoes, carrots and celery.

Add the drained barley to the cooked vegetables and stir in.

Sprinkle the soft brown sugar over the parsnip in the frying pan.

ROASTED APPLE AND PUMPKIN SOUP

Preparation time: 20 minutes
Total cooking time: 1 hour 30 minutes
Serves 4

2 red apples, unpeeled
1/4 cup (60 ml/2 fl oz) olive oil
1 onion, finely chopped
2 teaspoons ground cumin
1/4 teaspoon chilli powder
1 kg (2 lb) butternut pumpkin,
    roughly chopped
2 potatoes, chopped
2 teaspoons plain flour
4 cups (1 litre) vegetable stock
1 1/4 cups (315 ml/10 fl oz)
    cream

1 Preheat the oven to moderately hot 200°C (400°F/Gas 6). Cut the unpeeled apples into thick wedges and cut away the core. Lay in a baking dish and pour over 1 tablespoon of the oil. Roast for 25–30 minutes, turning occasionally, until golden brown. Set aside.

2 Heat the remaining oil in a large pan, add the onion, cumin and chilli and cook for 10 minutes over low heat, or until the onion is very soft and golden. Add the pumpkin and potato and cook for 15 minutes, over medium-high heat, tossing regularly, or until slightly brown. Add the flour and cook, stirring, for 1 minute.

3 Remove from the heat and gradually pour in the stock, stirring. Return to the heat, bring to the boil, then reduce the heat and simmer, covered, for 30 minutes. Drain, reserving the vegetables and stock.

4 Set aside 8 pieces of the roasted apple. Put the rest in a food processor, with half the vegetables and 1 cup (250 ml/8 fl oz) of the reserved stock. Purée until smooth and return to the pan. Repeat with the remaining vegetables and the same amount of stock; add to the pan with any remaining stock and the cream. Reheat and season well. Serve the soup with the remaining roasted apple as a garnish.

NUTRITION PER SERVE
Protein 9 g; Fat 50 g; Carbohydrate 40 g;
Dietary Fibre 5 g; Cholesterol 105 mg;
2700 kJ (645 cal)

Using a sharp knife, seed and roughly chop the pumpkin.

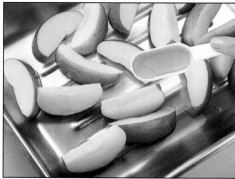

Lay the unpeeled apples in the baking tray and drizzle with the olive oil.

Cook the vegetables until they begin to brown a little.

Add some of the reserved stock to the vegetables and apple.

PASTA AND WHITE BEAN SOUP

Preparation time: 30 minutes
Total cooking time: 20 minutes
Serves 6

$^1/_3$ cup (50 g/1$^3/_4$ oz) pine nuts
1 cup (50 g/1$^3/_4$ oz) basil leaves
50 g (1$^3/_4$ oz) rocket leaves
2 cloves garlic, chopped
$^1/_3$ cup (35 g/1$^1/_4$ oz) finely
    grated Parmesan
$^1/_3$ cup (80 ml/2$^3/_4$ fl oz) olive
    oil
185 g (6 oz) spiral pasta

6 cups (1.5 litres) chicken or
    vegetable stock
2 x 300 g (10 oz) cans
    cannellini beans, drained

1 Put the pine nuts in a frying pan and dry fry them over moderate heat for 1–2 minutes, or until golden brown. Remove from the pan and allow to cool.
2 To make the pesto, mix the pine nuts, basil, rocket, garlic and Parmesan in a food processor and process until finely chopped. With the motor running, add the oil in a thin stream until well combined. Season to taste with salt and pepper. Set aside.

3 Cook the pasta until just underdone. Heat the chicken stock in a large pan until it begins to boil. Reduce the heat to simmering point. Drain the pasta and add to the stock with the cannellini beans. Reheat and serve with a spoonful of pesto.

NUTRITION PER SERVE
Protein 15 g; Fat 20 g; Carbohydrate 40 g; Dietary Fibre 4 g; Cholesterol 5 mg; 1770 kJ (425 cal)

COOK'S FILE

Note: Cannellini beans are small, white and slightly kidney-shaped and are used a lot in Italian cooking, particularly in Tuscany.

Dry fry the pine nuts until golden brown, but take care not to let them burn.

Put the pine nuts, basil, rocket, garlic and Parmesan in a food processor.

Add the drained cannellini beans to the simmering stock.

ORANGE-SCENTED, CURRIED PARSNIP SOUP

Preparation time: 25 minutes
Total cooking time: 40 minutes
Serves 6–8

50 g (1³⁄4 oz) butter
1 onion, chopped
800 g (1 lb 10 oz) parsnips, diced
2 teaspoons curry powder
¹⁄3 cup (80 ml/2³⁄4 fl oz) orange juice

¹⁄2 teaspoon grated orange rind
6 cups (1.5 litres) chicken or vegetable stock
strips of orange rind, to garnish

1 Melt the butter in a large pan. Cook the onion for 2–3 minutes, then stir in the parsnip. Cover the pan and cook over low heat, stirring occasionally, for 20 minutes, or until the parsnip has softened but not browned.
2 Add the curry powder and cook for a further 2–3 minutes. Add the orange juice and rind. Put the parsnip mixture in a blender and blend in batches until smooth. Return to the pan and pour on the stock. Bring to the boil and simmer for 15 minutes.
3 Season to taste and garnish with the orange rind. Serve with a spoonful of cream stirred through the soup.

NUTRITION PER SERVE (8)
Protein 2 g; Fat 5 g; Carbohydrate 10 g; Dietary Fibre 3 g; Cholesterol 15 mg; 445 kJ (105 cal)

COOK'S FILE

Serving suggestion: Both soups on this page are delicious served with Mini bagels, as shown.

Peel and cut the parsnips into strips then finely dice.

Peel the orange rind, remove the white pith, then cut the rind into thin strips.

Add the curry powder to the onion and parsnip and mix in well.

POTATO, PEA AND PARMESAN SOUP

Preparation time: 45 minutes
Total cooking time: 1 hour
Serves 4

750 g (1¹⁄2 lb) unshelled peas
¹⁄4 cup (60 ml/2 fl oz) olive oil
30 g (1 oz) butter
3 cloves garlic, thinly sliced
2 onions, very thinly sliced
500 g (1 lb) potatoes, chopped
2 teaspoons plain flour

2 cups (500 ml/16 fl oz) beef stock
2 teaspoons grated lemon rind
¹⁄4 cup (15 g/¹⁄2 oz) chopped flat-leaf parsley
¹⁄2 cup (125 ml/4 fl oz) cream
100 g (3¹⁄2 oz) grated Parmesan

1 Shell the peas and set aside.
2 Heat the oil and butter in a large, heavy-based pan. Add the garlic, onion and potato and cook, stirring regularly, for 15–20 minutes, or until the potato is golden. Add the flour and stir for 2 minutes. Add the stock and 3 cups (750 ml/24 fl oz) of water and bring to the boil, stirring until the mixture thickens slightly. Reduce the heat and simmer, covered, for 20 minutes.
3 Add the peas, lemon rind and parsley. Simmer for 10 minutes, or until the peas are just tender. Stir in the cream, half the Parmesan and season to taste. Serve the remaining Parmesan with the soup.

NUTRITION PER SERVE
Protein 25 g; Fat 40 g; Carbohydrate 40 g; Dietary Fibre 15 g; Cholesterol 90 mg; 2650 kJ (630 cal)

Using a sharp knife, slice the garlic and onion very thinly.

Cook the onion, garlic and potato until golden brown, stirring regularly.

Stir in the peas, grated lemon rind and chopped parsley.

Orange-scented, curried parsnip soup (top) with Potato, pea and Parmesan soup

HEARTY MINESTRONE

Preparation time: 30 minutes
Total cooking time: 1 hour 25 minutes
Serves 6–8

2 tablespoons olive oil
2 onions, chopped
2 rashers bacon, chopped
1 potato, chopped into large
   cubes
280 g (9 oz) sweet potato,
   chopped into large cubes
3 carrots, sliced
250 g (8 oz) pumpkin, cubed
400 g (13 oz) cabbage, shredded
280 g (9 oz) yellow squash,
   sliced

220 g (7 oz) green beans,
   chopped
2 x 400 g (13 oz) can chopped
   tomatoes
6 cups (1.5 litres) chicken or
   vegetable stock
1 teaspoon dried Italian herbs
1 teaspoon dried oregano
1/2 cup (80 g/2¾ oz) macaroni
300 g (10 oz) can butter beans
grated Parmesan, to serve

1 Heat the oil and cook the onion and bacon for 3–4 minutes over moderate heat, or until the onion is just brown. Reduce the heat slightly and add the potato and sweet potato. Stir and cook for 1–2 minutes. Add the carrot and pumpkin and cook for a further

1–2 minutes, stirring continuously.
2 Add the cabbage, squash, green beans, tomato, stock and herbs. Increase the heat and bring to the boil. Reduce the heat and simmer gently, covered, for 1 hour.
3 Add the macaroni and butter beans and cook for a further 10–12 minutes, or until the pasta is tender. Season to taste. Serve with the Parmesan.

NUTRITION PER SERVE (8)
Protein 9 g; Fat 6 g; Carbohydrate 30 g;
Dietary Fibre 8 g; Cholesterol 5 mg;
840 kJ (200 cal)

COOK'S FILE

Serving suggestion: This soup is traditionally served with Grissini, crisp Italian bread sticks.

Slice the squash, chop the green beans and finely shred the cabbage.

Cook the onion and bacon until the onion is just brown.

Add the macaroni to the soup and cook until tender.

Using a vegetable peeler, peel the Jerusalem artichokes, then roughly chop.

Add the onion, artichoke and potato and cook over low heat.

Add the brandy and flour and cook for 1 minute.

Once the cream is added, season to taste with salt and freshly ground black pepper.

CREAM OF JERUSALEM ARTICHOKE SOUP

Preparation time: 45 minutes
Total cooking time: 30 minutes
Serves 4

50 g (1³/4 oz) butter
2 onions, finely chopped
500 g (1 lb) Jerusalem
    artichokes, roughly chopped
2 potatoes, roughly chopped
1 tablespoon brandy
1 tablespoon plain flour
3 cups (750 ml/24 fl oz) chicken
    stock
³/4 cup (185 ml/6 fl oz) cream
chopped parsley, to serve

1 Melt the butter in a large pan over medium heat until foamy. Add the onion, artichoke and potato and cook, covered, over low heat for 10 minutes.

Uncover and cook, stirring regularly, for 8 minutes.
2 Stir in the brandy and flour, and cook for 1 minute. Gradually stir in about 2 cups (500 ml/16 fl oz) of the stock and cook, stirring continuously, until the soup boils and thickens. Simmer for a further 5 minutes. Transfer to a food processor and purée until smooth, adding more stock if needed.
3 Return to the pan, add the cream and season well with plenty of salt and freshly ground black pepper, then reheat. Sprinkle with the chopped parsley, to serve.

NUTRITION PER SERVE
Protein 7 g; Fat 30 g; Carbohydrate 20 g; Dietary Fibre 5 g; Cholesterol 100 mg; 1650 kJ (395 cal)

COOK'S FILE

Note: Jerusalem artichoke is a white-fleshed root related to the sunflower.

It is not related to the thistle-like globe artichoke, even though they share the same name and taste rather similar.

CREAM OF CELERY SOUP

Preparation time: 40 minutes
Total cooking time: 25 minutes
Serves 4

2½ cups (600 ml/20 fl oz) milk
1 onion, studded with 3 cloves
1⅔ cups (410 ml/13 fl oz)
    vegetable stock
4 celery tops and leaves
2 bay leaves, torn in half
3 stalks celery
60 g (2 oz) butter
1 onion, finely chopped
¼ cup (30 g/1 oz) plain flour
½ cup (125 ml/4 fl oz) cream

Blue cheese croutons
4 slices bread
80 g (2¾ oz) blue cheese, at
    room temperature
40 g (1¼ oz) finely grated
    mozzarella cheese

1 Put the milk, studded onion, stock, celery tops and leaves, bay leaves and ½ teaspoon each of salt and white pepper in a pan. Bring to the boil, then reduce the heat and simmer gently for 8 minutes. Allow to cool, then strain. Set aside, discarding the flavourings.
2 Cut the celery into matchsticks. Heat the butter in a large pan and, when foaming, add the onion and cook for 5 minutes, or until softened. Add the celery and cook for a further 2 minutes. Add the flour and cook for 1 minute, stirring continuously.
3 Remove from the heat and gradually stir in the stock. Return to the heat and cook, stirring, until the mixture boils and thickens. Simmer for 2 minutes. Stir in the cream and season to taste. Set aside and keep warm.
4 To make the blue cheese croutons, lightly toast the bread, then trim away the crusts. Spread the bread with the blue cheese and sprinkle with the mozzarella. Grill for 1–2 minutes, or until golden. Cut into 8 triangles and float a couple on top of the soup. Serve the rest alongside.

NUTRITION PER SERVE
Protein 15 g; Fat 40 g; Carbohydrate 30 g; Dietary Fibre 2 g; Cholesterol 125 mg; 2340 kJ (560 cal)

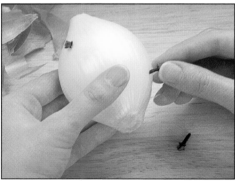
Peel the onion and stud with the cloves, pressing firmly to secure.

Using a sharp knife, cut the celery into even-sized lengths, then into matchsticks.

Remove the pan from the heat and pour in the stock.

Trim the crusts from the toasted bread and spread with the blue cheese.

92

ZUCCHINI CORN CHOWDER

Preparation time: 15 minutes
Total cooking time: 25 minutes
Serves 4

500 g (1 lb) desirée potatoes, diced
1 onion, chopped
2 sticks celery, finely chopped
4 cups (1 litre) chicken or vegetable stock
1 cup (200 g/6½ oz) corn kernels (either fresh or frozen)
4 zucchini, chopped

1 cup (125 g/4 oz) grated Cheddar
1½ cups (70 g/2¼ oz) roughly chopped rocket leaves
1 cup (250 ml/8 fl oz) milk
4 slices prosciutto, chopped, to serve

1 Place the potato, onion, celery and stock in a large pan and bring to the boil. Simmer, covered, for 20 minutes, or until the vegetables are tender. Leave to cool slightly.
2 Process the vegetables in a food processor until smooth. Return to a clean pan and bring gently to the boil.
3 Reduce the heat, add the corn and zucchini and cook until the zucchini is tender but still firm. Stir in the Cheddar, rocket leaves and milk. Reheat gently, while stirring, but do not allow the soup to boil.
4 Adjust the consistency of the soup with extra stock if necessary. Season to taste with salt and freshly ground black pepper and serve topped with the chopped prosciutto.

NUTRITION PER SERVE
Protein 20 g; Fat 15 g; Carbohydrate 30 g; Dietary Fibre 5 g; Cholesterol 55 mg; 1475 kJ (350 cal)

COOK'S FILE

Serving suggestion: This soup is delicious served with Chilli, corn and red capsicum muffins.

Using a sharp knife, roughly chop the rocket leaves.

Using a sharp knife, chop the prosciutto into small pieces.

Add the grated Cheddar and rocket leaves to the soup.

CHILLI, CHICKPEA AND CORIANDER SOUP

Preparation time: 20 minutes
Total cooking time: 25 minutes
Serves 2–4

30 g (1 oz) butter
1 onion, roughly chopped
3 cloves garlic, crushed
2 red chillies, seeded and finely
    chopped
2 teaspoons ground cumin
1 teaspoon ground turmeric
1 teaspoon ground coriander
425 g (14 oz) can chickpeas
1/3 cup (20 g/3/4 oz) chopped
    coriander leaves and stalks

1 teaspoon grated lemon rind
2 1/2 cups (600 ml/20 fl oz)
    chicken or vegetable stock

Crispy gremolata
2 slices of bread
30 g (1 oz) butter, melted
2 tablespoons chopped parsley
1 tablespoon grated lemon rind

1 Heat the butter in a large pan. Cook the onion, garlic and chilli for 2–3 minutes, or until softened but not browned. Add the spices and cook for 1–2 minutes, then add the chickpeas.
2 Process in a food processor until smooth. Add the coriander and lemon rind, pour on the stock and process until smooth. Reheat gently for 15 minutes, stirring frequently, but do not allow the soup to boil. Season to taste with salt and freshly ground black pepper.
3 To make the crispy gremolata, preheat the oven to moderate 180°C (350°F/Gas 4). Put the bread in a food processor and chop roughly. Lay the breadcrumbs on a baking tray and mix in the butter. Bake for 5 minutes, or until crisp. Mix the parsley and lemon rind together and mix with the breadcrumbs just before serving. Serve the gremolata sprinkled on top of the soup.

NUTRITION PER SERVE (4)
Protein 20 g; Fat 20 g; Carbohydrate 50 g; Dietary Fibre 15 g; Cholesterol 40 mg; 1870 kJ (450 cal)

Using a sharp knife, chop the coriander leaves and stalks.

Add the ground cumin, turmeric and coriander to the pan.

Mix through the melted butter with the breadcrumbs on the baking tray.

POTATO AND GARLIC SOUP

Preparation time: 15 minutes
Total cooking time: 1 hour 5 minutes
Serves 4–6

2 bulbs garlic
500 g (1 lb) potatoes
2 tablespoons olive oil
1 onion, finely chopped
8 cups (2 litres) chicken or
    vegetable stock
chopped chives, to serve

1 Separate the garlic bulbs into cloves and gently crush with the flat side of a knife to split the skin. Peel the cloves and cut in half. Chop the potatoes into small cubes.

2 Heat the olive oil in a large frying pan, add the onion and garlic and cook over medium-low heat for 5–10 minutes, or until the garlic is lightly golden. Add the potato and cook over low heat for 5 minutes. Add the chicken stock and simmer for 40–45 minutes, or until the garlic is very soft and the stock has reduced. Set aside to cool slightly.

3 Process the soup in batches in a food processor until smooth. Return to the pan and add ¹/₂ teaspoon of salt; taste before adding any more seasoning. Reheat gently before serving. Serve with a sprinkling of chopped chives.

NUTRITION PER SERVE (6)
Protein 3 g; Fat 7 g; Carbohydrate 15 g; Dietary Fibre 4 g; Cholesterol 0 mg; 540 kJ (130 cal)

COOK'S FILE

Note: If you don't have time to make stock, butchers or poultry shops may sell their own. Or try the carton stocks from supermarkets, which contain less salt and additives than cubes. If you are not using home-made stock, make sure you taste the soup before seasoning—some shop-bought stocks can be extremely salty. Season after cooking, as long simmering tends to concentrate the flavours of the soup.
Serving suggestion: Serve with Walnut bread, as shown.

Two bulbs may seem a lot, but once it is cooked garlic takes on a mellow flavour.

Crush each clove with the flat side of a knife to split the skin.

Simmer the stock until the garlic cloves are very soft.

POTAGE BONNE FEMME

Preparation time: 20 minutes
Total cooking time: 45 minutes
Serves 6

30 g (1 oz) butter
1 tablespoon olive oil
2 leeks, thinly sliced
500 g (1 lb) potatoes, finely
   chopped
2 carrots, finely chopped
7 cups (1.75 litres) vegetable
   stock
finely chopped flat-leaf parsley,
   to garnish

1 Melt the butter and oil in a large pan. Add the leek and cook over low heat for 5 minutes, or until softened. Add the potato and carrot and cook over medium heat for 5 minutes, stirring continuously.
2 Add the stock and slowly bring to the boil. Simmer, covered, for 25–30 minutes, or until the vegetables are tender. Allow to cool slightly.
3 Process the soup in a food processor in batches until smooth and return to the pan. Reheat gently over low heat and season well with salt and freshly cracked pepper. Serve sprinkled with chopped parsley.

NUTRITION PER SERVE
Protein 5 g; Fat 8 g; Carbohydrate 20 g; Dietary Fibre 5 g; Cholesterol 13 mg; 650 kJ (160 cal)

COOK'S FILE

Hint: If you don't have time to make your own stock, ask your butcher or poultry shop if they make their own. Alternatively, buy supermarket stock in cartons—these tend to be less salty than the cubes.

When using shop-bought stock be careful with the amount of seasoning you add, as they can be rather salty. Always taste before seasoning.
Note: Potage Bonne Femme is an old-fashioned traditional French soup. *Potage* is the French word for soup and *bonne femme* (literally, 'good wife') is the term applied to dishes that are prepared in a simple, family or rustic fashion.
Serving suggestion: This soup is delicious served with Mini wholemeal loaves.

Thinly slice the leeks and finely chop the potatoes and carrots.

Process the soup in batches in a food processor until smooth.

TORTELLINI VEGETABLE SOUP WITH PISTOU

Preparation time: 30 minutes
Total cooking time: 55 minutes
Serves 6–8

1 tablespoon olive oil
1 leek, finely chopped
1 onion, finely chopped
2 carrots, finely chopped
2 potatoes, finely chopped
2 zucchini, finely chopped
1 stick celery, finely chopped
2 tomatoes, chopped
10 cups (2.5 litres) vegetable
    stock

375 g (12 oz) tortellini pasta
2 cups (100 g/3¹/4 oz) basil
    leaves
3 cloves garlic, chopped
1 cup (100 g/3¹/4 oz) finely
    grated Parmesan
5 tablespoons olive oil, extra

1 Heat the oil in a very large pan, add the leek and onion and cook over low heat for 5 minutes, or until just soft. Add the carrot, potato, zucchini and celery and cook over medium heat for 5 minutes, stirring continuously. Add the tomato and stock and bring to the boil. Simmer, covered, over low heat for 20–30 minutes, or until the vegetables are tender.

2 Bring a large saucepan of salted water to the boil and cook the pasta for 6–8 minutes, until *al dente*. Drain, add to the soup and season well.

3 To make the pistou, place the basil in a food processor with the garlic and Parmesan. Process until chopped. With the motor running, add the extra oil. Add a spoonful to each bowl.

NUTRITION PER SERVE (8)
Protein 15 g; Fat 20 g; Carbohydrate 40 g; Dietary Fibre 6 g; Cholesterol 10 mg; 1640 kJ (390 cal)

COOK'S FILE

Serving suggestion: Serve with Olive oil and garlic griddle breads as shown.

Add the chopped tomato and stock to the softened vegetables.

Add the al dente *(semi-firm) tortellini to the soup.*

Process the basil, garlic and Parmesan until finely chopped.

PUMPKIN SOUP

Preparation time: 30 minutes
Total cooking time: 50 minutes
Serves 6–8

4–5 kg whole pumpkin,
  with 5 cm stem
30 g butter
1 onion, chopped
1 carrot, peeled and chopped
1 teaspoon ground cumin
1/2 teaspoon ground nutmeg
1 teaspoon soft brown sugar
3 cups chicken stock
salt and ground black pepper
1/2 cup cream
cream and fresh chives, to serve

1 Preheat the oven to 160°C. Use a small sharp knife to cut a circle from the top of the pumpkin. Scrape the seed material from inside the pumpkin and lid and discard. Scoop out the flesh with a spoon, leaving a thick border. Dice the flesh (you will have about 800 g) and wash and dry the inside and outside of the pumpkin.

2 Heat the butter in a large heavy-based pan. Add the onion, pumpkin flesh and carrot, cover and cook over low heat for 10 minutes, stirring occasionally. Add the cumin, nutmeg and sugar and cook for 5 minutes more.

3 Add the chicken stock and bring to the boil, reduce the heat and cover. Simmer for 30 minutes, stirring occasionally. Meanwhile, put the pumpkin shell, with its lid on, in the oven for 30 minutes to heat through.

4 Purée the soup, in batches, and return to the clean pan. Season to taste and stir in the cream. Reheat gently without boiling. Ladle into the pumpkin shell, garnish with cream and chives, replace the lid and serve.

NUTRITION PER SERVE (8)
Protein 14 g; Fat 12 g; Carbohydrate 45 g; Dietary Fibre 8 g; Cholesterol 30 mg; 1410 kJ (336 cal)

COOK'S FILE

Storage time: May be kept covered and refrigerated (not in the shell) for up to 3 days. Freeze for up to 1 month.
Variation: If you prefer, make the soup with 800 g pumpkin, peeled and cubed. Serve in soup bowls, instead of in the whole pumpkin.

Cut a circle from the top of the pumpkin using a small sharp knife.

Use paper towels to dry the pumpkin shell inside and out.

Add the cumin, nutmeg and sugar and cook for a further 5 minutes.

Carefully ladle the soup into the warmed pumpkin shell to serve.

MEXICAN CORN SOUP

Preparation time: 20 minutes
Total cooking time: 30 minutes
Serves 4–6

4 cups fresh corn kernels,
off the cob
4¹/2 cups vegetable stock
30 g butter
¹/2 cup chopped spring onions
1 teaspoon paprika

¹/2–1 teaspoon Tabasco
2 green chillies, chopped
¹/2 cup sour cream

1 Put 3 cups of the corn in a blender or food processor with the stock. Process for 30 seconds until smooth.
2 Heat the butter in a large heavy-based pan, add the spring onions and paprika and stir over medium heat for 2 minutes, or until soft.
3 Add the corn purée to the pan and bring to the boil. Reduce the heat to low and simmer for 10 minutes. Add the remaining cup of whole corn kernels and return to the boil. Reduce the heat to low and leave to simmer, uncovered, for a further 15 minutes, or until the soup is thick. Stir in the Tabasco sauce and serve topped with the chopped chillies and a dollop of sour cream.

NUTRITION PER SERVE (6)
Protein 5 g; Fat 14 g; Carbohydrate 25 g; Dietary Fibre 4 g; Cholesterol 40 mg; 995 kJ (238 cal)

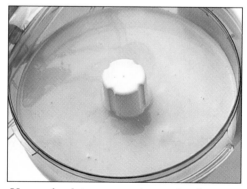

Use a food processor to purée the corn and stock until smooth.

Stir-fry the spring onions in the butter and paprika until soft.

Add the remaining cup of whole corn kernels to give texture to the soup.

CREAMY BEETROOT SOUP

Preparation time: 15 minutes
Total cooking time: 50 minutes
Serves 6

1 tablespoon oil
1 small onion, chopped
1.5 kg beetroot, peeled, chopped
5 cups vegetable stock
2 teaspoons caraway seeds
2 tablespoons horseradish
   cream
1 cup sour cream

1 Heat the oil in a large heavy-based pan. Cook the onion over medium heat for 5 minutes until soft.

2 Add the beetroot, vegetable stock and caraway seeds and bring to the boil. Reduce the heat and simmer, partially covered, for 40 minutes.

3 Cool, then process in batches until smooth. Reheat gently and stir in the horseradish and sour cream to serve.

NUTRITION PER SERVE
Protein 6 g; Fat 20 g; Carbohydrate 23 g; Dietary Fibre 8 g; Cholesterol 55 mg; 1245 kJ (295 cal)

COOK'S FILE

Storage time: Can be kept in the fridge for 1 day. Add the sour cream and horseradish when you reheat.

Peel the beetroot with a potato peeler before dicing the flesh.

Add the beetroot, stock and caraway seeds and bring to the boil.

Stir in the horseradish and sour cream after processing the soup.

WHOLE GREEN PEA SOUP

Preparation time: 20 minutes +
  1 hour soaking
Total cooking time: 40 minutes
Serves 6

1 kg green peas in the pod
4 cups vegetable stock
30 g butter
1 small onion, sliced
2 tablespoons finely chopped
    flat-leaf parsley
2 tablespoons olive oil
4 thick slices bread, cut
    into 1 cm cubes

1 Shell the peas and set them aside. Cut the stringy tops from the pods and discard them. Wash the pods thoroughly and place in a large bowl. Cover with cold water and leave to stand for 1 hour. Drain the pods well and put them in a large heavy-based pan. Add the stock and bring to the boil, reduce the heat and simmer, covered, for 15 minutes, or until the pods are tender. Leave to cool slightly.
2 Put the pods and stock in batches into a food processor or blender and process for 30 seconds until smooth. Strain the purée, discarding the pods.
3 Melt the butter in a pan, add the onion and cook over medium heat until soft. Add the peas, parsley and 1 cup of water, bring to the boil, reduce the heat to low and cook, covered, for 15 minutes or until tender.
4 Heat the oil in a frying pan, add the bread cubes and cook until lightly brown. Remove them from the pan and leave to drain on paper towels.
5 Add the purée of pea pods to the simmering peas and stir through. Bring to the boil, reduce the heat and simmer for 5 minutes to heat through. Season and serve with the croutons.

NUTRITION PER SERVE
Protein 12 g; Fat 12 g; Carbohydrate 23 g; Dietary Fibre 10 g; Cholesterol 23 mg; 1019 kJ (243 cal)

COOK'S FILE

Variation: Add 1/2 cup of cream at the end of cooking and heat through for a delicious creamy pea soup.
Hint: If the pea pods seem quite tough remove the tails as well as tops.

Shell the peas and set them aside but keep the pods.

Simmer the pods in stock for 15 minutes until they are tender.

Fry the bread cubes in hot oil until lightly brown and then drain on paper towels.

Add the strained purée of pea pods to the simmering peas.

CHEESE SOUP

Preparation time: 20 minutes
Total cooking time: 15 minutes
Serves 4–6

75 g butter
3 spring onions, finely chopped
1/2 cup plain flour
3 1/2 cups chicken stock
1 cup milk

100 g pumpkin, finely grated
150 g grated cheddar cheese
crusty bread rolls, to serve

1 Melt the butter in a heavy-based pan and cook the spring onion for 3 minutes, until soft. Add the flour and stir for 2 minutes until smooth. Add the combined stock and milk gradually, stirring until smooth.
2 Add the pumpkin and bring to the boil, then reduce the heat and simmer

for 10 minutes. Add the cheese to the pan and stir until melted and smooth.
3 Cut the tops from the bread rolls and hollow out the centres. Heat in a preheated 180°C oven for a few minutes until warm, then use as soup bowls. After drinking the soup, tear the rolls apart to eat.

NUTRITION PER SERVE (6)
Protein 11 g; Fat 20 g; Carbohydrate 20 g;
Dietary Fibre 1 g; Cholesterol 63 mg;
1270 kJ (305 cal)

Peel the pumpkin and finely grate it using the coarse side of a grater.

Add the stock and milk gradually and stir continuously to prevent lumps forming.

Add the grated cheese to the pan and stir until melted and smooth.

HOMESTYLE VEGETABLE SOUP

Preparation time: 25 minutes +
   overnight soaking
Total cooking time: 55 minutes
Serves 6

1 cup dried soup mix
2 tablespoons oil
1 large onion, finely chopped
1 green capsicum, chopped
2 zucchini, sliced
2 sticks celery, sliced

125 g button mushrooms, sliced
2 carrots, sliced
1 large potato, peeled, chopped
500 g pumpkin, peeled, chopped
8 cups vegetable stock

1 Soak the soup mix in water for 8 hours, then drain. Heat the oil in a large heavy-based pan and cook the onion for 5 minutes, until soft. Add the capsicum, zucchini, celery and mushrooms and cook for 5 minutes.
2 Add the sliced carrot, potato and pumpkin and stir to combine. Pour in the stock and add the soup mix; bring

to the boil, then reduce the heat.
3 Partially cover the pan and simmer for 45 minutes, until the vegetables and soup mix are very soft. For a thinner soup add a little water.

NUTRITION PER SERVE
Protein 5 g; Fat 7 g; Carbohydrate 15 g; Dietary Fibre 5 g; Cholesterol 0.5 mg; 595 kJ (140 cal)

COOK'S FILE

Storage time: Keep for 2 days in the refrigerator or freeze for 1 month.
Note: Soup mix consists of dried barley, lentils and split peas.

Cover the soup mix with water and leave to soak and rehydrate.

Pour the stock into the pan over the chopped vegetables.

Partially cover the pan and simmer until the vegetables are very soft.

SPINACH AND POTATO SOUP

Preparation time: 20 minutes
Total cooking time: 45 minutes
Serves 6

30 g butter
1 large leek, sliced
2 cloves garlic, crushed
1 bunch English spinach
4 potatoes, peeled, chopped
4 cups vegetable stock
1/2 cup sour cream

1 Melt the butter in a large heavy-based pan. Add the leek and cook over medium heat for 10 minutes, stirring occasionally, until very soft. Add the crushed garlic and cook for a further minute.
2 Wash the spinach very thoroughly to avoid any grittiness; discard the stalks and shred the leaves. Add to the pan with the potato and stock and bring to the boil. Reduce the heat and leave to simmer, partially covered, for about 30 minutes, until the potatoes are very soft.
3 Allow to cool a little for ease of handling, before processing in batches until smooth. Return to the pan and reheat gently without allowing to boil. Stir in the sour cream and add salt and pepper to taste.

NUTRITION PER SERVE
Protein 4 g; Fat 13 g; Carbohydrate 15 g; Dietary Fibre 2.5 g; Cholesterol 40 mg; 780 kJ (185 cal)

COOK'S FILE

Storage time: If necessary, soup can be refrigerated for 1 day.
Note: If you can't find English spinach, use silverbeet instead.

Cook the leek over medium heat until it is very soft.

Discard the stalks of the spinach and chop the leaves into shreds.

Partially cover with a loose-fitting lid and simmer until the potatoes are soft.

CREAM OF CAULIFLOWER SOUP

Preparation time: 20 minutes
Total cooking time: 15–20 minutes
Serves 4–6

750 g cauliflower
1 tablespoon oil
3 cups chicken stock
1 cup cream
1/4 teaspoon ground nutmeg
salt and ground black pepper, to taste

1 Cut the cauliflower into small even-sized florets. Heat the oil in a large heavy-based pan and stir-fry the cauliflower for 3 minutes, or until it is just starting to soften.
2 Add the stock to the pan, cover and simmer for 10–15 minutes until the cauliflower is tender.
3 Stir in the cream and set the soup aside to cool a little. Use a food processor or blender to process in batches until smooth. Return to the pan and add the nutmeg, salt and pepper to taste. Heat through gently and serve immediately.

NUTRITION PER SERVE (6)
Protein 4 g; Fat 21 g; Carbohydrate 4 g; Dietary Fibre 2 g; Cholesterol 55 mg; 915 kJ (220 cal)

COOK'S FILE

Note: Choose very fresh cauliflower with a firm head and no brown or black spots to make this delicately flavoured soup.
Variation: For an even richer soup, add 1 cup grated Cheddar cheese with the nutmeg and seasonings. Garnish with tiny steamed cauliflower florets, or a sprig of fresh chervil.

Use a sharp knife to cut the cauliflower into small, even-sized florets.

Stir-fry the cauliflower for 3 minutes until it is starting to soften.

Once the cauliflower is tender, stir in the cream and then process.

Spinach and Potato Soup (top) and Cream of Cauliflower Soup

GARLIC SOUP

Preparation time: 20 minutes
Total cooking time: 25 minutes
Serves 4

1 whole bulb garlic
  (about 20 cloves)
2 large sprigs thyme
4 cups chicken stock
1/3 cup cream
salt and white pepper
4 thick slices white bread
fresh thyme, to garnish

1 Crush each clove of garlic with the side of a knife. Discard the skin and place the garlic in a large pan with the thyme, stock and 1 cup water. Bring to the boil and then reduce the heat and simmer gently for 20 minutes, uncovered.
2 Strain the soup through a fine sieve into a clean pan. Add the cream and reheat gently, without allowing to boil. Season to taste.
3 Trim and discard the crusts from the bread and cut the bread into cubes about 3 cm square. Spread these out on a flat oven tray and cook in a pre-heated 180°C oven for 5–10 minutes, until lightly golden. Put the bread into 4 serving bowls. Pour the soup over the bread, garnish with extra thyme and serve immediately.

NUTRITION PER SERVE
Protein 4 g; Fat 10 g; Carbohydrate 15 g; Dietary Fibre 3 g; Cholesterol 28 mg; 705 kJ (170 cal)

COOK'S FILE

Storage time: Best served same day. The bread cubes may be cooked up to 4 hours in advance and kept in an airtight container until required.

Bruise the cloves of garlic with the side of a knife and then discard the skin.

Strain the soup through a fine sieve into a clean pan.

Bake the bread in the oven until toasted and lightly golden.

AUTUMN GARDEN SOUP

Preparation time: 35 minutes
Total cooking time: 55 minutes
Serves 6

30 g butter
1 large leek, sliced
1 clove garlic, crushed
1 teaspoon grated ginger
2 parsnips, peeled and chopped
1 medium celeriac,
    peeled and chopped

2 large carrots, chopped
3 potatoes, peeled and chopped
2 turnips, peeled and chopped
5 cups vegetable stock
2 tablespoons chopped chives

1 Melt the butter in a large heavy-based pan and add the leek. Cook over low heat for about 15 minutes until very soft and lightly golden.
2 Add the garlic and ginger and cook, stirring, for 1 minute further. Add the vegetables and stock to the pan and bring to the boil.

3 Reduce heat to simmer, partially covered, for about 40 minutes until very soft. Stir in the chives and serve.

NUTRITION PER SERVE
Protein 4 g; Fat 5 g; Carbohydrate 18 g; Dietary Fibre 6 g; Cholesterol 13 mg; 535 kJ (128 cal)

COOK'S FILE

Storage time: The soup will keep for up to 2 days in the refrigerator.
Hint: The soup becomes very thick on standing and may be thinned down with extra stock or water.

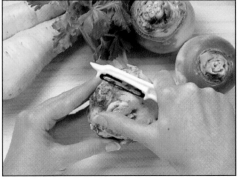

Peel away the outer rough surface of the celeriac with a potato peeler.

Cook the leek until soft and golden and then add the garlic and ginger.

Simmer for about 40 minutes, until the vegetables are very soft.

CURRIED SWEET POTATO SOUP

Preparation time: 20 minutes
Total cooking time: 40 minutes
Serves 6

1 tablespoon oil
1 large onion, chopped
2 cloves garlic, crushed
3 teaspoons curry powder
1.25 kg orange sweet potato, peeled and cubed
4 cups chicken stock
1 large apple, peeled, cored and grated
1/2 cup coconut cream

1 Heat the oil in a large heavy-based pan and cook the onion over medium heat for 10 minutes, stirring occasionally, until very soft. Add the garlic and curry powder and cook for a minute further.

2 Add the sweet potato, stock and apple and stir to combine. Bring to the boil, reduce the heat and simmer, partially covered, for 30 minutes, until the sweet potato is very soft.

3 Allow the soup to cool a little before processing in batches until smooth. Return to the pan, stir in the coconut cream and reheat gently without boiling. Delicious served with warmed pitta bread.

NUTRITION PER SERVE
Protein 5 g; Fat 8 g; Carbohydrate 35 g; Dietary Fibre 5.5 g; Cholesterol 0 mg; 975 kJ (233 cal)

COOK'S FILE

Storage time: Can be kept in the fridge for 1 day without the coconut cream: add this when you reheat.

Add the garlic and curry powder to the softened onion.

Stir in the stock with the cubed sweet potato and grated apple.

Once the soup has been processed stir in the coconut cream.

STILTON AND APPLE SOUP

Preparation time: 20 minutes
Total cooking time: 30 minutes
Serves 8

40 g butter
2 tablespoons plain flour
3 cups chicken or vegetable
stock

4 red apples
2 cups milk
250 g stilton cheese
2 tablespoons chopped chives

1 Melt the butter in a large heavy-based pan. Sprinkle with the flour and stir over low heat for 2 minutes, or until lightly golden. Gradually add the stock, stirring until smooth.

2 Peel, core and slice the apples and add to the pan. Cook, covered, over medium heat for 20 minutes, or until tender. Cool, then purée in a processor in batches until smooth.

3 Return the soup to the pan, add the milk and reheat, stirring. Simmer gently and add the crumbled stilton and chives. Stir well until the soup is smooth and serve immediately.

NUTRITION PER SERVE
Protein 9 g; Fat 17 g; Carbohydrate 15 g; Dietary Fibre 2 g; Cholesterol 50 mg; 1020 kJ (245 cal)

Add the stock gradually, stirring all the time to prevent lumps forming.

To test if the apples are tender insert the tip of a sharp knife.

Add the crumbled stilton while the soup simmers and stir until smooth.

Meat & Poultry Stews

NAVARIN OF LAMB

Preparation time: 25 minutes
Total cooking time: 1 hour 35 minutes
Serves 4

8 lamb noisettes
plain flour, seasoned
2 tablespoons oil
2 sticks celery, sliced
12 baby carrots, peeled
12 new potatoes, unpeeled
6 sprigs of thyme
1/4 cup (15 g/1/2 oz) parsley
2 onions, chopped
2 cloves garlic, crushed
1/3 cup (40 g/11/4 oz) plain flour
21/2 cups (625 ml/21 fl oz)
    chicken stock
1 cup (250 ml/8 fl oz) red wine
1/4 cup (60 g/2 oz) tomato paste

1 Toss the lamb in the seasoned flour, shaking off the excess. Preheat the oven to moderate 180°C (350°F/Gas 4).
2 Heat the oil in a heavy-based pan. In batches, brown the lamb well on both sides over medium-high heat.

Drain well on paper towels, then transfer to a greased, 3 litre ovenproof casserole dish. Top with the celery, carrots, potatoes, thyme and parsley.
3 Cook the onion and garlic in the same heavy-based pan, stirring over medium heat for about 5–10 minutes, or until the onion is soft.
4 Add the flour and stir for 1 minute, or until the onion is coated. Add the remaining ingredients and stir until the sauce boils and thickens. Pour over the lamb and vegetables. Bake, covered, for 11/4 hours, or until the lamb is tender. Remove the string from the lamb to serve.

NUTRITION PER SERVE
Protein 40 g; Fat 60 g; Carbohydrate 60 g; Dietary Fibre 10 g; Cholesterol 120 mg; 4050 kJ (970 cal)

COOK'S FILE

Notes: A noisette is a round slice of meat, cut from a boned loin and tied with string to hold its shape. For this recipe you could also use a boned leg of lamb, cut into 3 cm (11/4 inch) cubes.
Storage time: Cover and refrigerate for 2 days. Reheat gently to serve.

Add the lightly floured lamb to the hot oil and brown well all over.

Add the stock, wine and tomato paste to the softened onion mixture.

SPICED PORK WITH BUTTER BEANS

Preparation time: 25 minutes +
  30 minutes soaking
Total cooking time: 1 hour 50 minutes
Serves 4–6

200 g (6¹/₂ oz) dried butter or
    lima beans
1 large dried chilli
2 tablespoons oil
750 g (1¹/₂ lb) pork neck, cut
    into bite-sized pieces
2 teaspoons ground cumin
1 teaspoon ground coriander
2 onions, chopped
2 large potatoes, chopped
200 g (6¹/₂ oz) butternut pumpkin,
    peeled and cut into bite-sized
    pieces
1 large red apple, grated
3 cups (750 ml/24 fl oz) chicken
    stock
¹/₂ cup (125 ml/4 fl oz) cream

1 Soak the beans in boiling water for 30 minutes. In a separate bowl, soak the chilli in boiling water for 20 minutes. Drain the beans well and set aside. Chop the chilli and set aside.
2 Heat the oil in a large, heavy-based saucepan. Brown the meat in batches over medium-high heat. Remove from the pan with any juices and set aside.
3 Cook the spices, chopped chilli and onion in the pan for 5 minutes over medium heat, stirring often. Return the meat and any juices to the pan. Add the potato, pumpkin, apple and stock and season well with salt and freshly ground pepper. Cover and simmer over very low heat for 1 hour. Add the drained beans and simmer for 25 minutes, or until tender.

4 Stir through the cream and simmer, uncovered, for 10 minutes, or until the sauce is thick, stirring occasionally.

NUTRITION PER SERVE (6)
Protein 35 g; Fat 17 g; Carbohydrate 18 g; Dietary Fibre 4 g; Cholesterol 100 mg; 1520 kJ (365 cal)

COOK'S FILE

Notes: Pork neck, or pork scotch fillet, is a succulent cut, perfect for stews.
● During cooking, the vegetables will dissolve to thicken the stew. If you prefer to keep them chunky, add them 15 minutes after adding the stock.

Using separate bowls, cover the dried beans and dried chilli with boiling water.

Cook the spices, chopped chilli and onions over medium heat for about 5 minutes.

Add the drained beans to the casserole mixture. Simmer until tender.

In a bowl, combine the leeks, shallots, garlic, parsley, mint and zucchini.

Brush the veal with browned butter, then overlap a layer of veal over the vegetables.

Cut the bacon in half crossways and arrange over the top layer of vegetables.

Evenly pour the cream in around the edge of the dish.

SPRING VEAL WITH BACON AND ZUCCHINI

Preparation time: 20 minutes
Total cooking time: 1 hour 50 minutes
Serves 4–6

3 medium leeks, thinly sliced
6 French shallots, chopped
2 cloves garlic, crushed
2 tablespoons chopped parsley
2 tablespoons chopped mint
200 g (6½ oz) small young
    zucchini, thickly sliced
85 g (3 oz) butter
1 kg (2 lb) thin leg veal slices
4 rashers lean bacon
⅓ cup (80 ml/2½ fl oz) cream
4 baby zucchini, with flowers

1 Combine the leeks, shallots, garlic, parsley, mint and sliced zucchini. Spread a thin layer in a deep, oiled ovenproof dish; season well. Preheat the oven to warm 170°C (325°F/Gas 3).
2 Gently melt the butter in a pan until golden brown with a nutty aroma. Remove from the heat.
3 Cut the veal into 9 cm (3½ inch) pieces, brush with the browned butter and season well. Overlap a veal layer over the vegetables. Repeat the layers, finishing with a layer of vegetables.
4 Remove the rind from the bacon. Cut the bacon in half crossways and arrange over the vegetables. Cover and bake for 40 minutes. Pour the cream in around the edge, then bake, partially covered, for 40 minutes more.
5 Arrange the baby zucchini over the bacon rashers. Cover and bake for 15–20 minutes: the vegetables and veal will shrink in from the sides of the dish to form a mould. If the sauce is thin, simmer in a pan until thick. Cut the mould into portions and drizzle with the sauce to serve.

NUTRITION PER SERVE (6)
Protein 50 g; Fat 20 g; Carbohydrate 3 g; Dietary Fibre 3 g; Cholesterol 200 mg; 1640 kJ (390 cal)

BOSTON BAKED BEANS

Preparation time: 25 minutes +
6–8 hours soaking
Total cooking time: 1 hour 35 minutes
Serves 4–6

1³/4 cups (350 g/11 oz) dried
  cannellini beans
1 whole ham hock
2 onions, chopped
2 tablespoons tomato paste
1 tablespoon Worcestershire
  sauce
1 tablespoon molasses
1 teaspoon French mustard
¹/4 cup (45 g/1¹/2 oz) brown sugar
¹/2 cup (125 ml/4 fl oz) tomato
  juice

1 Cover the beans with cold water and soak for 6–8 hours, or overnight.
2 Drain the beans, rinse them well and place in a large pan. Add the ham hock and cover with cold water. Bring to the boil, then reduce the heat and simmer, covered, for 25 minutes, or until the beans are tender. Preheat the oven to warm 160°C (315°F/Gas 2–3).
3 Remove the ham hock from the pan and set aside to cool. Drain the beans, reserving 1 cup (250 ml/8 fl oz) of the cooking liquid. Trim the ham of all skin, fat and sinew, then roughly chop the meat and discard the bone.
4 Transfer the meat and beans to a 2 litre casserole dish. Add the reserved liquid and all remaining ingredients. Mix gently, then cover and bake for 1 hour. Serve with hot, buttered toast.

NUTRITION PER SERVE (6)
Protein 28 g; Fat 5 g; Carbohydrate 30 g; Dietary Fibre 2 g; Cholesterol 60 mg; 1090 kJ (260 cal)

COOK'S FILE

Notes: Any type of dried bean can be used in this recipe.
● To quick-soak beans, place them in a pan, add hot water to cover, bring slowly to the boil, then remove from the heat. Leave to soak for 1 hour before draining and using.
● Cooked beans can be frozen in 1 cup quantities and thawed as required.

Place the drained beans in a large pan. Add the ham hock and cover with cold water.

Trim the ham of all fat, skin and sinew, then roughly chop the meat.

Add the reserved liquid and remaining ingredients to the meat and beans.

SPICY BEEF, POTATO AND CAPSICUM STEW

Preparation time: 35 minutes
Total cooking time: 2 hours 20 minutes
Serves 4–6

300 g (10 oz) French shallots
2 tablespoons olive oil
1 kg (2 lb) gravy beef, cut into
    4 cm (1¹⁄₄ inch) cubes
4 cloves garlic, crushed
3 teaspoons paprika
1 teaspoon fennel seeds
¹⁄₂ teaspoon ground cumin
1 tablespoon plain flour
¹⁄₂ cup (125 ml/4 fl oz) red wine
2 tablespoons brandy

¹⁄₂ teaspoon dried thyme
¹⁄₂ teaspoon dried oregano
1 bay leaf
1¹⁄₂ cups (375 ml/12 fl oz) beef
    stock
1 tablespoon honey
400 g (13 oz) potatoes, cut into
    large chunks
2 red capsicums, chopped
¹⁄₂ cup (125 g/4 oz) sour cream
chopped chives, for serving

1 Preheat the oven to moderate 180°C (350°F/Gas 4). Place the shallots in a bowl, cover with boiling water and leave for 30 seconds. Drain and peel.
2 Heat the oil in a large, heavy-based pan, then brown the meat in batches over medium-high heat and transfer to a large casserole dish.

3 Add the shallots to the pan and cook over medium heat until soft and golden. Add the garlic, paprika, fennel seeds and cumin; cook until fragrant.
4 Add the flour, cook for 30 seconds, then remove from the heat. Stir in the red wine and brandy. Return to the heat and add the thyme, oregano, bay leaf and stock. Stir until the mixture bubbles, then add to the meat.
5 Cover and bake for 1¹⁄₂ hours, then add the honey, potato and capsicum. Cook, uncovered, for 30 minutes, or until the potato is tender. Season to taste. Serve with a dollop of sour cream and a sprinkling of chives.

NUTRITION PER SERVE (6)
Protein 40 g; Fat 20 g; Carbohydrate 30 g; Dietary Fibre 3 g; Cholesterol 140 mg; 1790 kJ (430 cal)

Remove the skin from the blanched and drained shallots.

Brown the meat in batches in the hot oil over medium-high heat.

Add the red wine and brandy to the spice mixture and stir well.

COUNTRY-STYLE CHICKEN WITH BABY VEGETABLES

Preparation time: 45 minutes
Total cooking time: 2 hours
Serves 4

1.5 kg (3 lb) chicken pieces
  (about 8 portions)
60 g (2 oz) clarified butter
12 baby pickling onions
1 cup (250 ml/8 fl oz) dry white
  wine
1 cup (250 ml/8 fl oz) chicken
  stock
1 cup (250 ml/8 fl oz) cream
12 baby carrots
16 snowpeas
16 asparagus spears
12 button mushrooms
1 tablespoon chopped chives

1 Season the chicken portions with a little salt and pepper. Heat half the butter in a frying pan, then brown the chicken in batches for 2–3 minutes on each side to seal the flavours. Place in a casserole dish and add the onions. Preheat the oven to moderately hot 200°C (400°F/Gas 6).

2 Pour the wine into the frying pan and stir over medium heat, scraping down the side and base of the pan. Add the stock and whisk in the cream. Bring to the boil, then reduce the heat and simmer for 20 minutes. Pour the sauce over the chicken; cover and bake for 1 hour 10 minutes.

3 Meanwhile, bring a pan of salted water to the boil. In separate batches, boil or steam the carrots, snowpeas and asparagus until just cooked, but still slightly crunchy. Plunge in iced water, then drain and set aside.

4 Heat the remaining butter in a frying pan. Sauté the mushrooms for 2–3 minutes, stirring constantly.

5 Place the mushrooms on top of the stew with the blanched vegetables and cook for another 20 minutes, or until the chicken is tender. Skim off any fat, stir carefully to mix all the vegetables through and sprinkle with the chives to serve.

NUTRITION PER SERVE
Protein 95 g; Fat 50 g; Carbohydrate 15 g; Dietary Fibre 4 g; Cholesterol 350 mg; 4040 kJ (965 cal)

Lightly brown the seasoned chicken in half the melted butter.

Plunge the blanched vegetables into a bowl of iced water to stop them cooking.

Place the drained blanched vegetables on top of the stew and cook for 20 minutes.

GINGERED DUCK CURRY

Preparation time: 30 minutes +
  30 minutes refrigeration + soaking
Total cooking time: 1 hour 30 minutes
Serves 4

1.8 kg (3 lb 10 oz) duck
1 clove garlic, crushed
1 teaspoon grated fresh ginger
1 tablespoon dark soy sauce
1/2 teaspoon sesame oil
8 dried Chinese mushrooms
5 cm (2 inch) piece fresh ginger,
  peeled and thinly sliced
2 tablespoons yellow curry paste
2 tablespoons chopped lemon
  grass, white part only

400 ml (13 fl oz) can coconut milk
4 Kaffir lime leaves, shredded
100 g (3½ oz) Thai pea eggplants
2 teaspoons soft brown sugar
2 teaspoons fish sauce
1 tablespoon lime juice

1 Cut the duck in half by cutting down
both sides of the backbone, through
the breastbone. Discard the backbone.
Cut each duck half into 4 portions,
removing any fat. Rub the duck with
the combined garlic, ginger, soy sauce
and oil. Refrigerate for 30 minutes.
2 Soak the mushrooms in boiling
water for 20 minutes. Drain, remove
the stalks and cut in half.
3 Heat a lightly oiled pan. Brown the
duck over medium heat. Leaving only

1 tablespoon of fat in the pan, stir-fry
the ginger, curry paste and lemon grass
for 3 minutes. Stir in the coconut milk,
lime leaves and 1/2 cup (125 ml/4 fl oz)
water. Add the duck; cover and simmer
gently for 45 minutes. Skim well.
4 Remove the eggplant stems; add the
eggplants to the pan with the sugar,
fish sauce and mushrooms. Simmer,
partly covered, for 30 minutes, or until
tender. Stir in lime juice to taste.

NUTRITION PER SERVE (6)
Protein 50 g; Fat 40 g; Carbohydrate 6 g;
Dietary Fibre 1 g; Cholesterol 300 mg;
2330 kJ (560 cal).

COOK'S FILE

Note: To reduce the fat in this dish, use
light coconut milk and skin the duck.

*Cut the duck down the middle. Cut the legs
and breasts in half to give 8 portions.*

*Stir the coconut milk, water and lime
leaves into the stir-fried spice mixture.*

*Remove the stems from the pea eggplants
and add the eggplants to the pan.*

TAGINE OF LAMB WITH QUINCE AND LEMON

Preparation time: 25 minutes
Total cooking time: 2 hours 10 minutes
Serves 4

1.5 kg (3 lb) boned shoulder of
  lamb, cut into 12 even pieces
1 onion, finely chopped
2 cloves garlic, crushed
1 cinnamon stick
1 teaspoon ground ginger
1/2 teaspoon saffron threads
1 large quince, peeled, seeded
  and cut into 12 pieces
1/4 cup (60 ml/2 fl oz) honey

1 teaspoon ground cinnamon
1/2 preserved lemon
chopped parsley, for serving

1 Trim the lamb of excess fat and place in a large pan. Add the onion, garlic, cinnamon stick, ginger and saffron and enough cold water to cover. Slowly bring to the boil, stirring occasionally. Reduce the heat, cover and simmer for 45 minutes. Transfer the meat to a large casserole dish and set aside.

2 Add the quince, honey and ground cinnamon to the cooking liquid and simmer for 15 minutes, or until the quince is tender. Discard the cinnamon stick; remove the quince and add to the meat, reserving the liquid.

3 Preheat an oven to moderate 180°C (350°F/Gas 4). Boil the cooking liquid for 30 minutes, or until reduced by half, then pour over the meat and quince. Remove and discard the flesh from the lemon. Slice the rind thinly, then add to the meat. Cover and bake for 40 minutes, or until the meat is tender. Sprinkle with parsley to serve.

NUTRITION PER SERVE
Protein 80 g; Fat 15 g; Carbohydrate 20 g; Dietary Fibre 3 g; Cholesterol 250 mg; 2160 kJ (515 cal)

COOK'S FILE

Hint: As you work, place the peeled quince in water with a little lemon juice to prevent discolouring.

Add the onion, garlic, cinnamon stick, ginger, saffron and cold water to the lamb.

Add the quince, honey and ground cinnamon to the cooking liquid.

Remove and discard the flesh from the preserved lemon and slice the rind thinly.

VEAL, LEMON AND CAPER STEW

Preparation time: 30 minutes
Total cooking time: about 2 hours
Serves 4–6

1 tablespoon olive oil
50 g (1³/4 oz) butter
1 kg (2 lb) stewing veal, cut into
    4 cm (1¹/4 inch) chunks
300 g (10 oz) French shallots
3 leeks, cut into large chunks
2 cloves garlic, crushed
1 tablespoon plain flour
2 cups (500 ml/16 fl oz) chicken
    stock
1 teaspoon grated lemon rind
¹/3 cup (80 ml/2³/4 fl oz) lemon
    juice
2 bay leaves
2 tablespoons capers, drained
    and well rinsed
chopped parsley, for serving
caper berries, to garnish

1 Preheat the oven to moderate 180°C (350°F/Gas 4). Heat the oil and half the butter in a large, heavy-based pan. Brown the veal in batches over medium-high heat and transfer to a large casserole dish.
2 Blanch the shallots in boiling water for 30 seconds, then peel and add to the pan with the leeks. Gently cook for 5 minutes, or until soft and golden. Add the garlic, cook for 1 minute, then transfer to the casserole dish.
3 Melt the remaining butter in the pan, add the flour and cook for 30 seconds. Remove from the heat, add the stock and stir until well combined. Return to the heat and cook, stirring, until the sauce begins to bubble.
4 Pour the sauce into the casserole dish and stir in the lemon rind, lemon juice and bay leaves. Cover and bake for 1–1¹/2 hours, or until the veal is tender. During the last 20 minutes of cooking, remove the lid to allow the sauces to reduce a little.
5 To serve, stir in the capers and season with salt and freshly cracked black pepper. Sprinkle with parsley and garnish with caper berries.

NUTRITION PER SERVE (6)
Protein 40 g; Fat 13 g; Carbohydrate 5 g; Dietary Fibre 2 g; Cholesterol 160 mg; 1300 kJ (300 cal)

COOK'S FILE

Notes: Caper berries are sold in jars of brine or vinegar in speciality stores.

● If possible, use tiny capers in this dish as they have a superb flavour. Regular capers can be used instead.

Add the leeks and peeled shallots to the pan and gently fry until soft and golden.

Remove the pan from the heat and stir in the stock, scraping up the brown bits.

CHICKEN WITH SHERRY, RAISINS AND PINE NUTS

Preparation time: 30 minutes
Total cooking time: 50 minutes
Serves 4

1.5 kg (3 lb) chicken pieces
    (about 8 portions)
plain flour, seasoned with salt
    and freshly ground pepper
¼ cup (60 ml/2 fl oz) olive oil
2 onions, thinly sliced
2 red capsicums, sliced

4 cloves garlic, finely sliced
1 cup (250 ml/8 fl oz) chicken stock
½ cup (125 ml/4 fl oz) dry sherry
½ cup (125 ml/4 fl oz) orange
    juice
125 g (4 oz) raisins
125 g (4 oz) pine nuts, toasted

1 Toss the chicken in the seasoned flour to coat. Heat the oil in a large, heavy-based pan. Brown the chicken in batches over medium heat until crisp and golden all over. Remove from the pan and set aside.

2 Drain the pan of excess oil and add the onion, capsicum and garlic. Cover the pan tightly and cook for about 3 minutes.

3 Add the chicken, chicken stock, sherry, orange juice and raisins and season to taste with salt and freshly ground pepper. Cover and simmer for about 35 minutes, turning the chicken now and then in the sauce.

4 Remove the chicken, keep warm and simmer the sauce for 5 minutes to thicken. Pour the sauce over the chicken and scatter with pine nuts to serve.

NUTRITION PER SERVE
Protein 93 g; Fat 45 g; Carbohydrate 35 g; Dietary Fibre 6 g; Cholesterol 190 mg; 3980 kJ (950 cal).

Toss the chicken in the seasoned flour to coat evenly all over.

Add the onion, capsicum and garlic to the pan. Cover and cook for 3 minutes.

Add the chicken, stock, sherry, orange juice and raisins to the capsicum mixture.

CHICKEN CACCIATORE

Preparation time: 20 minutes
Total cooking time: 1 hour 15 minutes
Serves 4

1.25 kg (2 lb 8 oz) chicken pieces
2 tablespoons plain flour
1 tablespoon olive oil
1 large onion, finely chopped
2 cloves garlic, chopped
2 x 425 g (14 oz) cans tomatoes,
    roughly chopped

2 cups (500 ml/16 fl oz) chicken
    stock
½ cup (125 ml/4 fl oz) white wine
2 tablespoons tomato paste
1 teaspoon caster sugar
2 tablespoons chopped basil
2 tablespoons chopped parsley
½ cup (90 g/3 oz) black olives

1 Toss the chicken in the flour to coat. Heat the oil in a large, heavy-based pan and brown the chicken in batches over medium heat. Remove from the pan and drain on paper towels.

2 Cook the onion and garlic in the pan for 10 minutes over low heat, stirring. Add the tomatoes, stock and wine. Bring to the boil, reduce the heat and simmer for 15 minutes. Add the tomato paste, sugar and chicken; mix well.

3 Cover and simmer for 30 minutes, then add the herbs and olives and season to taste. Simmer for another 15 minutes, stirring occasionally.

NUTRITION PER SERVE
Protein 60 g; Fat 10 g; Carbohydrate 15 g; Dietary Fibre 4 g; Cholesterol 125 mg; 1800 kJ (480 cal).

Brown the chicken in batches in the hot oil and drain on paper towels.

Add the tomatoes, stock and wine to the softened onion and garlic mixture.

Stir in the herbs, olives and salt and pepper to taste.

Chicken with sherry, raisins and pine nuts (top) and Chicken cacciatore

RICH STEAK AND KIDNEY STEW

Preparation time: 35 minutes
Total cooking time: 2 hours 30 minutes
Serves 4–6

1 kg (2 lb) chuck steak, trimmed
8 lamb kidneys
1/4 cup (60 ml/2 fl oz) oil
1 rasher bacon, rind removed,
    and cut into long, thin strips
40 g (1 1/4 oz) butter
1 large onion, chopped
300 g (10 oz) button mushrooms,
    halved
1 cup (250 ml/8 fl oz) Muscat
2–3 cloves garlic, crushed
1/4 teaspoon ground allspice
1/2 teaspoon paprika
2 teaspoons coriander seeds,
    lightly crushed
1 tablespoon wholegrain mustard
1 cup (250 ml/8 fl oz) beef stock
2–3 tablespoons soft brown sugar
1–2 teaspoons thyme
1–2 teaspoons rosemary

1 Cut the steak into 2–3 cm (1 inch) cubes. Cut the kidneys in half, remove the core and fat, then slice them in half again.

2 Heat 1 teaspoon of the oil in a large, heavy-based pan. Add the bacon and cook over medium heat until just crisp. Remove and set aside.

3 Heat 2 tablespoons of the oil and 30 g (1 oz) of the butter in the pan. Brown the steak in batches and set aside.

4 Add the onion to the pan and cook for 3 minutes, or until soft and golden. Add the mushrooms and cook, stirring, for 3 minutes, until starting to brown. Stir in half the Muscat and simmer for 3–4 minutes. Remove and set aside.

5 Add the remaining oil and butter to the pan. Stir in the garlic, allspice, paprika and coriander and cook for 1 minute. Add the kidneys and cook until just starting to brown. Stir in the mustard and remaining Muscat and simmer for 2 minutes.

6 Stir in the bacon, steak, onion and mushrooms. Stir in the stock, bring to the boil, then reduce the heat, cover and simmer for 1 hour. Add the sugar.

7 Simmer, covered, for 40 minutes, then uncovered for 20 minutes, stirring in the herbs during the last 10 minutes.

NUTRITION PER SERVE (6)
Protein 40 g; Fat 20 g; Carbohydrate 15 g; Dietary Fibre 2 g; Cholesterol 155 mg; 1830 kJ (440 cal)

Halve the kidneys and remove the cores and fat. Slice in half again.

Add half the Muscat to the onions and mushrooms and simmer for 3–4 minutes.

Add the kidneys to the pan-fried spices and cook until just starting to brown.

LAMB WITH BORLOTTI BEANS

Preparation time: 20 minutes +
overnight soaking
Total cooking time: 2 hours
Serves 6

1 cup (200 g /6¹/2 oz) dried
   borlotti beans
1 tablespoon olive oil
12 lamb loin chops
1 onion, finely chopped
1 stick celery, chopped
1 carrot, chopped
3 cloves garlic, finely chopped

¹/2 teaspoon dried chilli flakes
1 teaspoon cumin seeds
2 cups (500 ml/16 fl oz) lamb or
   chicken stock
2 bay leaves
3 tablespoons lemon juice
¹/3 cup (20 g/³/4 oz) chopped
   parsley
1 tablespoon shredded mint

1 Soak the beans overnight in cold water. Drain, rinse well and set aside.
2 Preheat the oven to moderate 180°C (350°F/Gas 4). Heat the oil in a large heavy-based pan. Brown the lamb over high heat in batches and transfer to a casserole dish.

3 Add the onion, celery and carrot to the pan and cook over low heat for about 10 minutes, or until soft and golden. Add the garlic, chilli and cumin seeds and cook for 1 minute, then transfer to the casserole dish.
4 Add the stock, beans and bay leaves. Cover tightly; bake for 1¹/2–1³/4 hours, or until the lamb is very tender and the beans are cooked. Season with salt and freshly cracked black pepper. Stir in the lemon juice, parsley and mint just before serving.

NUTRITION PER SERVE
Protein 30 g; Fat 8 g; Carbohydrate 20 g;
Dietary Fibre 5 g; Cholesterol 65 mg;
1185 kJ (280 cal)

When the oil is hot, brown the lamb over high heat in batches.

Add the onion, celery and carrot to the pan and cook until soft and golden.

Add the stock, drained borlotti beans and bay leaves to the casserole.

CREAMY TOMATO AND CHICKEN STEW

Preparation time: 35 minutes
Total cooking time: 50 minutes
Serves 4–6

4 rashers bacon
2 tablespoons oil
50 g (1¾ oz) butter
300 g (10 oz) small button
 mushrooms, halved
1.5 kg (3 lb) chicken pieces
2 onions, chopped
2 cloves garlic, crushed
400 g (13 oz) can tomatoes
1 cup (250 ml/8 fl oz) chicken
 stock
1 cup (250 ml/8 fl oz) cream
2 tablespoons chopped parsley
2 tablespoons lemon thyme
 leaves

1 Chop the bacon into large pieces. Place a large, heavy-based pan over medium heat. Brown the bacon, then remove and set aside on paper towels.
2 Heat half the oil and a third of the butter in the pan until foaming, then stir in the mushrooms and cook until softened and golden brown. Remove from the pan with a slotted spoon.
3 Add the remaining oil to the pan with a little more butter. When the oil is hot, brown the chicken pieces in batches over high heat until the skin is golden all over and a little crisp. Remove from the pan.
4 Heat the remaining butter in the pan. Add the onion and garlic and cook over medium-high heat for about 3 minutes, or until softened. Pour in the tomatoes, stock and cream. Return the bacon, mushrooms and chicken pieces to the pan and simmer over medium-low heat for 25 minutes. Stir in the herbs, season with salt and freshly ground pepper and simmer for another 5 minutes before serving.

NUTRITION PER SERVE (6)
Protein 70 g; Fat 40 g; Carbohydrate 7 g; Dietary Fibre 3 g; Cholesterol 215 mg; 2650 kJ (630 cal)

When the oil and butter are foaming, add the mushrooms and cook until soft.

Brown the chicken pieces in batches over high heat until the skin is golden and crisp.

Add the tomatoes, stock and cream to the softened onion and garlic.

BRAISED CHICKEN WITH CHICKPEAS

Preparation time: 35 minutes
Total cooking time: 1 hour 35 minutes
Serves 4

50 g (1³/4 oz) butter
1 onion, roughly chopped
3 cloves garlic, crushed
1 carrot, finely chopped
¹/2 stick celery, finely chopped
1.5 kg (2 lb) chicken pieces
     (about 8 portions)
¹/3 cup (80 ml/2³/4 fl oz) Marsala
1 cup (250 ml/8 fl oz) chicken
     stock
2 tablespoons lemon juice

¹/2 cup (40 g/1¹/4 oz) fresh
     breadcrumbs
300 g (10 oz) can chickpeas,
     rinsed and drained
200 g (6¹/2 oz) button mushrooms,
     sliced
2 tablespoons shredded mint
2 tablespoons chopped parsley

1 Heat half the butter in a large, heavy-based pan and cook the onion over medium heat until soft and golden. Add the garlic, carrot and celery and cook over gentle heat for 5 minutes. Remove from the pan and set aside.
2 Melt the remaining butter in the pan and brown the chicken in batches over high heat. Return all the chicken to the pan with the carrot and celery mixture. Quickly add the Marsala and stir well, scraping the sides and base of the pan. Add the stock and lemon juice, bring to the boil, then reduce the heat and simmer gently for 1 hour, stirring occasionally.
3 Remove the chicken; keep warm. In a food processor, purée the contents of the pan, then add the breadcrumbs and blend for another 15 seconds.
4 Return the chicken to the pan, pour in the purée, add the chickpeas and mushrooms and simmer, covered, for 15 minutes. Season to taste, and scatter with mint and parsley to serve.

NUTRITION PER SERVE
Protein 120 g; Fat 30 g; Carbohydrate 50 g; Dietary Fibre 15 g; Cholesterol 260 mg; 3900 kJ (930 cal)

Gently fry the garlic, carrot and celery in the butter for 5 minutes.

Pour the Marsala over the vegetables and chicken, stirring well.

Add the fresh breadcrumbs to the puréed pan mixture and process until smooth.

BEEF AND GLOBE ARTICHOKE STEW

Preparation time: 30 minutes
Total cooking time: 2 hours 15 minutes
Serves 4–6

2 tablespoons olive oil
1 kg (2 lb) stewing beef, cut into
  large cubes
2 red onions, sliced
4 cloves garlic, crushed
1 teaspoon cumin seeds
2 teaspoons ground cumin
1 teaspoon ground coriander
2 teaspoons sweet paprika
1 tablespoon plain flour
2 cups (500 ml/16 fl oz) beef
  stock
1 teaspoon grated lemon rind
1 tablespoon soft brown sugar
1 tablespoon tomato paste
1/4 cup (60 ml/2 fl oz) lemon juice
4 fresh globe artichokes
3 tablespoons small black olives

1 Preheat the oven to moderate 180°C (350°F/Gas 4). Heat half the oil in a large heavy-based pan. Brown the meat in batches over medium-high heat and transfer to a large casserole dish.
2 Add the remaining oil to the pan and cook the onion over medium heat for 5 minutes, or until soft. Add the garlic, cumin seeds, cumin, coriander and paprika and cook for 1 minute.
3 Add the flour, cook for 30 seconds and remove from the heat. Add the stock, return to the heat and stir until the mixture bubbles. Add to the meat with the rind, sugar and tomato paste. Cover tightly and bake for 1 1/2 hours.
4 Meanwhile, add the lemon juice to a bowl of water. Cut the top third from each artichoke, trim the stem to 5 cm

(2 inches) and cut away the dark outer leaves. Cut the artichokes lengthways in half. Remove the prickly lavender-topped leaves in the centre and scoop out the hairy choke. Drop into the lemon-water until ready to use.
5 Drain the artichokes and add to the casserole, covering them in the liquid. Cover and cook for 30 minutes, or until tender. For a thicker gravy, cook

uncovered for 15 minutes more. Season and stir in the olives to serve.

NUTRITION PER SERVE (6)
Protein 40 g; Fat 12 g; Carbohydrate 8 g; Dietary Fibre 2 g; Cholesterol 112 mg; 1212 kJ (290 cal)

COOK'S FILE

Note: Tiny black olives have a great flavour and are sold in delicatessens.

Add the garlic and spices to the fried onion and cook for 1 minute.

Cut the trimmed artichokes lengthways in half and place them in the lemon-water.

Drain the artichokes and add them to the casserole, covering them with the liquid.

STUFFED PORK CHOPS WITH WILD RICE

Preparation time: 15 minutes
Total cooking time: 2 hours 30 minutes
Serves 6

Stuffing
90 g (3 oz) butter
1/2 cup (40 g/1 1/4 oz) fresh
   breadcrumbs
1 small onion, finely chopped
5 button mushrooms, finely
   chopped
2 tablespoons pine nuts
1/2 teaspoon chopped thyme
2 tablespoons chopped parsley

6 pork loin chops, trimmed
plain flour, seasoned with salt
   and freshly ground pepper
2 tablespoons olive oil
60 g (2 oz) butter
1 large tomato, sliced into rounds
1 onion, sliced into rounds
1 cup (190 g/6 1/2 oz) wild rice
1/2 cup (125 ml/4 fl oz) cider
1 cup (250 ml/8 fl oz) chicken
   stock
1 clove garlic, crushed
1/4 teaspoon paprika

1 Preheat the oven to warm 170°C (325°F/Gas 3). To make the stuffing, heat a third of the butter in a pan. Add the breadcrumbs and stir over medium heat until golden; remove and set aside. Heat the remaining butter and fry the onion for 5 minutes, or until soft. Add the remaining stuffing ingredients and fry for 3 minutes. Remove from the heat, add the breadcrumbs and season well.
2 Cut a pocket in the meaty part of each pork chop, then fill with the stuffing. Secure with a toothpick and coat in the seasoned flour.
3 Heat the oil and half the butter in the pan. Brown the chops over high heat; transfer to an oiled ovenproof dish wide enough to fit them in a single layer. Place a slice of tomato and onion on each; secure with a toothpick. Scatter the rice around and pour on the cider.
4 Add the stock, garlic and paprika to the same pan the pork was browned in. Cook over high heat for 1 minute, scraping the base and side of the pan. Pour the sauce over the chops, adding

water if needed to cover the rice. Dot with the remaining butter; cover tightly and bake for 1 1/2 hours. Check the liquid: you may need to add more water to cover the rice. Cover tightly and bake for 30 minutes more, or until the pork is very tender. Remove the toothpicks before serving.

NUTRITION PER SERVE
Protein 30 g; Fat 30 g; Carbohydrate 15 g; Dietary Fibre 2 g; Cholesterol 112 mg; 1925 kJ (460 cal)

COOK'S FILE
Serving suggestion: This dish is lovely served with a purée of fresh peas and sour cream.

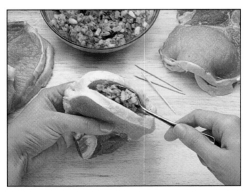

Fill each pork chop with the prepared stuffing and secure with a toothpick.

Scatter the rice around the pork and pour the cider over the top.

BEEF AND PEPPERCORN STEW

Preparation time: 15 minutes
Total cooking time: 2 hours
Serves 4

1 kg (2 lb) chuck steak, cut into
    3 cm (1¼ inch) cubes
2 teaspoons cracked black
    peppercorns
40 g (1¼ oz) butter
2 tablespoons oil
1 large onion, thinly sliced
2 cloves garlic, sliced
1½ tablespoons plain flour
2 tablespoons brandy

3 cups (750 ml/24 fl oz) beef
    stock
1 tablespoon Worcestershire
    sauce
2 teaspoons Dijon mustard
500 g (1 lb) baby new potatoes
¼ cup (60 ml/2 fl oz) cream
2 tablespoons chopped parsley

1 Toss the steak in the peppercorns. Heat half the butter and half the oil in a large heavy-based pan. Brown half the steak over high heat; remove and set aside. Heat the remaining butter and oil and brown the remaining steak. Remove and set aside.

2 Add the onion and garlic to the pan and cook, stirring, until the onion is golden. Add the flour and stir until browned. Remove from the heat.

3 Combine the brandy, beef stock, Worcestershire sauce and mustard, and gradually stir into the onion mixture. Return to the heat, add the steak and any juices, then simmer, covered, for 1¼ hours.

4 Add the potatoes and simmer, uncovered, for a further 30 minutes, or until the meat and potatoes are tender. Stir in the cream and parsley and season to taste with salt and freshly ground pepper.

NUTRITION PER SERVE
Protein 60 g; Fat 30 g; Carbohydrate 20 g; Dietary Fibre 3 g; Cholesterol 215 mg; 2580 kJ (615 cal)

Cut the steak into 3 cm (1¼ inch) cubes, using a sharp knife.

Add the brandy, stock, Worcestershire sauce and mustard to the onion mixture.

Add the potatoes and simmer, uncovered, for a further 30 minutes, or until tender.

VEAL AND FENNEL CASSEROLE

Preparation time: 20 minutes
Total cooking time: 2 hours 15 minutes
Serves 4–6

1 tablespoon oil
30 g (1 oz) butter
4 veal shanks, cut into 4 cm
(1½ inch) pieces
1 large onion, sliced
1 clove garlic, crushed
2 sticks celery, thickly sliced
3 carrots, thickly sliced
2 small fennel bulbs, quartered
¼ cup (30 g/1 oz) plain flour

425 g (14 oz) can crushed
tomatoes
⅓ cup (80 ml/2¾ fl oz) white
wine
1 cup (250 ml/8 fl oz) chicken
stock
1 tablespoon chopped thyme
12 black olives

1 Preheat the oven to moderate 180°C (350°F/Gas 4). Heat the oil and butter in a large heavy-based pan and brown the meat quickly in batches on both sides over high heat. Transfer to a large, shallow casserole dish.
2 Add the onion and garlic to the pan and cook over medium heat until soft. Add the celery, carrot and fennel and

cook for 2 minutes. Add the flour, stir until golden, then add the tomatoes, wine, stock and thyme. Bring to the boil, reduce the heat and simmer for 5 minutes, or until thickened. Season with salt and freshly ground pepper.
3 Add the sauce to the veal; cover and bake for 1½–2 hours, or until tender. Scatter with olives to serve.

NUTRITION PER SERVE (6)
Protein 20 g; Fat 8 g; Carbohydrate 10 g; Dietary Fibre 3 g; Cholesterol 80 mg; 840 kJ (200 cal)

COOK'S FILE

Note: Many butchers sell veal shanks already cut into pieces. You will need 12 medium pieces for this recipe.

Trim the leaves and base from the celery stalks and thickly cut the stalks.

Heat the oil and butter, then brown the meat in batches over high heat.

Add the celery, carrots and fennel to the onion and garlic and cook for 2 minutes.

HUNGARIAN VEAL GOULASH

Preparation time: 20 minutes
Total cooking time: 2 hours
Serves 4

2 tablespoons olive oil
2 onions, chopped
500 g (1 lb) stewing veal, cubed
1 tablespoon Hungarian paprika
¼ teaspoon caraway seeds

425 g (14 oz) can tomatoes
2 cups (500 ml/16 fl oz) beef stock
1 large potato, diced
1 large carrot, thickly sliced
1 green capsicum, chopped
½ cup (125 g/4 oz) sour cream

1 Heat the oil in a large, heavy-based pan. Cook the onion for 10 minutes over medium heat, stirring from time to time, until soft and golden. Remove from the pan, increase the heat, then brown the veal in batches.

2 Return all the veal to the pan with the onion. Add the paprika, caraway seeds, chopped tomatoes and stock. Bring to the boil, reduce the heat, then cover and simmer for 1¼ hours.
3 Add the vegetables. Cook uncovered for 20 minutes, or until tender. Season to taste with salt and freshly cracked black pepper, and stir in the sour cream. Serve with rice or pasta.

NUTRITION PER SERVE
Protein 35 g; Fat 25 g; Carbohydrate 18 g; Dietary Fibre 5 g; Cholesterol 144 mg; 1805 kJ (430 cal)

Heat the oil and fry the onions over medium heat until soft and golden.

Add the paprika, caraway seeds, chopped tomatoes and stock to the fried onions.

Add the vegetables and cook, uncovered, for 20 minutes, or until tender.

IRISH STEW

Preparation time: 20 minutes
Total cooking time: 1 hour 15 minutes
Serves 4

8 lamb neck chops
4 thick rashers bacon, rind removed
30 g (1 oz) butter
1 kg (2 lb) potatoes, thickly sliced
3 carrots, sliced
3 onions, sliced into thick rounds
2 cups (500 ml/16 fl oz) beef or vegetable stock

sprigs of thyme or lemon thyme, to taste
chopped parsley, to garnish

1 Trim the chops of excess fat; cut the bacon into short strips. Melt the butter in a large heavy-based pan and brown the chops on both sides over high heat. Remove and set aside. Add the bacon to the pan and cook until crisp. Drain on paper towels.
2 Arrange half the potato, carrot and onion in a deep heavy-based pan. Season with cracked pepper, then add half the bacon. Layer the chops on top and cover with the remaining potato,

carrot, onion and bacon. Add the stock and thyme.
3 Cover and bring to the boil, then reduce the heat and simmer for about 1 hour, or until the lamb is tender. Serve sprinkled with parsley.

NUTRITION PER SERVE
Protein 40 g; Fat 15 g; Carbohydrate 40 g; Dietary Fibre 7 g; Cholesterol 110 mg; 1870 kJ (450 cal)

COOK'S FILE

Note: Irish stew is traditionally made from mutton, without potatoes or carrots. Adding vegetables makes a satisfying one-pot meal.

Brown the chops on both sides in the hot butter over high heat.

Hungarian veal goulash (top) and Irish stew

Arrange half the potato, carrot and onion in a deep, heavy-based pan.

When the layers are complete, add the stock and thyme.

CHICKEN MARSALA

Preparation time: 20 minutes
Total cooking time: 1 hour 10 minutes
Serves 4

1/4 cup (60 ml/2 fl oz) olive oil
3 leeks, finely sliced
1 teaspoon finely chopped
    rosemary
3 bay leaves, torn
1 kg (2 lb) chicken pieces
plain flour, seasoned with salt
    and freshly ground pepper
1 large eggplant, cut into cubes
2 zucchini, roughly chopped
1/2 cup (125 ml/4 fl oz) Marsala
300 ml (10 fl oz) chicken stock

2 cups (500 ml/16 fl oz) tomato
    purée
200 g (6½ oz) button mushrooms,
    halved

1 Heat the oil in a large, heavy-based pan. Fry the leek, rosemary and bay leaves over low heat for 5 minutes, or until soft, stirring occasionally. Remove with a slotted spoon, leaving as much oil in the pan as possible.

2 Toss the chicken pieces in the seasoned flour. Add the chicken to the pan and brown well in batches over medium heat. Return all the chicken to the pan with the leek mixture.

3 Add the eggplant and zucchini and cook, stirring, for 2–3 minutes, or until softened, turning the chicken pieces

over. Add the Marsala and stock and cook for about 15 minutes over medium-high heat.

4 Add the tomato purée and season well with salt and pepper. Bring to the boil, turning the chicken pieces in the sauce. Reduce the heat to a very gentle simmer, then cover and cook for 35 minutes. Add the mushrooms and cook, uncovered, for 5 minutes.

NUTRITION PER SERVE
Protein 63 g; Fat 20 g; Carbohydrate 13 g; Dietary Fibre 9 g; Cholesterol 125 mg; 2200 kJ (530 cal)

COOK'S FILE

Note: Marsala is a famous Italian fortified wine. It has a smoky, rich flavour and ranges from dry to sweet.

Remove the softened leeks and herbs from the pan with a slotted spoon.

Add the chopped eggplant and zucchini to the chicken and leek mixture.

Stir in the tomato purée and season well with salt and pepper.

CHICKEN CALVADOS WITH GLAZED APPLES

Preparation time: 15 minutes
Total cooking time: 1 hour 10 minutes
Serves 4

1.25 kg (2 lb 8 oz) chicken pieces
plain flour, seasoned with salt
   and freshly ground pepper
2 tablespoons light olive oil
30 g (1 oz) butter
1 large onion, roughly chopped
1 tablespoon chopped marjoram
1 chicken stock cube, crumbled
3/4 cup (185 ml/6 fl oz) apple juice
1/3 cup (80 ml/2³/4 fl oz) Calvados
3/4 cup (185 ml/6 fl oz) cream

Glazed Apples
2 red apples
40 g (1¹/4 oz) butter
2 teaspoons sugar

1 Preheat the oven to moderate 180°C (350°F/Gas 4). Trim the chicken of excess fat and sinew, then toss in the flour to coat, shaking off any excess. In a large, heavy-based pan, heat the oil and butter and brown the chicken all over, in batches if necessary. Transfer to a large casserole dish.
2 Add the onion to the pan and cook over low heat until soft but not brown. Add the marjoram, stock cube, apple juice and Calvados and bring to the boil, stirring. Season well and simmer for 5 minutes.

3 Pour the sauce over the chicken and bake, covered, for 45 minutes or until the chicken is tender. Stir in the cream and bake for 5 minutes—the sauce will be thin but delicious.
4 Meanwhile, core (but do not peel) the apples, then cut into wedges. Melt the butter in a pan, add the apples and sugar and cook over very low heat, turning occasionally, until tender and glazed. Serve with the casserole.

NUTRITION PER SERVE
Protein 70 g; Fat 50 g; Carbohydrate 20 g; Dietary Fibre 2 g; Cholesterol 265 mg; 3615 kJ (860 cal)

COOK'S FILE

Note: Calvados is a French apple brandy. Cognac may be used instead.

Toss the trimmed chicken lightly in the flour to coat, shaking off any excess.

Add the marjoram, stock cube, apple juice and Calvados to the fried onions.

Glaze the apple wedges in the sugar and butter and cook on both sides until tender.

MOROCCAN LAMB SHANKS

Preparation time: 25 minutes
Total cooking time: 3 hours 15 minutes
Serves 4

Spicy Paste
30 g (1 oz) bunch coriander,
    roots intact
1 teaspoon ground turmeric
2 teaspoons ground cumin
1 teaspoon paprika
1 teaspoon ground coriander
1/2 teaspoon ground cinnamon
1 dried red chilli
2 cloves garlic, crushed
2 tablespoons honey
1/4 cup (60 ml/2 fl oz) olive oil

light olive oil, for cooking
8 lamb shanks
3 onions, sliced into thick rings
sugar, for sprinkling
1 cup (250 ml/8 fl oz) white wine
2 cups (500 ml/16 fl oz) chicken
    stock
4 lime quarters, to garnish
coriander leaves, to garnish

1 In a food processor, blend the spicy paste ingredients (including coriander roots) to a smooth paste. Set aside.
2 Heat 3 tablespoons of oil in a large, heavy-based pan. Brown the shanks in batches over high heat and transfer to a large, ovenproof dish. Preheat the oven to moderate 180°C (350°F/Gas 4).
3 Heat a tablespoon of oil in the pan. Add the onion rings, sprinkle with sugar and sauté over medium heat for 10–15 minutes, or until golden.
4 Add the spicy paste and sauté for 2 minutes. Season well, add the wine and stock and simmer for 15 minutes.

5 Pour the wine sauce over the lamb shanks. Cover and bake for 1 hour, then turn the shanks over and bake for another 1 1/2 hours, or until the meat is tender. Spoon any fat from the surface, transfer to plates and garnish with lime quarters and coriander leaves. Serve with couscous.

NUTRITION PER SERVE
Protein 60 g; Fat 20 g; Carbohydrate 15 g; Dietary Fibre 2 g; Cholesterol 170 mg; 2214 kJ (530 cal)

COOK'S FILE

Serving suggestion: Couscous is a traditional Moroccan accompaniment.

Blend all the spicy paste ingredients in a food processor until smooth.

Heat the oil in a large pan. Brown the shanks over high heat.

Add the spicy paste to the fried onion and sauté for 2 minutes.

BEEF IN BEER WITH CAPERS AND ANCHOVIES

Preparation time: 25 minutes
Total cooking time: 3 hours 20 minutes
Serves 4–6

1 kg (2 lb) gravy beef
plain flour, seasoned with salt
    and freshly ground pepper
olive oil, for cooking
4 cloves garlic, finely chopped
2 cups (500 ml/16 fl oz) beef
    stock
1½ cups (375 ml/12 fl oz) beer
2 onions, chopped
3 bay leaves

⅓ cup (55 g/2 oz) stuffed or
    pitted green olives, sliced
6 anchovies
2 tablespoons capers, drained

1 Cut the beef into 4 cm (1½ inch) chunks, following the sinew and separation of the meat. Lightly coat in the flour. Heat 3 tablespoons of oil in a deep heavy-based pan, add the garlic, then brown the beef over high heat.
2 Add the stock, beer, onions and bay leaves, season well and bring to the boil. Reduce the heat; cover and gently simmer for 2½ hours, stirring about three times during cooking. Remove the lid and simmer for 30 minutes more. Stir, then mix in the olives.

3 Heat 2 teaspoons of oil in a small pan. Add the anchovies and capers, gently breaking up the anchovies. Cook over medium heat for 4 minutes, or until brown and crisp. To serve, place the meat on serving plates, drizzle with the sauce, sprinkle with anchovies and capers, and season with salt and freshly cracked pepper.

NUTRITION PER SERVE (6)
Protein 40 g; Fat 6 g; Carbohydrate 4 g; Dietary Fibre 1 g; Cholesterol 115 mg; 965 kJ (230 cal)

COOK'S FILE

Note: The capers should be squeezed very dry before being added to the pan, or they will spit in the hot oil.

Cut the beef into large chunks, following the sinew and separation of the meat.

Add the stock, beer, onions and bay leaves to the browned beef.

Fry the anchovies and capers in a little hot oil until brown and crisp.

OSSO BUCO WITH GREMOLATA AND MILANESE RISOTTO

Preparation time: 40 minutes
Total cooking time: 2 hours 20 minutes
Serves 4

Gremolata
1 tablespoon finely shredded or
    zested lemon rind
1–2 cloves garlic, finely chopped
1/4 cup (7 g/1/4 oz) finely chopped
    parsley

Osso Buco
4 veal shank pieces, each
    5 cm (2 inches) thick
plain flour, seasoned with salt
    and freshly ground pepper
2 tablespoons olive oil
2 large onions, sliced
6 egg tomatoes, finely chopped
2 tablespoons tomato paste
1 1/2 cups (375 ml/12 fl oz) white
    wine
1 tablespoon cornflour
2–3 cloves garlic, crushed
1 cup (30 g/1 oz) finely chopped
    parsley

Milanese Risotto
1 litre chicken stock
50 g (1 3/4 oz) butter
2 tablespoons olive oil
1 onion, finely chopped
1–2 cloves garlic, crushed
1/4 teaspoon saffron threads
1 1/4 cups (250 g/8 oz) arborio rice
1/2 cup (50 g/1 2/3 oz) freshly
    grated Parmesan

1 To make the gremolata, combine the lemon rind, garlic and parsley and set aside.

2 Coat the veal with seasoned flour, shaking off any excess. Heat half the oil in a heavy-based pan large enough to fit the meat in a single layer. When the oil is hot, brown the veal well on all sides. Remove and set aside.

3 Heat the remaining oil in the pan and cook the onion for 2–3 minutes, or until soft but not brown. Add the meat in a single layer, sitting snugly in the pan. Season to taste.

4 Mix together the chopped tomatoes, tomato paste and wine and pour over the meat. Bring to the boil, reduce the heat, cover and simmer for 1 1/2 hours.

5 Remove 1 cup (250 ml/8 fl oz) of the cooking liquid and allow to cool a little. Place the cornflour in a small bowl and whisk in the liquid, then stir in the garlic and chopped parsley and add the mixture to the dish. Simmer, uncovered, for about 30 minutes, or until the meat is very tender and the sauce has thickened. Sprinkle with the gremolata just before serving.

6 While the sauce is simmering, make the risotto. Heat the stock in a pan and keep it at a simmer. In another heavy-based pan, heat the butter and oil. Add the onion, garlic and saffron and cook, stirring, for 2–3 minutes without browning. Add the rice and stir for 1–2 minutes, or until well coated.

7 Add the stock, about 1/2 cup (125 ml/4 fl oz) at a time, stirring constantly over low heat until all the liquid is absorbed before adding more stock. Repeat until all the stock is absorbed and the rice is tender—this will take 25–30 minutes, and requires constant stirring. Stir in the Parmesan, season and serve at once.

NUTRITION PER SERVE
Protein 30 g; Fat 35 g; Carbohydrate 30 g; Dietary Fibre 5 g; Cholesterol 114 mg; 2580 kJ (615 cal)

To make the gremolata, combine the lemon rind, garlic and parsley.

When the oil is hot, brown the veal shanks well all over.

Pour the chopped tomatoes, tomato paste and wine over the meat and onions.

In a bowl, blend some of the cornflour with a cup of the cooled liquid.

Add the rice to the fried onion, garlic and saffron mixture; stir until coated.

Add the stock a little at a time, stirring until absorbed before adding more stock.

COQ AU VIN

Preparation time: 20 minutes
Total cooking time: 1 hour
Serves 6

2 sprigs of thyme
4 sprigs of parsley
2 bay leaves
2 kg (4 lb) chicken pieces
plain flour, seasoned with salt
   and freshly ground pepper
1/4 cup (60 ml/2 fl oz) oil
4 thick bacon rashers, sliced
12 pickling onions
2 cloves garlic, crushed
2 tablespoons brandy

1 1/2 cups (375 ml/12 fl oz) red
   wine
1 1/2 cups (375 ml/12 fl oz)
   chicken stock
1/4 cup (60 g/2 oz) tomato paste
250 g (8 oz) button mushrooms
fresh herbs, for sprinkling

1 To make the bouquet garni, wrap the thyme, parsley and bay leaves in a small square of muslin and tie well with string, or tie them between two 5 cm (2 inch) lengths of celery.

2 Toss the chicken in flour to coat, shaking off any excess. In a heavy-based pan, heat 2 tablespoons of oil and brown the chicken in batches over medium heat. Drain on paper towels.

3 Wipe the pan clean with paper towels and heat the remaining oil. Add the bacon, onions and garlic and cook, stirring, until the onions are browned. Add the chicken, brandy, wine, stock, bouquet garni and tomato paste. Bring to the boil, reduce the heat and simmer, covered, for 30 minutes.

4 Stir in the mushrooms and simmer, uncovered, for 10 minutes, or until the chicken is tender and the sauce has thickened. Remove the bouquet garni, sprinkle with fresh herbs and serve with crusty French bread.

NUTRITION PER SERVE
Protein 80 g; Fat 20 g; Carbohydrate 7 g; Dietary Fibre 2 g; Cholesterol 180 mg; 2420 kJ (580 cal)

Wrap the thyme, parsley and bay leaves in a small square of muslin.

In batches, brown the chicken in the hot oil over medium heat.

Return the chicken to the pan with the liquids, bouquet garni and tomato paste.

Peel two strips of orange rind. Remove the pith and slice the orange into rounds.

Combine the chicken stock and wine and add to the softened onion mixture.

Grill the capsicum, skin-side-up, until the skin is blistered and black.

Stir the capsicum strips, orange slices, olives and parsley into the sauce.

MAJORCAN CHICKEN

Preparation time: 30 minutes
Total cooking time: 1 hour 30 minutes
Serves 4

2 tablespoons olive oil
30 g (1 oz) butter
1.5 kg (3 lb) chicken pieces
1 orange
1 red onion, thinly sliced
2 cloves garlic, chopped
3/4 cup (185 ml/6 fl oz) chicken
   stock
1/2 cup (125 ml/4 fl oz) white
   wine
1 tablespoon plain flour
1 red capsicum, quartered
12 stuffed green olives
3 tablespoons chopped parsley

1 Preheat the oven to moderate 180°C (350°F/Gas 4). Heat the oil and butter in a large pan. Brown the chicken in batches over high heat and transfer to a flameproof casserole dish.

2 Cut two large strips of rind from the orange and set aside. Remove the pith from the orange, then slice the orange into thin rounds. Set aside.

3 Cook the onion and garlic in the pan for 3 minutes over medium heat, or until softened. Combine the stock and wine. Stir the flour into the pan, then slowly add the stock and wine and stir until the mixture comes to the boil. Add the orange rind strips, then pour over the chicken. Cover and bake for 1 hour.

4 Meanwhile, grill the capsicum, skin-side-up, for 8 minutes, or until black and blistered. Place in a plastic bag, seal and allow to cool. Peel away the skin and cut the flesh into strips.

5 Remove the chicken from the dish; cover and keep warm. Bring the sauce to the boil on the stove top, skimming off the fat. Boil for 5 minutes to thicken slightly. Add the capsicum strips, orange slices, olives and parsley. To serve, remove the orange rind, season to taste and spoon the sauce over the chicken.

NUTRITION PER SERVE
Protein 90 g; Fat 25 g; Carbohydrate 10 g; Dietary Fibre 4 g; Cholesterol 205 mg; 2700 kJ (645 cal)

SMOKED SAUSAGE AND KIDNEY BEAN STEW

Preparation time: 20 minutes
Total cooking time: 2 hours 30 minutes
Serves 4–6

1 small red capsicum, halved
2 tablespoons olive oil
2–3 cloves garlic, crushed
1 large onion, thinly sliced
1 carrot, cut into cubes
420 g (14 oz) can kidney beans,
    rinsed and drained
2 cups (500 ml/16 fl oz) beef
    stock
1 tablespoon treacle
600 g (1¼ lb) piece speck or bacon
425 g (14 oz) can chopped
    tomatoes, juice reserved
2 tablespoons tomato paste
150 g (5 oz) smoked sausages

1 Grill the capsicum halves, skin-side-up, under a hot grill until the skin is black and blistered. Cool, then peel off the skin and dice the flesh.
2 Heat the oil in a large, heavy-based pan. Add the garlic, onion and carrot and cook, stirring, over low heat for 4–5 minutes without browning.
3 Add the beans, stock, treacle and freshly ground black pepper to taste. Slowly bring to the boil, then add the speck or bacon. Reduce the heat; cover and simmer for 1 hour. Stir through the undrained tomatoes and tomato paste and simmer for 30 minutes.
4 Place the sausages in a pan of cold water. Slowly bring to the boil, then drain and add to the stew. Simmer, uncovered, for 45 minutes, or until the sauce is thick and rich.
5 Remove the speck or bacon and sausages, using tongs. Slice them,

removing any fat and skin, and return to the stew for serving. Serve hot.

NUTRITION PER SERVE (6)
Protein 25 g; Fat 15 g; Carbohydrate 20 g; Dietary Fibre 8 g; Cholesterol 50 mg; 1370 kJ (330 cal)

COOK'S FILE
Note: Speck is a kind of smoked bacon, often sold in delicatessens.
Serving suggestion: This stew is lovely with a pumpkin and white bean purée.

Add the beans, stock, treacle and pepper to the onion mixture.

Simmer the stew until rich and thick, then remove the speck and sausages.

Remove the skin and excess fat from the speck. Slice the sausages and speck.

LAMB STEW WITH ROSEMARY DUMPLINGS

Preparation time: 25 minutes
Total cooking time: 2 hours
Serves 4

8 lamb neck chops
plain flour, seasoned with salt and freshly ground pepper
2 tablespoons oil
2 rashers bacon, finely chopped
1 large onion, sliced
2 cups (500 ml/16 fl oz) beef stock
1 tablespoon chopped thyme
2 carrots, thickly sliced
2 potatoes, chopped

Rosemary Dumplings
1 cup (125 g/4 oz) self-raising flour
20 g (3/4 oz) butter, chopped
1 tablespoon chopped rosemary
1/3 cup (80 ml/23/4 fl oz) milk

1 Trim the lamb of fat and sinew and toss lightly in the flour, shaking off any excess. Heat the oil in a large, heavy-based pan, then brown the lamb in batches over medium-high heat. Remove and set aside.
2 Add the bacon to the pan and cook over medium heat for 2 minutes, or until brown. Add the onion and cook for about 5 minutes, or until soft.
3 Return the browned lamb to the pan. Add the stock, thyme and 1/2 cup (125 ml/4 fl oz) of water, then simmer, covered, over low heat for 30 minutes. Add the carrot and potato and simmer for 1 hour more.
4 To make the rosemary dumplings, sift the flour into a bowl, then rub in the butter with your fingertips until

the mixture is fine and crumbly. Mix in the rosemary. Add most of the milk and mix to a soft dough with a knife, adding more milk if needed. Turn out onto a lightly floured surface and gently knead until smooth. Divide the dough into 12 portions and form into rough balls. Place the dumplings on top of the stew, then cover and cook for 15 minutes. Serve immediately.

NUTRITION PER SERVE
Protein 30 g; Fat 20 g; Carbohydrate 35 g; Dietary Fibre 4 g; Cholesterol 95 mg; 1930 kJ (460 cal)

COOK'S FILE

Storage time: The stew may be made a day ahead, but the dumplings should be made just before serving. Simply reheat the stew to simmering point, then add the fresh dumplings.

Lightly toss the trimmed lamb in the seasoned flour, shaking off any excess.

Sift the flour into a bowl. Rub in the butter with your fingertips until fine.

Divide the dough into 12 portions, then form into rough balls.

DUCK WITH JUNIPER BERRIES

Preparation time: 35 minutes
Cooking time: 1 hour 50 minutes
Serves 4

1.8 kg (3 lb 10 oz) duck
1 Granny Smith apple, peeled
  and thinly sliced
1 leek, cut into large chunks
1/2 small red cabbage, shredded
2 bay leaves
2 sprigs of fresh thyme
6 juniper berries, lightly crushed
1/4 teaspoon whole black
  peppercorns
1 1/2 cups (375 ml/12 fl oz)
  chicken stock
1 cup (250 ml/8 fl oz) orange
  juice
50 g (1 3/4 oz) butter, chopped
2 tablespoons soft brown sugar
1/3 cup (80 ml/2 3/4 fl oz) cider
  vinegar
1 1/2 teaspoons cornflour
sprigs of chervil, to serve

1 Preheat the oven to moderate 180°C (350°F/Gas 4). Cut the duck in half by cutting down both sides of the backbone and through the breastbone. Discard the backbone. Cut each duck half into 4 portions, removing any fat. Brown the duck portions in a lightly oiled, heavy-based pan over medium heat; remove and set aside.
2 Drain the pan of all but 1 tablespoon of oil, reserving the excess. Cook the apple until golden all over; remove and set aside. Add 1 tablespoon of the fat to the pan and lightly brown the leek.
3 Add the cabbage, bay leaves, thyme, juniper berries and peppercorns and cook, stirring, for 10 minutes, or until

the cabbage softens. Transfer to a large flameproof casserole dish. Add the stock and orange juice and bring to the boil. Add the duck, pressing gently into the liquid, then cover and bake for 1 1/2 hours.
4 Remove the duck and keep warm. Drain the liquid into a pan; simmer for 5 minutes, or until reduced to 1 cup (250 ml/8 fl oz). Stir in the butter, sugar and vinegar. Blend the cornflour with

1 tablespoon water and stir into the mixture until it boils and thickens.
5 Stir the apple and half the sauce into the cabbage mixture and season to taste. Spoon onto a serving plate, top with the duck, drizzle with sauce and garnish with chervil to serve.

NUTRITION PER SERVE
Protein 50 g; Fat 30 g; Carbohydrate 25 g; Dietary Fibre 4 g; Cholesterol 335 mg; 2250 kJ (540 cal).

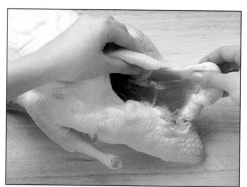

Remove the excess fat from the inside of the duck.

Add the duck portions to the cabbage mixture, pressing them into the liquid.

Stir the sugar, vinegar and butter into the reduced sauce.

SPICY VENISON AND VEGETABLE HOTPOT

Preparation time: 45 minutes
Total cooking time: 2 hours
Serves 6

1 tablespoon olive oil
25 g (³/4 oz) butter
100 g (3¹/2 oz) pancetta, chopped
1 kg (2 lb) trimmed shoulder
    of venison, cut into 4 cm
    (1¹/2 inch) cubes
2 onions, each cut into 8 wedges
2 cloves garlic, crushed
1 tablespoon chopped fresh ginger
1 teaspoon ground cinnamon

¹/2 teaspoon allspice
1 teaspoon dried thyme
1 bay leaf
500 g (1 lb) tomatoes, peeled,
    seeded and diced
1 cup (250 ml/8 fl oz) beef stock
¹/3 cup (80 ml/2³/4 fl oz) orange
    juice
¹/3 cup (80 ml/2³/4 fl oz) port
200 g (6¹/2 oz) turnip
200 g (6¹/2 oz) parsnip
200 g (6¹/2 oz) carrot
chopped chives, to garnish

1 Heat the oil and butter in a large, heavy-based pan. Cook the pancetta over medium heat until lightly golden. Remove and set aside.

2 Brown the venison in batches and set aside. Cook the onion until golden; add the garlic and ginger and cook for 1 minute. Add the pancetta and venison and all ingredients except the root vegetables. Bring to the boil, then reduce the heat, cover tightly and very gently simmer for 1 hour.

3 Peel the turnip, parsnip and carrot, cut into even-sized wedges and add to the pan. Cover and cook for 40 minutes, or until tender, then uncover to reduce the sauce. Season to taste, scatter with the chives and serve.

NUTRITION PER SERVE
Protein 40 g; Fat 25 g; Carbohydrate 14 g; Dietary Fibre 5 g; Cholesterol 90 mg; 1895 kJ (460 cal)

Brown the venison in batches in the hot oil and butter.

Add the pancetta and venison with all the ingredients except the root vegetables.

Peel and cut the turnip, parsnip and carrot into wedges about the same size.

143

HEARTY PORK AND RED LENTILS

Preparation time: 35 minutes
Total cooking time: 2 hours
Serves 4–6

1 kg (2 lb) lean pork neck,
    sliced 2 cm (3/4 inch) thick
plain flour, seasoned with salt
    and freshly ground pepper
50 g (1 3/4 oz) butter
1 tablespoon olive oil
1 large onion, finely chopped
3 cloves garlic, finely chopped
2 tablespoons chopped sage
1 1/4 cups (310 ml/10 fl oz)
    vegetable stock
1 1/4 cups (310 ml/10 fl oz) red
    wine
1 cup (250 g/8 oz) red lentils,
    rinsed
2 carrots, chopped
2 potatoes, chopped
3 sticks celery, chopped
1 bay leaf, torn in three
2 teaspoons finely grated lemon
    rind
2 tablespoons chopped parsley

1 Coat the pork in the flour, shaking off any excess. In a large, deep, heavy-based pan, heat the butter and oil over medium heat until foamy. Brown the pork well, in batches if necessary.
2 Return all the pork to the pan. Add the onion, garlic, sage, stock and wine; season well. Bring to the boil, turning the pork to coat in the liquid. Reduce the heat, cover and simmer for 1 hour, turning the pork during cooking. If the sauce becomes too thick, add about 1 cup (250 ml/8 fl oz) of water.
3 Add the lentils, carrots, potatoes, celery and bay leaf to the stew with

2 cups (500 ml/16 fl oz) of water, and plenty of salt and pepper. Bring to the boil, then reduce the heat to low. Simmer, covered, for 40 minutes.
4 Add the rind. Cook, uncovered, for 30 minutes, or until the sauce is thick and mash-like. If the pork is falling apart, remove and keep warm. To

serve, pile the sauce onto the plates, rest some pork on top and sprinkle with parsley. Serve with mashed potato and steamed green beans.

NUTRITION PER SERVE (6)
Protein 50 g; Fat 13 g; Carbohydrate 20 g; Dietary Fibre 8 g; Cholesterol 110 mg; 1884 kJ (450 cal)

Brown the pork well in the foamy butter and oil mixture.

When the wine mixture boils, turn the pork over to coat in the cooking liquid.

Add the lemon rind to the stew and cook, covered, for 30 minutes.

VEAL WITH SWEET VEGETABLES

Preparation time: 30 minutes
Total cooking time: 2 hours 30 minutes
Serves 4

olive oil, for cooking
8 veal shank pieces, each 2 cm
    (3/4 inch) thick
2 cloves garlic, finely chopped
2 onions, chopped
2 carrots, chopped
1 stick celery, chopped
2 bay leaves, torn
750 ml (24 fl oz) beef stock
50 g (1¾ oz) butter
200 g (6½ oz) white sweet potato
200 g (6½ oz) parsnips
150 g (5 oz) baby turnips
150 g (5 oz) new potatoes
2 teaspoons soft brown sugar
2 tablespoons balsamic vinegar

1 Preheat the oven to warm 160°C (315°F/Gas 2–3). Heat 3 tablespoons of oil in a roasting pan over medium heat and brown the veal all over. Remove and set aside. Add the garlic, onion, carrot and celery and brown lightly for 10 minutes. Add the veal, bay leaves and stock and stir well. Bring to the boil, cover tightly with foil, then bake for 1½ hours.

2 Towards the end of baking, cut the sweet potato and parsnips into large chunks; trim the turnips and cut in half. Heat the butter and a little oil in a deep frying pan until foamy. Toss all the root vegetables over medium heat for 5–6 minutes, or until the edges are golden. Sprinkle with sugar and vinegar and toss well. Cook gently for 10 minutes, or until the vegetables soften and the juices caramelise.

3 Turn the veal in the stock, add the vegetables and toss well. If the meat is drying out, stir in 1 cup (250 ml/8 fl oz) water. Season well, then cover and cook for 20 minutes. This dish is delicious served with steamed rice or creamy polenta.

NUTRITION PER SERVE
Protein 5 g; Fat 10 g; Carbohydrate 30 g; Dietary Fibre 6 g; Cholesterol 30 mg; 930 kJ (220 cal)

Heat the oil in a roasting pan, add the veal shanks and brown all over.

Add the root vegetables to the foaming butter. Cook until the edges are golden.

Add the caramelised vegetables to the veal mixture and toss well.

PORK AND EGGPLANT POT

Preparation time: 20 minutes
Total cooking time: 1 hour 40 minutes
Serves 4

olive oil, for cooking
375 g (12 oz) slender eggplant,
    cut into 3 cm (1¼ inch) slices
8 bulb spring onions
400 g (13 oz) can chopped
    tomatoes
2 cloves garlic, crushed
2 teaspoons ground cumin
500 g (1 lb) pork fillet, sliced
    3 cm (1¼ inches) thick
plain flour, seasoned with salt
    and freshly ground pepper

⅔ cup (170 ml/5½ fl oz) cider
1 sprig of rosemary
2 tablespoons finely chopped
    toasted almonds

1 Heat 3 tablespoons of oil in a large, heavy-based pan. Brown the eggplant in batches over high heat, adding oil as needed. Remove and set aside.
2 Quarter the spring onions along their length. Add some oil to the pan and fry over medium heat for 5 minutes. Add the tomatoes, garlic and cumin; cook for 2 minutes. Remove and set aside.
3 Coat the pork in the flour, shaking off any excess. Brown in batches over medium-high heat until golden, adding oil as needed. Remove and set aside.
4 Add the cider to the pan and stir well, scraping down the side and base.

Allow to boil for 1–2 minutes, then add ½ cup (125 ml/4 fl oz) water. Reduce the heat and stir in the spring onions and tomatoes. Add the pork, season to taste and poke the rosemary sprig into the stew. Partially cover and simmer gently for 20 minutes.
5 Layer the eggplant on top, partially cover and cook for 25 minutes, or until the pork is tender. Just before serving, gently toss the almonds through.

NUTRITION PER SERVE
Protein 30 g; Fat 7 g; Carbohydrate 10 g; Dietary Fibre 5 g; Cholesterol 60 mg; 980 kJ (235 cal)

COOK'S FILE

Serving suggestion: This dish is lovely with a cauliflower and fennel purée.

Fry the eggplant in batches over high heat until browned on both sides.

Add the cider to the frying pan, scraping the brown bits from the side and base.

Layer the eggplant over the top of the pork and tomato mixture.

BEEF SAUSAGE AND MUSHROOM STEW

Preparation time: 20 minutes +
   30 minutes standing
Cooking time: 1 hour
Serves 4–6

15 g (1/2 oz) packet dried
   porcini mushrooms
12 thick beef sausages
300 g (10 oz) piece speck or bacon
2 teaspoons oil
2 onions, cut into eighths
8 cloves garlic
1 sprig of thyme
3 bay leaves
1 1/2 cups (375 ml/12 fl oz)
   red wine

1 cup (250 ml/8 fl oz) beef stock
1 teaspoon Dijon mustard
1 bunch baby carrots
100 g (3 1/2 oz) Swiss brown
   mushrooms, halved
100 g (3 1/2 oz) button
   mushrooms, halved
1 tablespoon cornflour
chopped parsley, for serving

1 Soak the mushrooms for 30 minutes in enough boiling water to cover.
2 Brown the sausages well all over in a lightly oiled pan over medium heat. Drain on paper towels and place in a large, flameproof casserole dish.
3 Remove the rind from the speck or bacon; cut the meat into small strips. Heat the oil in a pan and add the speck, onions and garlic. Cook, stirring, until the onions are golden, then place in the casserole dish with the thyme, bay leaves, wine, stock and mustard. Cover, bring to the boil, then reduce the heat and simmer for 20 minutes.
4 Reserving 3 tablespoons of liquid, drain the mushrooms. Add the carrots and all mushrooms to the stew. Cover and simmer for 20 minutes. Mix the cornflour into the reserved liquid; stir into the stew until it boils and thickens. Sprinkle with parsley to serve.

NUTRITION PER SERVE (6)
Protein 30 g; Fat 40 g; Carbohydrate 10 g; Dietary Fibre 7 g; Cholesterol 115 mg; 2455 kJ (590 cal)

COOK'S FILE

Note: Speck is a type of smoked bacon sold in delicatessens.

Cover the porcini mushrooms with boiling water and soak for 30 minutes.

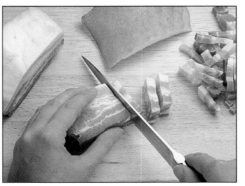

Remove the rind from the speck and cut the meat into small strips.

Add the carrots and all the mushrooms to the sausages. Simmer for 20 minutes.

CHICKEN CHASSEUR

Preparation time: 20 minutes
Total cooking time: 1 hour 30 minutes
Serves 4

1 kg (2 lb) chicken thigh fillets
2 tablespoons oil
1 clove garlic, crushed
1 large onion, sliced
100 g (3¼ oz) button mushrooms,
    sliced
1 teaspoon thyme leaves
400 g (13 oz) can chopped
    tomatoes

¼ cup (60 ml/2 fl oz) chicken
    stock
¼ cup (60 ml/2 fl oz) white wine
1 tablespoon tomato paste

1 Preheat the oven to moderate 180°C (350°F/Gas 4). Trim the chicken of excess fat and sinew. Heat the oil in a heavy-based frying pan and brown the chicken in batches over medium heat. Drain on paper towels, then transfer to a casserole dish.
2 Add the garlic, onion and mushrooms to the pan and cook over medium heat for 5 minutes, or until soft. Add to the chicken with the thyme and tomatoes.

3 Combine the stock, wine and tomato paste and pour over the chicken. Cover and bake for 1¼ hours, or until the chicken is tender.

NUTRITION PER SERVE
Protein 60 g; Fat 15 g; Carbohydrate 6 g; Dietary Fibre 2 g; Cholesterol 125 mg; 1710 kJ (410 cal)

COOK'S FILE

Storage time: This dish may be cooked a day ahead. Refrigerate in an airtight container overnight.
Note: Don't be tempted to use poor quality wine for cooking, as the taste will affect the flavour of the dish.

Brown the chicken in the hot oil over medium heat and drain on paper towels.

Add the garlic, onion and mushrooms to the pan and cook until soft.

Pour the combined stock, wine and tomato paste over the chicken mixture.

Using sharp scissors, cut the forelegs off the rabbit through the connective tissue.

Cutting where the hind legs join the body, remove the legs and cut in half to separate.

Cut the ribcage and body of the rabbit into 4 even pieces.

Add the peeled and chopped tomatoes to the pan and simmer for 45 minutes.

COUNTRY RABBIT IN RED WINE

Preparation time: 15 minutes
Total cooking time: 1 hour 30 minutes
Serves 4

1.25 kg (2 lb 8 oz) rabbit
1/2 cup (125 ml/4 fl oz) olive oil
2 cloves garlic, crushed
1 sprig of rosemary, finely chopped
1 cup (250 ml/8 fl oz) red wine
1/2 cup (125 ml/4 fl oz) chicken stock
4 tomatoes, peeled and chopped

1 Cut the forelegs from the rabbit by cutting through the connective tissue joining the body. Cut across the back of the rabbit just above the legs, then cut the legs in half. Cut the body (saddle) of the rabbit into 2 pieces, then cut the ribcage and backbone into 4 pieces, to form 8 portions.

2 Heat the oil in a heavy-based pan. Add the rabbit, garlic and rosemary and brown the rabbit over medium heat on all sides.

3 Add the wine and stock; season with salt and freshly ground black pepper. Cover and simmer gently for 30 minutes. Add the tomatoes and cook, covered, for another 45 minutes over low heat, or until the rabbit is tender. Serve with crusty Italian bread to mop up the juices.

NUTRITION PER SERVE
Protein 75 g; Fat 40 g; Carbohydrate 4 g; Dietary Fibre 2 g; Cholesterol 190 mg; 3020 kJ (720 cal)

COOK'S FILE

Note: To save time, ask your butcher or poulterer to cut the rabbit for you.

RED WINE AND PORK STEW

Preparation time: 30 minutes +
   overnight marinating
Total cooking time: 1 hour 30 minutes
Serves 4–6

750 g (1¹/₂ lb) pork, cut into
   3 cm (1¹/₄ inch) cubes
¹/₄ cup (60 ml/2 fl oz) oil
plain flour, seasoned with salt
   and freshly ground pepper
12 bulb spring onions, trimmed
3 rashers bacon, cut into strips
2 carrots, chopped
200 g (6¹/₂ oz) button mushrooms
2 sticks celery, sliced

1¹/₂ cups (375 ml/12 fl oz)
   chicken stock
1 teaspoon thyme leaves
1 tablespoon chopped parsley

Marinade
1 cup (250 ml/8 fl oz) red wine
1 tablespoon olive oil
4 cloves garlic, crushed
1 tablespoon thyme leaves
2 teaspoons rosemary leaves
2 tablespoons chopped parsley

1 Combine the marinade ingredients
in a large bowl. Add the pork and mix
well. Cover and refrigerate overnight.
2 Reserving the marinade, drain the
pork. Heat 2 tablespoons of the oil in a
large, deep saucepan. Coat the pork in

the flour and brown in batches over
high heat. Remove and set aside.
3 Heat the remaining oil. Cook the
onions and bacon over medium-high
heat for 5 minutes. Add the carrots,
mushrooms and celery and cook for
5 minutes, stirring constantly.
4 Add the pork, chicken stock and
reserved marinade. Bring to the boil,
then reduce the heat and simmer for
1¹/₄ to 1¹/₂ hours, or until the pork is
very tender, stirring often to prevent
sticking. Season well with salt and
freshly ground pepper. Stir in the
herbs and serve.

NUTRITION PER SERVE (6)
Protein 35 g; Fat 15 g; Carbohydrate 3.5 g;
Dietary Fibre 3 g; Cholesterol 70 mg;
1340 kJ (320 cal)

*Combine the marinade ingredients and
the pork in a large bowl.*

*Lightly coat the drained pork in the
seasoned flour.*

*Add the reserved marinade to the meat
and vegetables.*

ROSEMARY-INFUSED LAMB AND LENTIL CASSEROLE

Preparation time: 20 minutes
Total cooking time: 2 hours 30 minutes
Serves 6

25 g (³/4 oz) butter
2 tablespoons olive oil
1 onion, finely sliced
2 cloves garlic, crushed
1 small carrot, finely chopped
2 teaspoons cumin seeds
¹/4 teaspoon chilli flakes
2 teaspoons finely chopped
   fresh ginger
1 kg (2 lb) boned leg of lamb,
   cut into 4 cm (1¹/2 inch)
   cubes
2 teaspoons rosemary leaves
3 cups (750 ml/24 fl oz) lamb
   or chicken stock
1 cup (185 g/6 oz) green or
   brown lentils
3 teaspoons soft brown sugar
2 teaspoons balsamic vinegar
sprigs of rosemary, to garnish

1 Preheat the oven to moderate 180°C (350°F/Gas 4). Heat the butter and half the oil in a large, heavy-based pan. Add the onion, garlic and carrot and cook over medium heat for about 5 minutes, or until soft and golden. Add the cumin seeds, chilli flakes and ginger, cook for 1 minute, then transfer to a large casserole dish.
2 Heat the remaining oil in the pan and brown the lamb in batches over high heat. Transfer to the casserole dish.
3 Add the rosemary to the pan and stir in 2¹/2 cups (625 ml/20 fl oz) of the stock, scraping up all the brown bits from the base and side of the pan.

Heat until the stock is bubbling, then pour into the casserole dish. Cover and bake for 1 hour.
4 Add the lentils, sugar and vinegar and cook for 1 hour more, or until the lentils are cooked. If the mixture is too thick, stir in the remaining stock.

Season with salt and freshly ground pepper and garnish with rosemary sprigs to serve.

NUTRITION PER SERVE
Protein 45 g; Fat 15 g; Carbohydrate 15 g; Dietary Fibre 5 g; Cholesterol 120 mg; 1618 kJ (385 cal)

When the oil is hot, add the onion, garlic and carrot and cook until soft and golden.

After browning the lamb, add the rosemary and stock, scraping up the brown bits.

Bake the casserole for 1 hour, then add the lentils, sugar and vinegar.

VIETNAMESE CHICKEN AND NOODLE CASSEROLE

Preparation time: 40 minutes
Total cooking time: 25 minutes
Serves 4

1 stem lemon grass
4 Kaffir lime leaves
1 litre chicken stock
400 ml (13 fl oz) coconut cream
¼ cup (30 g/1 oz) coconut milk
   powder
2 tablespoons peanut oil
400 g (13 oz) chicken breast
   fillet, cut into strips
12 raw king prawns, peeled and
   deveined, tails intact
8 spring onions, sliced
2 teaspoons finely chopped
   fresh ginger
4 cloves garlic, finely chopped
2 small red chillies, seeded and
   finely chopped
500 g (1 lb) Hokkien noodles
1 teaspoon dried shrimp paste
2 tablespoons lime juice
1 cup (90 g/3 oz) bean sprouts
mint leaves, to garnish
coriander leaves, to garnish

1 Finely chop the white stem of the lemon grass. Remove the centre stem from the Kaffir lime leaves, then finely shred the leaves.
2 Place the lemon grass and lime leaves in a large, heavy-based pan with the stock, coconut cream and coconut milk powder. Bring to the boil, stirring constantly to dissolve the coconut milk powder. Reduce the heat and simmer, covered, for 15 minutes.
3 Heat a wok over high heat and add the peanut oil. Toss in the chicken, prawns, spring onion, ginger, garlic and chillies. Stir-fry for 5–10 minutes, or until the chicken and prawns are cooked through.
4 Place the noodles in the simmering coconut cream, then add the chicken and prawn mixture from the wok. Add the shrimp paste and lime juice. Allow the noodles to heat through.

5 Divide the sprouts among warmed deep bowls and place the noodles, chicken and prawns on top. Ladle the sauce over, scatter with mint and coriander and serve at once.

NUTRITION PER SERVE
Protein 40 g; Fat 35 g; Carbohydrate 10 g; Dietary Fibre 4 g; Cholesterol 135 mg; 2150 kJ (515 cal)

Using a sharp knife, finely chop the white stem of the lemon grass.

Stir-fry the chicken, prawns, spring onions, ginger, garlic and chilli.

Add the noodles to the simmering coconut cream mixture.

RABBIT, CHORIZO AND OLIVE CASSEROLE

Preparation time: 35 minutes
Total cooking time: 2 hours 30 minutes
Serves 4–6

150 g (5 oz) French shallots
2 tablespoons olive oil
2 kg (4 lb) rabbit pieces
2 chorizo sausages, sliced
12 pickling onions
2 cloves garlic, crushed
1 teaspoon dried thyme
1 teaspoon paprika
1 tablespoon plain flour
1/2 cup (125 ml/4 fl oz) white wine
1 1/2 cups (375 ml/12 fl oz)
   chicken stock

1 tablespoon tomato paste
1/2 teaspoon grated orange rind
1/3 cup (80 ml/2 3/4 fl oz) orange
   juice
12 Kalamata olives
2 tablespoons chopped parsley
2 tablespoons chopped chives

1 Soak the shallots in boiling water for 30 seconds; drain and peel. Preheat the oven to moderate 180°C (350°F/Gas 4).

2 In a large, heavy-based pan, heat half the oil and brown the rabbit in batches over high heat, then transfer to a large casserole dish. Heat the remaining oil; fry the chorizo, shallots and onions over medium heat until soft and golden.

3 Add the garlic, thyme and paprika and cook for 1 minute. Add the flour and cook for 30 seconds.

4 Remove from the heat, pour in the wine and stir well, scraping up any bits in the pan. Return to the heat, add the stock and stir until bubbling. Add the tomato paste, rind and orange juice, then add to the rabbit and mix well. Cover and cook for 2–2 1/4 hours, or until the rabbit is tender. Season to taste, stir in the olives and parsley and scatter with chives to serve.

NUTRITION PER SERVE (6)
Protein 95 g; Fat 28 g; Carbohydrate 12 g; Dietary Fibre 1.5 g; Cholesterol 264 mg; 3052 kJ (730 cal)

C O O K ' S   F I L E

Note: Chorizo is a spicy Spanish pork sausage flavoured with cayenne.
Serving suggestion: Lovely with creamy parsnip mash.

Place the shallots in a bowl and cover with boiling water, then drain and peel.

Heat half the oil in a large pan. Brown the rabbit in batches over high heat.

Heat the remaining oil in the pan and add the chorizo, shallots and onions.

PORK WITH SOUR CHERRIES

Preparation time: 15 minutes
Total cooking time: 1 hour 35 minutes
Serves 4

1.5 kg (3 lb) pork neck (pork
    scotch fillet)
plain flour, seasoned with salt
    and freshly ground pepper
1/4 cup (60 ml/2 fl oz) olive oil
30 g (1 oz) butter
2 onions, sliced
1/2 cup (125 ml/4 fl oz) chicken
    stock
1/2 cup (125 ml/4 fl oz) red wine
2 tablespoons chopped tarragon
    leaves
700 g (1 lb 7 oz) jar pitted
    cherries, syrup reserved

1 Preheat the oven to warm 160°C
(315°F/Gas 2–3). Cut the pork into 4 cm
(1½ inch) cubes and toss lightly in the
seasoned flour, shaking off any excess.
Heat the oil in a large heavy-based
pan. In batches, quickly brown the
pork over medium heat and transfer
to a large, shallow casserole dish.
2 Melt the butter in the pan. Cook the
onion over low heat for 10 minutes, or
until soft but not brown.
3 Add the stock, wine, tarragon and
1 cup (250 ml/8 fl oz) of the reserved
cherry syrup. Stirring, bring to the
boil and season to taste. Pour the
mixture over the pork, then cover and
bake for 1 hour. Drain the cherries,
stir them through the mixture and
bake for 15 minutes to heat through.

NUTRITION PER SERVE
Protein 90 g; Fat 25 g; Carbohydrate 30 g;
Dietary Fibre 4 g; Cholesterol 190 mg;
3050 kJ (730 cal)

*Add the pork to the hot oil and cook over
medium heat until well browned.*

*Add the onions to the melted butter and
cook until soft but not brown.*

*Add the stock, wine, tarragon and the
cherry syrup to the softened onions.*

KIDNEYS IN CREAMY MUSTARD SAUCE

Preparation time: 15 minutes
Total cooking time: 25 minutes
Serves 4

8 lamb kidneys
50 g (1³/₄ oz) butter
6 French shallots, finely sliced
1 cup (250 ml/8 fl oz) cream
2 teaspoons wholegrain mustard
2 teaspoons Dijon mustard
¹/₃ cup (20 g/³/₄ oz) chopped
   parsley

1 To prepare the kidneys, slice them in half lengthways. Using a pair of small sharp scissors, carefully snip out the core of each kidney and remove any membrane.
2 Melt half the butter in a small pan. Add the shallots and gently cook for 5 minutes, or until soft and golden. Add the cream and simmer for 10 minutes, or until reduced by one-quarter. Remove from the heat and stir in both mustards; mix well and set aside.
3 Melt the remaining butter in a frying pan over medium heat. When the butter foams, cook the kidney halves for 2 minutes on each side.

4 Pour the creamy mustard sauce over the kidneys and simmer, stirring, for 2 minutes. Stir in the chopped parsley and serve.

NUTRITION PER SERVE
Protein 20 g; Fat 40 g; Carbohydrate 2 g; Dietary Fibre 0 g; Cholesterol 455 mg; 1820 kJ (435 cal)

COOK'S FILE

Note: When buying kidneys, select those that are firm and have a rich, even colour.
Serving suggestion: This dish is delicious served with mashed potato and steamed green beans.

Cut the kidneys in half lengthways and remove the core and membrane.

Add the two mustards to the cream and stir until well combined.

Pour the cream and mustard sauce over the kidneys.

BEEF BOURGUIGNON

Preparation time: 10 minutes
Total cooking time: 2 hours
Serves 4–6

1 kg (2 lb) topside or round steak
plain flour, seasoned with salt
    and freshly ground pepper
3 rashers bacon, rind removed
oil, for cooking
12 pickling onions
1 cup (250 ml/ 8 fl oz) red wine
2 cups (500 ml/16 fl oz) beef
    stock

1 teaspoon dried thyme
200 g (6½ oz) button mushrooms
2 bay leaves

1 Trim the steak of fat and sinew and cut into 2 cm (3/4 inch) cubes. Lightly toss in the seasoned flour to coat, shaking off the excess.
2 Cut the bacon into 2 cm (3/4 inch) squares. Heat some oil in a large pan and quickly cook the bacon over medium heat. Remove the bacon from the pan, then add the meat and brown well in batches. Remove and set aside. Add the onions to the pan and cook until golden.

3 Return the bacon and meat to the pan with the remaining ingredients. Bring to the boil, reduce the heat and simmer, covered, for 1½ hours, or until the meat is very tender, stirring now and then. Remove the bay leaves to serve. Mashed potato and steamed green beans are a nice accompaniment.

NUTRITION PER SERVE (6)
Protein 40 g; Fat 7 g; Carbohydrate 5 g; Dietary Fibre 1 g; Cholesterol 90 mg; 1150 kJ (275 cal)

COOK'S FILE

Storage time: Refrigerate in an airtight container for up to 3 days.

Trim the meat of fat and sinew and cut into cubes.

Fry the bacon in the hot oil over medium heat until lightly browned.

Return the bacon and meat to the pan and add the remaining ingredients.

PORK AND MUSTARD STEW

Preparation time: 15 minutes
Total cooking time: 1 hour 10 minutes
Serves 4–6

2 tablespoons oil
1 kg (2 lb) pork neck, cut into
    3 cm (1¼ inch cubes)
20 g (3/4 oz) butter
1 large onion, sliced
1 clove garlic, crushed

250 g (8 oz) button mushrooms,
    halved
1 tablespoon plain flour
1/3 cup (80 ml/2¾ fl oz) lemon
    juice
1 cup (250 ml/8 fl oz) chicken
    stock
2 tablespoons wholegrain mustard
2 teaspoons honey
½ teaspoon ground cumin

1 Preheat the oven to warm 170°C (325°F/Gas 3). Heat the oil in a large, heavy-based pan and brown the pork

in batches over high heat. Transfer to a large casserole dish.
2 Add the butter to the pan and cook the onion and garlic until soft but not brown. Add the mushrooms and cook for 1 minute. Stir in the flour, then the remaining ingredients. Stirring, bring to the boil. Season to taste and spoon the mixture over the pork. Cover and bake for 45 minutes, or until tender.

NUTRITION PER SERVE (6)
Protein 40 g; Fat 10 g; Carbohydrate 5 g; Dietary Fibre 2 g; Cholesterol 85 mg; 1195 kJ (285 cal)

Using a sharp knife, cut the pork neck into large cubes.

In the same pan, melt the butter, add the onion and garlic and cook until soft.

Stir the flour into the onion and garlic mixture. Add the remaining ingredients.

Beef bourguignon (top)
with Pork and mustard stew

TRADITIONAL LAMB SHANKS

Preparation time: 30 minutes
Total cooking time: 2 hours 25 minutes
Serves 4–6

8 lamb shanks
1 tablespoon olive oil
1 orange
1 large onion, sliced
4 cloves garlic
1 large carrot, cut into chunks
1 parsnip, cut into chunks
1 stick celery, cut into chunks
2 bay leaves
3 cups (750 ml/24 fl oz) chicken
    stock
2 cups (500 ml/16 fl oz) red wine
1 tablespoon redcurrant jelly
3 teaspoons cornflour
sprigs of thyme, to garnish

1 Preheat the oven to warm 160°C (315°F/Gas 2–3). Pat the shanks dry with paper towels. Heat the oil in a flameproof casserole or baking dish large enough to fit the shanks in a single layer, then brown the shanks over high heat for 3 minutes, turning frequently. Remove and set aside.

2 Peel three 5 cm (2 inch) strips of rind from the orange, avoiding the bitter white pith. Set aside.

3 Add the onion and garlic cloves to the dish and cook over medium heat for 2 minutes, stirring. Add the carrot, parsnip and celery and place the shanks snugly on top. Add the rind strips and bay leaves, then pour in the stock and red wine. Cover and bake for 2 hours, or until the meat is very tender and comes away from the bone.

4 Using tongs, carefully remove the shanks from the dish; cover with foil to keep warm. Remove the rind and bay leaves and strain the juices into a pan. Set the vegetables aside.

5 Add the redcurrant jelly to the dish and stir to dissolve. Boil rapidly for 20 minutes, or until the sauce is reduced to 1½ cups (375 ml/12 fl oz). Combine the cornflour with a little water and whisk into the sauce, stirring until thickened and glossy.

6 To serve, place the lamb shanks on serving plates, arrange the vegetables on top, drizzle with the sauce and garnish with thyme.

NUTRITION PER SERVE (6)
Protein 40 g; Fat 7 g; Carbohydrate 9 g; Dietary Fibre 2.5 g; Cholesterol 112 mg; 1355 kJ (325 cal)

COOK'S FILE

Note: This dish can be refrigerated for 2 days, or frozen for 2 months.

Heat the oil in a baking dish and brown the shanks over high heat.

Peel strips of rind from the orange, avoiding the bitter white pith.

VEAL WITH ALMONDS AND MUSHROOMS

Preparation time: 20 minutes
Total cooking time: 1 hour 50 minutes
Serves 4–6

75 g (2½ oz) blanched
    almonds
olive oil, for cooking
2 onions, chopped
1 kg (2 lb) diced veal
plain flour, seasoned with salt
    and freshly ground pepper
½ cup (125 ml/4 fl oz) red wine
500 g (1 lb) very ripe tomatoes,
    chopped
2 tablespoons chopped oregano
50 g (1¾ oz) butter
400 g (13 oz) mushrooms (such
    as tiny buttons, shiitake or
    porcini)

1 Preheat the oven to slow 150°C (300°F/Gas 2). Scatter the almonds on a baking tray and bake for 10 minutes, or until golden. Cool and roughly chop.
2 Heat 2 tablespoons of oil in a deep, heavy-based pan. Cook the onion over low heat for 15 minutes, stirring often. Remove and set aside, leaving as much oil as possible in the pan.
3 Toss the veal in the flour, shaking off any excess. Reheat the pan and brown the veal over medium heat in batches, adding more oil if necessary.
4 Return all the veal to the pan with any juices; add the onion and wine. Bring to the boil and stir well. Reduce the heat to very low, cover with foil and a tightly fitting lid, then simmer very gently for 1 hour.
5 Stir well, then mix in the tomatoes and oregano. Cover and simmer for another 20 minutes. Season to taste.

6 Melt the butter until foamy in a frying pan over medium heat. Cut any large mushrooms and cook until just wilted, tossing well.
7 To serve, dish the stew onto serving plates, top with the mushrooms, drizzle over any juices and sprinkle with the chopped toasted almonds.

NUTRITION PER SERVE (6)
Protein 45 g; Fat 17 g; Carbohydrate 6 g; Dietary Fibre 4 g; Cholesterol 160 mg; 1565 kJ (375 cal)

Gently cook the onion for 15 minutes, or until golden. Remove and set aside.

Return the browned veal to the pan with any juices. Add the onions and red wine.

When the butter is foaming, add all the mushrooms and cook until just wilted.

CHILLI CON CARNE

Preparation time: 10 minutes
Total cooking time: 50 minutes
Serves 4

1 tablespoon olive oil
1 onion, chopped
3 cloves garlic, crushed
1 stick celery, sliced
500 g (1 lb) lean beef mince
2 teaspoons chilli powder
pinch of cayenne pepper
1 tablespoon chopped oregano

400 g (13 oz) can crushed
   tomatoes
2 tablespoons tomato paste
1 teaspoon soft brown sugar
1 tablespoon cider vinegar or
   red wine vinegar
420 g (13 oz) can red kidney
   beans, drained and rinsed

1 Heat the oil in a large, heavy-based pan. Add the onion, garlic and celery and cook, stirring, over medium heat for 5 minutes, or until softened.
2 Add the mince and stir over high heat for 5 minutes, or until well browned. Add the chilli powder, cayenne and oregano. Stir well and cook over medium heat for 5 minutes.
3 Mix in the tomatoes, tomato paste and 1/2 cup (125 ml/4 fl oz) of water. Simmer for 30 minutes, stirring now and then.
4 Add the sugar, vinegar and beans and season to taste with salt and freshly ground black pepper. Heat through for 5 minutes before serving.

NUTRITION PER SERVE
Protein 35 g; Fat 20 g; Carbohydrate 20 g; Dietary Fibre 10 g; Cholesterol 80 mg; 1640 kJ (390 cal)

Add the mince to the onion, garlic and celery mixture. Stir until well browned.

Add the crushed tomatoes, tomato paste and water to the mince mixture.

Stir in the sugar, vinegar and drained kidney beans and simmer for 5 minutes.

LEMON LAMB WITH JUNIPER BERRIES

Preparation time: 30 minutes
Total cooking time: 2 hours
Serves 4

¼ cup (60 ml/2 fl oz) olive oil
2 large onions, chopped
2 cloves garlic, chopped
1 kg (2 lb) diced lamb
2 cups (500 ml/16 fl oz) chicken
  stock
4 large carrots
3 sticks celery
15 juniper berries
¾ cup (185 ml/7 fl oz) dry white
  wine
1 wedge preserved lemon

1 Heat 1 tablespoon of the oil in a large, heavy-based pan. Add the onion and garlic, cover and cook gently, shaking the pan to prevent sticking, for 12 minutes or until the onion is very soft, sweet and starting to colour. Remove and set aside.

2 Heat some more oil in the pan. In batches, brown the lamb over high heat, adding oil as needed; remove and set aside. Return the onion to the pan with any juices from the lamb.

3 Over high heat, stir in ½ cup (125 ml/ 4 fl oz) of the stock and allow it to reduce by half. Repeat this process twice, until the liquid is rich and dark: do not rush this step, as it produces a superb flavour.

4 Chop the carrots and celery to an even size, and bruise the juniper berries with the flat side of a large knife. Add them to the pan with the lamb, wine and remaining stock. Season well. Cover and simmer for 1 hour, or until the lamb is tender.

5 Rinse the preserved lemon. Discard the salty flesh and cut the rind into strips. Add to the pan, then cover and simmer for 20 minutes, or until the stew has thickened. Season to taste with salt and freshly ground pepper and serve.

NUTRITION PER SERVE
Protein 60 g; Fat 24 g; Carbohydrate 8 g; Dietary Fibre 4 g; Cholesterol 165 mg; 2104 kJ (500 cal)

COOK'S FILE

Note: Juniper berries are sold in the spice section of good supermarkets.

Add the onion and garlic to the oil. Cover and gently cook until very soft.

Chop the carrots and celery into evenly sized pieces.

Using the flat side of a large knife, bruise the juniper berries.

BOMBAY LAMB CURRY

Preparation time: 25 minutes
Total cooking time: 1 hour 25 minutes
Serves 4–6

1.5 kg leg lamb, boned (ask
    your butcher to do this)
2 tablespoons ghee or oil
2 onions, finely chopped
2 cloves garlic, crushed
2 small green chillies,
    finely chopped
5 cm piece ginger, grated
1¹/₂ teaspoons turmeric
2 teaspoons ground cumin
3 teaspoons ground coriander
¹/₂–1 teaspoon chilli powder
1–1¹/₂ teaspoons salt
425 g can crushed tomatoes
2 tablespoons coconut cream

1 Cut the meat into cubes, removing any skin and fat. You will have about 1 kg meat remaining. Heat the ghee or oil in a large heavy-based frying pan (with a lid). Add the onion and cook, stirring frequently, over medium high heat for 10 minutes until golden brown. Add the garlic, chillies and ginger and stir for a further 2 minutes, taking care not to burn them.

2 Mix together the turmeric, cumin, coriander and chilli powder in a small bowl. Stir to a smooth paste with 2 tablespoons water and add to the frying pan. Stir constantly for 2 minutes, taking care not to burn them.

3 Add the meat a handful at a time, stirring well to coat with spices. It is important to make sure all the meat is well-coated and browned.

4 Add the salt to taste and stir in the undrained tomatoes. Bring to the boil, cover and reduce the heat to low. Simmer for 45–60 minutes, until the lamb is tender. Stir in the coconut cream 30 minutes before the end of the cooking time.

NUTRITION PER SERVE (6)
Protein 58 g; Fat 13 g; Carbohydrate 5 g; Dietary Fibre 1.5 g; Cholesterol 165 mg; 1565 kJ (375 cal)

COOK'S FILE

Storage time: Keep covered and refrigerated for up to 3 days. The flavour of curry improves if kept for at least 1 day.

Cut the meat into bite-sized chunks, about 3 cm square.

Once the onion is golden brown, stir in the garlic, chilli and ginger.

Blend the ground spices to a smooth paste with a little water.

Add the meat a handful at a time to make sure it is thoroughly coated.

PERSIAN CHICKEN

Preparation time: 20 minutes
Total cooking time: 1 hour
Serves 6

1.5 kg small chicken thighs
1/2 cup plain flour
2 tablespoons olive oil
1 large onion, chopped
2 cloves garlic, chopped
1/2 teaspoon ground cinnamon
4 ripe tomatoes, chopped
6 fresh dates, stones removed, halved
2 tablespoons currants

2 cups rich chicken stock
2 teaspoons finely grated lemon rind
salt and freshly ground black pepper
1/2 cup almonds, toasted and roughly chopped
2 tablespoons chopped fresh parsley

1 Coat the chicken pieces with flour and shake off any excess. Heat the oil in a large heavy-based pan over moderate heat. Brown the chicken on all sides, turning regularly, and then remove from the pan. Drain any excess oil from the pan.

2 Add the onion, garlic and ground cinnamon to the pan and cook for 5 minutes, stirring regularly, until the onion is soft.

3 Add the tomatoes, dates, currants and stock. Bring to the boil, return the chicken to the pan, cover with sauce, lower the heat and simmer uncovered for 30 minutes. Add the lemon rind and season to taste. Bring back to the boil and boil for 5 minutes, or until thickened. Garnish with almonds and parsley and serve with buttered rice.

NUTRITION PER SERVE
Protein 56 g; Fat 20 g; Carbohydrate 17 g; Dietary Fibre 3.5 g; Cholesterol 175 mg; 1975 kJ (470 cal)

An easy way to coat the chicken with flour is to toss them both in a bag.

Brown the chicken on all sides, turning it regularly to prevent sticking.

Add the tomatoes, dates, currants and stock to the softened onion.

BEEF OLIVES

Beef olives can be filled with the traditional sage filling or the sun-dried tomato filling below. Each filling will serve 4 people.

Preparation time: 20 minutes
Total cooking time: 1 hour 30 minutes
Serves 4

1 kg skirt steak, cut into thin
   slices lengthways
1/4 cup plain flour
1 tablespoon olive oil
1 carrot, finely chopped
1 cup red wine
425 g can crushed tomatoes
2 bay leaves

Traditional sage filling:
1 tablespoon olive oil
1 small onion, chopped
2 cloves garlic, chopped
2 large tomatoes, diced
1/2 cup fresh breadcrumbs
2 tablespoons chopped sage

Sun-dried tomato, mushroom
* and olive filling:*
1 tablespoon olive oil
4 spring onions, chopped
2 cloves garlic, crushed
100 g mushrooms, chopped
8 sun-dried tomatoes, chopped
60 g black olives, chopped
1/2 cup fresh breadcrumbs
2 tablespoons chopped basil

1 Put the steak between sheets of plastic wrap and pound with a meat mallet until very thin, taking care not to tear the meat. Set aside.
2 To make the Sage Filling: Heat the oil in a deep heavy-based pan and cook the onion and garlic, stirring, for 3 minutes. Transfer the mixture to a bowl and add the tomatoes, breadcrumbs, sage and salt and pepper to taste. Mix well and set aside.

To make the Sun-dried Tomato Filling: Heat the oil in a heavy-based pan, add the spring onion, garlic and mushrooms and cook for 3 minutes, stirring continuously, over medium heat. Transfer to a bowl, add the tomatoes, olives, breadcrumbs, basil and salt and pepper, to taste. Mix well and set aside.

3 Lay a slice of meat on a board and place about 1/3 cup of filling neatly along the short edge. Roll up firmly, folding in a little of the sides as you roll, and tie with string to secure.

4 Repeat with the remaining meat and filling. Roll the Beef Olives lightly in flour, shaking off any excess.

5 Wipe out the pan with paper towels and add the oil. Brown the carrots and Beef Olives in batches over medium heat, turning regularly, and then return them all to the pan.

6 Add the wine, undrained tomatoes and bay leaves to the pan and turn the Olives to coat them. Cover and simmer very gently over low heat for 1 hour, or until tender. Remove from the sauce, trim away the string and slice the Olives. Remove the bay leaves and purée the sauce in a food processor or blender until smooth. Serve poured over the Beef Olives.

NUTRITION PER SERVE
Protein 65 g; Fat 25 g; Carbohydrate 30 g; Dietary Fibre 6.5 g; Cholesterol 170 mg; 2695 kJ (645 cal)

COOK'S FILE

Storage time: Beef Olives may be prepared to the end of step 4 and refrigerated for up to 1 day.

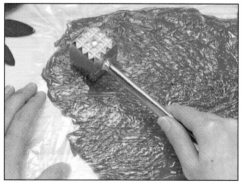

Pound the steak with a meat mallet between two sheets of plastic wrap.

For the Sage Filling add the breadcrumbs with the other ingredients and mix well.

Roll the Olives firmly, folding in a little from the sides as you roll.

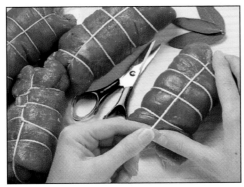

Once they are rolled up, secure the Olives with string.

Brown the Olives in batches and then return them all to the pan.

Use a pair of tongs to lift the Beef Olives from the sauce.

LAMB CHOP CASSEROLE

Preparation time: 15 minutes
Total cooking time: 1 hour 15 minutes
Serves 4

6–8 lamb chump chops
1 teaspoon oil
1 large onion, finely chopped
1/3 cup redcurrant jelly
1 teaspoon grated lemon rind
1 tablespoon lemon juice
1 tablespoon barbecue sauce
1 tablespoon tomato sauce
1/2 cup chicken stock

1 Trim any fat from the lamb. Preheat the oven to 170°C. Heat the oil in a large heavy-based frying pan; add the chops and cook over medium-high heat for 2–3 minutes, turning once, until well browned. Remove from the pan and put in a casserole dish.
2 Add the onion to the frying pan and cook over medium heat, stirring frequently, for 5 minutes or until the onion is softened. Add the jelly, lemon rind and juice, barbecue and tomato sauces and stock. Stir for 2–3 minutes until heated through. Pour over the chops and stir well, cover and place in the oven. Cook for 1 hour, or until the

meat is tender, turning 2–3 times. Lift out the chops onto a side plate and leave them to keep warm.
3 Pour the sauce into a pan and boil rapidly for 5 minutes until the sauce has thickened and reduced. Return the chops to the sauce before serving.

NUTRITION PER SERVE
Protein 30 g; Fat 11 g; Carbohydrate 13 g; Dietary Fibre 1 g; Cholesterol 95 mg; 1150 kJ (275 cal)

COOK'S FILE

Storage time: Keep covered and refrigerated for up to 2 days. Suitable to freeze for up to 1 month.

Once the chops have been well browned put them in a casserole dish.

Pour the sauce over the chops in the dish and stir to combine.

Use a pair of tongs to turn the chops a couple of times during cooking.

POACHER'S RABBIT

Preparation time: 30 minutes
Total cooking time: 2 hours 15 minutes
Serves 4

1 tablespoon vinegar
1 tablespoon salt
1 rabbit, about 1 kg, cut
   into 12 portions
   (ask your butcher to do this)
1/4 cup plain flour
salt and freshly ground pepper
1/3 cup olive oil
2 rashers bacon, roughly
   chopped
8 bulb spring onions, trimmed
2 medium carrots, finely sliced
1 1/2 cups cider
2 teaspoons French mustard
1/2 teaspoon dried rosemary
1/2 teaspoon dried thyme
1 bay leaf
1/3 cup finely chopped parsley

1 Add the vinegar and salt to a bowl of water and leave the rabbit portions to soak overnight. Drain, rinse well and dry on paper towels. Combine the flour, salt and pepper in a large bowl and toss the rabbit in seasoned flour. Preheat the oven to moderate 180°C.

2 Heat 1/4 cup of the oil in a large heavy-based frying pan and brown the rabbit quickly in batches over medium heat. Transfer to a 2 litre casserole dish.

3 Add the remaining oil to the pan; add the bacon, onions and carrot and fry over medium heat for 5 minutes, or until lightly browned. Add to the casserole dish.

4 Pour the cider into the frying pan and stir in the mustard, herbs and bay leaf. Bring to the boil and then pour over the rabbit. Cover with a tight-fitting lid and bake for 2 hours, or until tender. Remove the bay leaf and stir in the parsley.

NUTRITION PER SERVE
Protein 65 g; Fat 40 g; Carbohydrate 13 g; Dietary Fibre 2 g; Cholesterol 160 mg; 2864 kJ (684 cal)

COOK'S FILE

Storage time: Refrigerate for up to 2 days. Freeze for up to 1 month.
Hint: For more sauce, add more cider or water towards the end of cooking.

Use paper towels to dry the drained and rinsed rabbit portions.

Cut the tops and tails from the bulb spring onions.

Fry the bacon, onions and carrot until lightly browned.

Add the mustard, herbs and bay leaf to the cider in the frying pan.

KASHMIR LAMB WITH SPINACH

Preparation time: 20 minutes
Total cooking time: 1 hour 30 minutes
Serves 4

2 tablespoons oil
750 g diced leg of lamb
2 large onions, chopped
3 cloves garlic, crushed
4 cm fresh ginger, grated
2 teaspoons ground cumin
2 teaspoons ground coriander
2 teaspoons turmeric
1/4 teaspoon ground cardamom

1/4 teaspoon ground cloves
3 bay leaves
11/2 cups chicken stock
1/2 cup cream
2 bunches English spinach
  leaves, washed and chopped

1 Heat the oil in a heavy-based pan and brown the lamb in batches, stirring regularly. Remove from the pan. Add the onions, garlic and ginger and cook for 3 minutes, stirring regularly. Add the cumin, coriander, turmeric, cardamom and cloves and cook, stirring, for 1–2 minutes or until fragrant. Return the lamb to the pan with any juices. Add the bay leaves and stock.

2 Bring to the boil and then reduce the heat, stir well, cover and simmer for 35 minutes. Add the cream and cook, covered, for a further 20 minutes or until the lamb is very tender.

3 Add the spinach and cook until the spinach has softened. Season to taste and serve with steamed rice.

NUTRITION PER SERVE
Protein 45 g; Fat 25 g; Carbohydrate 3 g; Dietary Fibre 2 g; Cholesterol 165 mg; 1820 kJ (435 cal)

COOK'S FILE

Storage time: Curry is best cooked a day in advance and refrigerated. Do not add the spinach until reheating.

Return the browned lamb to the pan and add the bay leaves.

Stir in the cream and simmer until the lamb is very tender.

It will only take a few minutes for the spinach to soften and reduce.

ROMAN CHICKEN

Preparation time: 10 minutes
Total cooking time: 45 minutes
Serves 2–4

1 tablespoon olive oil
1 small onion, sliced
4 thick rashers bacon, diced
4 large or 8 small chicken legs
1 clove garlic, crushed
1/3 cup chopped fresh parsley

1 cup chicken stock
1 tablespoon chopped fresh
  marjoram
440 g can crushed tomatoes

1 Heat the oil in a large heavy-based pan and cook the onion and bacon over medium heat for 5 minutes. Increase the heat and add the chicken in batches. Brown the chicken on all sides, turning often and taking care not to overcook the onion and bacon, for about 5 minutes.

2 Reduce the heat, add the garlic and parsley and cook for 2–3 minutes. Add the stock and marjoram, stirring well. Add the tomatoes, stir well and season to taste.

3 Bring to the boil, cover the pan and simmer gently for 30 minutes, turning the chicken legs occasionally, until they are cooked through.

NUTRITION PER SERVE (4)
Protein 37 g; Fat 10 g; Carbohydrate 5 g; Dietary Fibre 2 g; Cholesterol 80 mg; 1080 kJ (258 cal)

Brown the chicken well, taking care not to burn the onion.

Add the stock and marjoram. Stir well to prevent anything sticking to the pan base.

Turn the chicken legs occasionally to ensure even cooking on all sides.

Kashmir Lamb with Spinach (top) and Roman Chicken

OXTAIL RAGOUT

Preparation time: 20 minutes +
 3 hours soaking
Total cooking time: 4 hours
Serves 4

1 kg oxtail, cut into short pieces
 (ask your butcher to do this)
¼ cup plain flour
1 tablespoon ghee or oil
2 rashers bacon, chopped
1 small onion, peeled and
 studded with 6 whole cloves
2 cloves garlic, peeled
2 carrots, quartered lenghways
1½ cups beef or chicken stock
425 g can tomato purée
1 parsnip, peeled and
 quartered lengthways
1 leek, thickly sliced

1 Trim any fat from the oxtail and discard. Put the oxtail in a large bowl, cover with water and set aside for 3 hours. Drain and transfer the meat to a large heavy-based pan, cover with fresh water and bring to the boil. Reduce the heat and simmer for 10 minutes, skimming any froth from the surface with a spoon or absorbent paper towel. Drain the meat, allow to cool and pat dry with paper towels.

2 Preheat the oven to 150°C. Put the flour, salt and pepper in a large plastic bag; put the oxtail in the bag and shake to coat it with flour. Heat the ghee or oil in a large frying pan, add the bacon and cook over medium heat for 3 minutes, stirring frequently. Remove from the pan.

3 Add the oxtail and cook, stirring continuously over medium-high heat for 2–3 minutes, or until browned. Transfer to a casserole dish.

4 Add the bacon, onion, garlic and half the carrot. Stir in the stock and tomato purée. Cover and bake for 3 hours. Add the remaining carrot, parsnip and leek; cook for 40 minutes, or until the vegetables are tender.

NUTRITION PER SERVE
Protein 30 g; Fat 37 g; Carbohydrate 20 g; Dietary Fibre 5 g; Cholesterol 75 mg; 2300 kJ (545 cal)

COOK'S FILE

Storage time: Best made a day in advance and refrigerated.

Press the cloves firmly into the onion so they don't fall out during cooking.

Put the oxtail in a plastic bag with the flour and shake to coat evenly.

Cook the oxtail over medium-high heat until browned.

Add the remaining carrot with the parsnip and leek.

Use a couple of wooden spoons to toss the lamb cubes in the marinade.

Remove the cardamom pods and cinnamon stick and discard.

Add the marinade and apricot nectar to the meat in the pan.

Add the apricots and prunes and stir through gently.

LAMB AND APRICOT STEW

Preparation time: 30 minutes +
  marinating
Total cooking time: 1 hour 30 minutes
Serves 4–6

2 kg leg lamb, boned (ask your
  butcher to do this)
1 onion, thickly sliced
1/2 cup white wine
1 tablespoon grated lemon rind
1/4 cup lemon juice
1 tablespoon ground coriander
4 cardamom pods
1 cinnamon stick
salt and freshly ground
  black pepper
2 tablespoons oil
170 ml can apricot nectar
1/2 cup dried apricots
1/2 cup pitted prunes
1 tablespoon cornflour
1 tablespoon water
1/2 cup roasted unsalted
  cashew nuts
1/4 cup finely chopped
  fresh parsley

1 Trim away the skin and excess fat and cut the meat into 3 cm cubes. In a large ceramic or glass bowl, combine the onion, wine, lemon rind, juice, coriander, cardamom pods, cinnamon stick, salt and pepper. Toss the lamb cubes in the marinade, cover and refrigerate for a minimum of 8 hours or overnight. Stir 2 or 3 times.

2 Drain the meat and onion mixture, reserving the marinade, and dry on paper towels. Discard the cardamom and cinnamon. Heat the oil in a large heavy-based frying pan and brown the meat and onion, in batches, over high heat for 2–3 minutes.

3 Return all the meat and onion to the pan; add the marinade and apricot nectar. Bring to the boil, cover with a tight-fitting lid, reduce the heat to low and simmer for 30 minutes, stirring once. Add the apricots and prunes, stir gently through, cover and simmer for a further 30 minutes.

4 Combine the cornflour and water and mix to a smooth paste. Add to the pan and stir until thickened; simmer for a further 15 minutes, or until the lamb is tender. Scatter with cashews and parsley and serve with rice.

NUTRITION PER SERVE (6)
Protein 75 g; Fat 23 g; Carbohydrate 19 g; Dietary Fibre 3 g; Cholesterol 210 mg; 2510 kJ (600 cal)

CHICKEN AND ORANGE CASSEROLE

Preparation time: 50 minutes
Total cooking time: 1 hour 30 minutes
Serves 4–6

2 small chickens
1 tablespoon olive oil
2 thick rashers bacon, rind
    removed and thinly sliced
50 g butter
16 small pickling onions, peeled
    (ensure ends are intact)
2–3 cloves garlic, crushed
3 teaspoons grated fresh ginger
2 teaspoons grated orange rind
2 teaspoons ground cumin
2 teaspoons ground coriander
2 tablespoons honey
1 cup fresh orange juice
1 cup white wine
1/2 cup chicken or
    vegetable stock
1 bunch baby carrots
1 large parsnip, peeled
fresh coriander and orange zest,
    to serve

1 Using a sharp knife or a pair of kitchen scissors, cut each chicken into 8 pieces discarding the backbone. Remove any excess fat and discard (remove the skin as well, if preferred).
2 Heat about a teaspoon of the oil in a large, deep heavy-based pan. Add the bacon and cook over medium heat for 2–3 minutes or until just crisp. Remove from the pan and set aside to drain on paper towels. Add the remaining oil and half the butter to the pan. Cook the onions over medium heat until dark golden brown. Shake the pan occasionally to ensure even cooking and browning. Remove from the pan and set aside.
3 Add the chicken pieces to the pan and brown in small batches over medium heat. Remove from the pan and drain on paper towels.
4 Add the remaining butter to the pan. Stir in the garlic, ginger, orange rind, cumin, coriander and honey and cook, stirring, for 1 minute. Add the orange juice, wine and stock to the pan. Bring to the boil and then reduce the heat and simmer for 1 minute. Return the chicken pieces to the pan, cover and leave to simmer over low heat for 40 minutes.
5 Return the onions and bacon to the pan and simmer, covered, for a further 15 minutes. Remove the lid and leave to simmer for a further 15 minutes.
6 Trim the carrots, leaving a little green stalk, and wash well or peel if necessary. Cut the parsnip into small batons. Add the carrots and parsnip to the pan. Cover and cook for 5–10 minutes or until the carrots and parsnip are just tender. Do not over-cook the carrots or they will lose their bright colouring. When you are ready to serve, arrange 2–3 chicken pieces on each plate. Put a couple of carrots and a few parsnip batons on top and spoon over a little juice. Garnish with coriander leaves and orange zest.

NUTRITION PER SERVE (6)
Protein 40 g; Fat 18 g; Carbohydrate 22 g; Dietary Fibre 2 g; Cholesterol 145 mg; 1790 kJ (430 cal)

COOK'S FILE

Storage time: Can be refrigerated for up to 1 day at the end of stage 5. Reheat the casserole gently over low heat and add the carrots and parsnip just prior to serving.

Cut each chicken into 8 even-sized pieces using a knife or pair of scissors.

Cook the pickling onions until they are dark golden brown.

Brown the chicken pieces in batches and drain on paper towels.

Add the orange juice, wine and stock to the pan.

Return the browned pickling onions and cooked bacon to the pan.

Cut the parsnip into batons and leave the stalks on the carrots to provide colour.

HAM, BEAN AND SWEDE CASSEROLE

Preparation time: 35 minutes
Total cooking time: 1 hour 45 minutes
Serves 4

1 cup black-eyed beans, soaked
  in cold water overnight
1 smoked ham hock
18 small pickling onions
30 g butter
2 tablespoons oil
2 cloves garlic, crushed
2 tablespoons golden syrup

3 teaspoons ground cumin
1 tablespoon German or
  French mustard
1 swede or turnip, peeled, diced
2 tablespoons tomato paste

1 Drain the beans and put them in a large heavy-based pan. Add the ham hock and 2 litres water, cover and bring to the boil. Reduce the heat to low and simmer for 25–30 minutes. Drain, reserving 2 cups of the stock. Remove the skin from the hock and chop the meat into bite-sized pieces.

2 Peel the onions, leaving the bases intact. Heat the butter, oil, garlic and syrup in the cleaned pan. Add the onions and cook for 5–10 minutes, or until just starting to turn golden.

3 Stir in the ham, cumin, mustard and swede or turnip and cook for 2 minutes until golden. Season to taste and return the beans to the pan. Add the reserved stock and tomato paste, bring to the boil, reduce the heat and simmer, covered, for 1 hour. Uncover and simmer for 5–10 minutes longer, or until reduced and thickened.

NUTRITION PER SERVE
Protein 20 g; Fat 17 g; Carbohydrate 65 g;
Dietary Fibre 11 g; Cholesterol 26 mg;
2140 kJ (510 cal)

Remove the skin and chop the cooked ham hock into bite-sized pieces.

Peel the onions, leaving the bases intact so that they hold their shape.

Stir in the ham, cumin, mustard and swede or turnip.

MEXICAN BEEF STEW

Preparation time: 30 minutes
Total cooking time: 1 hour 30 minutes
Serves 6

500 g plum tomatoes, halved
6 flour tortillas
1–2 red chillies, finely chopped
1 tablespoon olive oil
1 kg stewing beef, cubed
1/2 teaspoon black pepper
2 onions, thinly sliced
11/2 cups beef stock
1/4 cup tomato paste

375 g can kidney beans, drained
1 teaspoon chilli powder
1/2 cup sour cream

1 Preheat the oven to 180°C. Grill the tomatoes, skin-side-up, under a hot grill for 6–8 minutes, or until the skin is black and blistered. Cool, remove the skin and roughly chop the flesh.

2 Bake 2 of the tortillas in the oven for 4 minutes, or until crisp. Break into pieces and put in a food processor with the tomato and chilli. Process for 30 seconds until almost smooth.

3 Heat the oil in a large heavy-based pan. Brown the beef in batches, season with pepper, then remove. Add the onion to the pan and cook for 5 minutes. Return the meat to the pan. Stir in the processed mixture, stock and tomato paste and bring to the boil. Reduce the heat, cover and simmer for 11/4 hours. Add the beans and chilli powder and heat through.

4 Grill the remaining tortillas for 2–3 minutes on each side, cool and cut into wedges. Serve the stew with sour cream and toasted tortilla wedges.

NUTRITION PER SERVE
Protein 50 g; Fat 20 g; Carbohydrate 40 g; Dietary Fibre 8 g; Cholesterol 125 mg; 2235 kJ (535 cal)

Grill the tomatoes until the skin is black and blistered and it will peel away easily.

Once the tortillas are crisp, break into pieces and put in the food processor.

Stir in the processed mixture, stock and tomato paste.

LANCASHIRE HOTPOT

Preparation time: 20 minutes
Total cooking time: 2 hours
Serves 8

8 forequarter chops,
  cut 2.5 cm thick
4 lamb kidneys, cut in quarters,
  cores removed
50 g dripping or butter
1/4 cup plain flour
4 medium potatoes, thinly sliced
2 large brown onions, sliced
2 sticks celery, chopped
1 large carrot, peeled and chopped
1³/4 cups chicken or beef stock
200 g button mushrooms, sliced
salt and ground black pepper
2 teaspoons chopped fresh thyme
1 tablespoon Worcestershire
  sauce

1 Preheat the oven to 160°C. Brush a large casserole dish with melted butter or oil. Trim the meat of excess fat and sinew and toss the chops and kidneys in flour, shaking off the excess. Heat the dripping or butter in a large frying pan and brown the chops quickly on both sides. Remove the chops from the pan and brown the kidneys. Layer half the potato slices in the base of the dish and place the chops and kidneys on top of them.
2 Add the onions, celery and carrot to the pan and cook until the carrot begins to brown. Layer on top of the chops and kidneys. Sprinkle the remaining flour over the base of the pan and cook, stirring, until dark brown. Gradually pour in the stock and bring to the boil, stirring. Add the mushrooms, salt, pepper, thyme and Worcestershire sauce, reduce the heat

and leave to simmer for 10 minutes. Pour into the casserole dish.
3 Layer the remaining potato over the top of the casserole, to cover the meat and vegetables. Cover and cook in the oven for 1¹/4 hours. Remove the

lid and cook for a further 30 minutes, or until the potatoes are brown.

NUTRITION PER SERVE
Protein 40 g; Fat 10 g; Carbohydrate 11 g; Dietary Fibre 3 g; Cholesterol 170 mg; 1227 kJ (295 cal)

Brown the kidneys in the hot dripping or butter, stirring regularly.

Stir in the mushrooms, seasoning, herbs and Worcestershire sauce.

Layer the remaining potato over the top of the casserole.

GAME CASSEROLE

Preparation time: 30 minutes
Total cooking time: 2 hours
Serves 6

1 kg venison shoulder
2 tablespoons oil
3 rashers bacon, chopped
3 medium onions, thickly sliced
2 tablespoons plain flour
1 cup red wine
1/2 cup chicken stock
2 tablespoons port
2 medium carrots, chopped
1 stick celery, chopped

1 clove garlic, crushed
1 bay leaf
1 cinnamon stick
2 cloves
1/2 teaspoon ground nutmeg
1/2 teaspoon dried thyme
1/2 teaspoon chopped chilli
150 g button mushrooms, halved

1 Preheat the oven to 180°C. Trim the excess fat and sinew from the venison and cut into cubes. Heat half the oil in a large heavy-based pan, add the bacon and fry over medium heat until brown. Remove with a slotted spoon. Add the onion and cook until soft and golden. Remove and set aside.

2 Add the remaining oil to the pan. Brown the venison in small batches, return it all to the pan, sprinkle with flour and cook, stirring, for 1 minute. Remove from the heat and add the wine, stock, port, bacon, onion, carrot, celery, garlic, bay leaf, cinnamon stick, cloves, nutmeg, thyme and chilli. Stir until well combined.

3 Pour into a casserole dish, cover and cook in the oven for 1 1/2 hours. Add the mushrooms and cook for a further 30 minutes.

NUTRITION PER SERVE
Protein 40 g; Fat 15 g; Carbohydrate 9 g; Dietary Fibre 3 g; Cholesterol 105 mg; 1550 kJ (370 cal)

Cook the onion slices until they are soft and golden.

Return all the browned venison to the pan and sprinkle with flour.

Add the mushrooms to the casserole and cook for a further 30 minutes.

PORK AND APPLE BRAISE

Preparation time: 20 minutes
Total cooking time: 40 minutes
Serves 4

2 tablespoons oil
1 large onion, thinly sliced
1 clove garlic, chopped
2 teaspoons soft brown sugar
2 green apples, cut into wedges
4 pork loin steaks or medallions
2 tablespoons brandy

2 tablespoons seeded mustard
1 cup rich chicken stock
1/2 cup pitted prunes
3/4 cup cream

1 Heat the oil in a large heavy-based pan. Cook the onion and garlic for 10 minutes over low heat, stirring often, until softened and golden brown. Add the sugar and apple and cook, stirring regularly, until the apple begins to brown. Remove from the pan.
2 Reheat the pan and lightly brown the pork steaks, two at a time; return to the pan. Add the brandy and stir until it has nearly all evaporated. Add the mustard and stock. Simmer over low heat, covered, for 15 minutes.
3 Return the apple to the pan with the prunes and cream and simmer for 10 minutes, or until the pork is tender. Season to taste before serving.

NUTRITION PER SERVE
Protein 25 g; Fat 12 g; Carbohydrate 22 g; Dietary Fibre 4 g; Cholesterol 55 mg; 1250 kJ (298 cal)

COOK'S FILE

Hint: Take care not to overcook pork or it can become tough and dry.

Stir the apple regularly over the heat until it begins to brown.

Brown the pork steaks two at a time and then return them all to the pan.

Put the browned apple back in the pan with the prunes and cream.

BEEF STEW WITH PECANS

Preparation time: 15 minutes
Total cooking time: 2 hours
Serves 4

1/4 cup olive oil
1 onion, sliced
120 g mushrooms, sliced
1–2 cloves garlic, crushed
1 1/2 tablespoons plain flour
1 teaspoon ground cinnamon
1/2 teaspoon black pepper
1/2 teaspoon ground nutmeg
1/2 teaspoon ground coriander
1 1/2 teaspoons salt
pinch cayenne pepper

1 teaspoon grated ginger
750 g lean stewing beef, cubed
3/4 cup beef stock
1/4 cup red wine
1 tablespoon soy sauce
12 prunes, pitted, soaking in
    1/2 cup extra beef stock
1 tablespoon soft brown sugar
60 g pecan nuts

1 Heat half the oil in a large, heavy-based pan. Fry the onion for 3 minutes until soft, add the mushrooms and garlic and cook for 2 minutes. Remove from the pan. Mix together the flour, 1/2 teaspoon cinnamon, pepper, nutmeg, coriander, 1 teaspoon salt, cayenne and ginger and use to coat the meat. Add the remaining oil to the pan and brown the meat in batches. Remove from the pan.

2 Add the stock, wine, soy sauce and extra stock (from soaking the prunes) to the pan. Bring to the boil, return the onions, mushrooms, garlic and meat to the pan. Simmer for 2 hours. Add the sugar and cook for 10 minutes, or until the meat is tender.

3 Heat the remaining oil in a small pan and fry the pecans for 4 minutes, or until golden brown. Add the rest of the salt and cinnamon and toss to coat the pecans. Add these to the stew with the prunes 5 minutes before serving.

NUTRITION PER SERVE
Protein 45 g; Fat 35 g; Carbohydrate 20 g; Dietary Fibre 6 g; Cholesterol 100 mg; 2452 kJ (585 cal)

To coat the meat toss it in a plastic bag with the seasoned flour.

Return the onions, mushrooms, garlic and meat to the pan.

Make sure the pecans are well coated with the cinnamon and salt.

Seafood Stews

MOROCCAN SEAFOOD

Preparation time: 50 minutes
Total cooking time: 50 minutes
Serves 6

2 tablespoons olive oil
2 red onions, roughly chopped
1 red capsicum, chopped
4 cloves garlic, crushed
2 teaspoons ground cumin
1 teaspoon ground coriander
2 teaspoons sweet paprika
1/2 teaspoon dried chilli flakes
1 cup (250 ml/8 fl oz) fish stock
425 g (14 oz) can chopped
    tomatoes
4 tablespoons orange juice
1 tablespoon sugar
1/4 cup (30 g/1 oz) raisins
375 g (12 oz) baby new potatoes
12 raw king prawns
500 g (1 lb) baby octopus, cleaned
1 kg (2 lb) white fish, cubed

Coriander Purée
30 g (1 oz) coriander leaves
2 tablespoons ground almonds
1/3 cup (80 ml/2 3/4 fl oz) extra
    virgin olive oil
1/2 teaspoon ground cumin
1 teaspoon honey

1 Heat the olive oil in a large pan and cook the onion for 5 minutes, or until soft. Add the capsicum and garlic and cook for 1 minute. Add the ground cumin, ground coriander, paprika and chilli flakes and cook until fragrant.

2 Pour in the stock, tomatoes, orange juice, sugar and raisins and bring to the boil. Add the potatoes, reduce the heat to low and gently simmer for 20–30 minutes, or until the potatoes are just tender. Season to taste.

3 Peel and devein the prawns, leaving the tails intact. Use a small sharp knife to cut off the octopus heads; slit the heads open and remove the gut. Grasp the body firmly and push the beak out with your finger; remove and discard. Add the prawns, octopus and fish to the pan and cook, covered, for 10 minutes, or until the fish flakes when tested with a fork.

4 To make the coriander purée, place the coriander and ground almonds in a food processor. With the motor running, drizzle in the oil and process until smooth, then add the cumin, honey and salt to taste. Process to combine and serve with the fish stew.

NUTRITION PER SERVE
Protein 60 g; Fat 30 g; Carbohydrate 25 g; Dietary Fibre 4 g; Cholesterol 175 mg; 2415 kJ (580 cal)

Peel and devein the prawns and cut the cleaned octopus into bite-sized pieces.

Process the coriander leaves and ground almonds, gradually drizzling in the oil.

LEMON GRASS, CORIANDER AND FISH STEW

Preparation time: 15 minutes
Total cooking time: 40 minutes
Serves 4

4 fish cutlets (200 g/6½ oz each)
plain flour, seasoned with salt
    and freshly ground pepper
2–3 tablespoons peanut oil
2 stems lemon grass
4 Kaffir lime leaves
2 onions, sliced
1 teaspoon ground cumin
1 teaspoon ground coriander
1 teaspoon finely chopped red
    chilli
¾ cup (180 ml/6 fl oz) chicken
    stock
1½ cups (375 ml/12 fl oz)
    coconut milk
¼ cup (15 g/½ oz) chopped
    coriander
2 teaspoons fish sauce

1 Preheat the oven to moderate 180°C (350°F/Gas 4). Toss the fish lightly in the flour. Heat half the oil in a large heavy-based frying pan and cook the fish over medium heat until lightly browned on both sides. Transfer to a shallow ovenproof dish.
2 Finely chop the white part of the lemon grass stems, and finely shred the lime leaves.
3 Heat the remaining oil in the pan. Add the onion and lemon grass and cook, stirring, for 5 minutes, or until the onion softens. Add the lime leaves, ground spices and chilli and stir for about 2 minutes, or until fragrant.
4 Add the stock and coconut milk and bring to the boil. Pour over the fish, then cover and bake for 30 minutes, or until the fish is tender.
5 Transfer the fish to a serving plate. Stir the chopped coriander and the fish sauce into the remaining sauce, and season to taste with salt and freshly ground pepper. Pour the sauce over the fish to serve.

NUTRITION PER SERVE
Protein 35 g; Fat 40 g; Carbohydrate 6 g; Dietary Fibre 1 g; Cholesterol 105 mg; 2040 kJ (490 cal)

COOK'S FILE

Note: Kaffir lime leaves are glossy and dark green, with double leaves and a floral citrus smell. They can be frozen.

Heat half the peanut oil and brown the lightly floured fish over medium heat.

Finely chop the white part of the lemon grass stems; shred the lime leaves.

Add the lime leaves, ground spices and chilli to the fried onions.

SEAFOOD STEW WITH FETA AND OLIVES

Preparation time: 20 minutes
Total cooking time: 35 minutes
Serves 4

500 g (1 lb) fresh mussels
12 raw king prawns
750 g (1¹/2 lb) firm white fish
    fillets
2 tablespoons olive oil
1 large onion, sliced
2 x 400 g (13 oz) cans tomatoes,
    chopped
2 strips lemon rind
1 tablespoon chopped lemon
    thyme

¹/3 cup (80 ml/2³/4 fl oz) dry
    vermouth or white wine
1 teaspoon sugar
12 black olives
125 g (4 oz) feta cheese, cubed

1 Discard any open mussels; scrub the rest and remove the beards. Place the mussels in a pan of simmering water: as soon as the shells open, place the mussels in a bowl of cold water, discarding any unopened ones. Open them up and leave on their half shells, discarding the other half.

2 Peel and devein the prawns, leaving the tails intact. Cut the fish into bite-sized pieces, removing any bones. Cover and refrigerate. Preheat the oven to moderate 180°C (350°F/Gas 4).

3 Heat the oil in a large, heavy-based pan and cook the onion over low heat for 5 minutes, or until soft but not brown. Add the tomatoes, lemon rind, lemon thyme, vermouth and sugar. Bring to the boil and season to taste. Reduce the heat, cover and simmer for 10 minutes.

4 Place the seafood in a shallow, ovenproof dish and cover with the hot sauce. Bake, covered, for 10 minutes. Add the remaining ingredients, covering the seafood with the sauce. Bake for 10 minutes, or until heated through. Serve immediately.

NUTRITION PER SERVE
Protein 70 g; Fat 25 g; Carbohydrate 10 g; Dietary Fibre 4 g; Cholesterol 313 mg; 2430 kJ (580 cal)

Scrub the mussels, remove the beards, then place in a pan of simmering water.

Peel and devein the prawns and cut the fish into bite-sized pieces.

Add the tomatoes, lemon rind, thyme, vermouth and sugar to the softened onion.

ZARZUELA

Preparation time: 40 minutes
Total cooking time: 1 hour 10 minutes
Serves 4

Sofrito Sauce
1 tablespoon olive oil
2 onions, finely chopped
2 large tomatoes, peeled, seeded
    and chopped
1 tablespoon tomato paste

Picada Sauce
3 slices white bread, crusts
    removed
10 blanched almonds, toasted
3 cloves garlic
1 tablespoon olive oil

1 raw lobster tail
750 g (1¹/₂ lb) white boneless
    fish, cut into bite-size pieces
plain flour, seasoned with salt
    and freshly ground pepper
1 tablespoon olive oil
125 g (4 oz) calamari rings
12 raw king prawns
¹/₂ cup (125 ml/4 fl oz) white wine
12 mussels, scrubbed and
    beards removed
¹/₂ cup (125 ml/4 fl oz) brandy
¹/₄ cup (15 g/¹/₂ oz) chopped
    parsley

1 To make the sofrito sauce, heat the oil in a pan over medium heat. Add the onion and cook, stirring, for 5 minutes without browning. Add the tomato, tomato paste and ¹/₂ cup (125 ml/4 fl oz) water and cook, stirring, over medium heat for a further 10 minutes. Stir in another ¹/₂ cup (125 ml/4 fl oz) water, season with salt and freshly ground pepper and set aside.

2 To make the picada sauce, finely chop the bread, almonds and garlic in a food processor. With the motor running, gradually add the oil to form a paste, adding another ¹/₂ tablespoon of oil if necessary.

3 Preheat the oven to moderate 180°C (350°F/Gas 4). Cut the lobster tail into rounds through the membrane that separates the shell segments. Set the rounds aside.

4 Lightly coat the fish in the flour. Heat the oil in a large pan and fry the fish over medium heat for 2–3 minutes, or until cooked and golden all over. Transfer to a large casserole dish.

5 Add the calamari to the pan and cook, stirring, for 1–2 minutes, then remove and add to the fish. Cook the lobster rounds and unshelled prawns for 2–3 minutes, or until just pink, then add to the casserole.

6 Add the wine to the pan and, when hot, add the mussels, discarding any which are already open. Cover and steam the mussels for 2–3 minutes. Discard any that do not open and add the rest to the casserole.

7 Ensuring nothing flammable is nearby, pour the brandy into one side of the pan and, when it has warmed, carefully ignite the brandy. Gently shake the pan until the flames have died down. Pour this mixture over the seafood in the casserole.

8 Pour over the sofrito sauce. Cover the casserole and bake for 20 minutes. Stir in the picada sauce and cook for a further 10 minutes, or until warmed through—do not overcook, or the seafood will toughen. Sprinkle with parsley to serve.

NUTRITION PER SERVE
Protein 90 g; Fat 30 g; Carbohydrate 15 g; Dietary Fibre 4 g; Cholesterol 410 mg; 3095 kJ (790 cal)

Add the tomatoes, tomato paste and water to the softened onions.

Finely chop the bread, almonds and garlic in a food processor. Gradually add the oil.

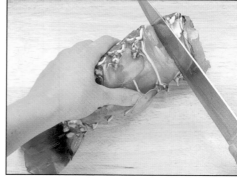

Cut the lobster tail into rounds through the membrane, separating the shell segments.

Transfer the lightly fried seafood to the casserole dish.

Add the mussels to the hot wine. Cover and steam for 2–3 minutes.

Remove the mussels and carefully pour the brandy into one side of the pan.

CIOPPINO

Preparation time: 30 minutes +
 30 minutes soaking
Total cooking time: 1 hour
Serves 4

2 dried mushrooms
1 kg (2 lb) firm white fish fillets
375 g (12 oz) raw king prawns
1 raw lobster tail
12 mussels
1/4 cup (60 ml/2 fl oz) olive oil
1 large onion, finely chopped
1 green capsicum, finely
 chopped
2–3 cloves garlic, crushed
425 g (14 oz) can crushed
 tomatoes
1 cup (250 ml/8 fl oz) white wine
1 cup (250 ml/8 fl oz) tomato
 juice
1 cup (250 ml/8 fl oz) fish stock
bay leaf
2 sprigs of parsley
6 basil leaves, chopped
1 tablespoon chopped parsley

1 Soak the mushrooms for 20 minutes. Cut the fish into bite-size pieces, removing any bones. Peel and devein the prawns, leaving the tails intact. Remove the meat from the lobster shell and cut into small pieces. Discard any open mussels; scrub the rest, remove the beards, then soak in cold water for 10 minutes. Drain the mushrooms, squeeze dry and chop finely.
2 Heat the oil in a heavy-based pan. Stirring, cook the onion, capsicum and garlic over medium heat for about 5 minutes, or until the onion is soft. Add the mushrooms, tomatoes, wine, tomato juice, stock, bay leaf, parsley sprigs and chopped basil. Bring to the

boil, reduce the heat, then cover and simmer for 30 minutes.
3 Layer the fish and prawns in a large pan. Add the sauce mixture, then cover and leave on low heat for 10 minutes, or until the prawns are pink and the fish is cooked. Add the lobster and mussels and simmer for 2–3 minutes. Season to taste. Discard any unopened mussels, sprinkle with parsley, and serve with crusty bread.

NUTRITION PER SERVE
Protein 100 g; Fat 25 g; Carbohydrate 8 g; Dietary Fibre 3 g; Cholesterol 460 mg; 2905 kJ (695 cal)

COOK'S FILE

Note: You can make your own fish stock for this recipe by simmering the trimmings from the fish, lobster and prawns in 1 1/4 cups (310 ml/10 fl oz) of water for about 20 minutes, then straining the liquid.

Remove the lobster meat from the shell and cut into small pieces.

When the onion is soft, add the chopped mushroom, tomatoes, liquids and herbs.

Add the lobster and mussels when the prawns are pink and the fish is cooked.

SEAFOOD, FENNEL AND POTATO STEW

Preparation time: 10 minutes
Total cooking time: 30 minutes
Serves 6

1 large fennel bulb
2 tablespoons olive oil
2 leeks, thinly sliced
2 cloves garlic, crushed
1/2 teaspoon paprika
2 tablespoons Pernod or Ricard
200 ml (6 1/2 fl oz) dry white wine
18 mussels, scrubbed and
   beards removed
1/4 teaspoon saffron threads
1/4 teaspoon thyme leaves
6 baby octopus
16 raw prawns, peeled and
   deveined
500 g (1 lb) swordfish steaks,
   cut into large chunks
400 g (13 oz) baby new potatoes
fennel greens, to garnish

1 Trim and thinly slice the fennel. Heat the oil in a large pan over medium heat. Add the fennel, leek and garlic. Stir in the paprika, season lightly and cook for 8 minutes, or until softened. Add the Pernod and wine and stir for 1 minute, or until reduced by a third.
2 Add the mussels, discarding any open ones. Cover and cook for 1 minute or until opened, discarding any which do not. Remove from the pan to cool; remove from the shells and set aside.
3 Add the saffron and thyme to the pan and cook for 1–2 minutes, stirring. Adjust the seasoning and transfer to a large, flameproof casserole dish.
4 Use a small sharp knife to remove the octopus heads. Grasp the bodies and push the beaks out with your index finger; remove and discard. Slit the heads and remove the gut. Mix the octopus, prawns, fish and potatoes into the stew. Cover and cook gently for 10 minutes, or until tender. Add the mussels, cover and heat through. Garnish with fennel greens and serve.

Trim the ends from the fennel and slice the bulb thinly.

Add the Pernod and wine to the softened fennel, leek and garlic mixture.

When the mussels are cool, remove them from their shells.

Cut off the octopus heads. Grasp the body firmly and push out the beak.

NUTRITION PER SERVE
Protein 65 g; Fat 10 g; Carbohydrate 15 g; Dietary Fibre 5 g; Cholesterol 390 mg; 1840 kJ (440 cal)

CAJUN SPICED FISH BRAISE

Preparation time: 15 minutes
Total cooking time: 25 minutes
Serves 4

750 g ling fillets or other firm
   meaty white-fleshed fish
2 tablespoons plain flour
2 tablespoons Cajun spice mix
2 tablespoons olive oil
30 g butter
1 large onion, thickly sliced
1 red capsicum, sliced

1/2 cup white wine
2 cups good-quality bottled
   tomato pasta sauce
1 wide strip lemon rind
8 fresh raw prawns, peeled
   and deveined

1 Cut the fish into bite-sized, thick pieces. Mix together the flour and Cajun spice mix and use to lightly coat the fish. Heat the oil and butter in a heavy-based pan over medium heat. Cook the fish, turning occasionally, until browned on all sides. Remove from the pan.

2 Add the onion and capsicum to the pan and cook, stirring regularly, for 5 minutes. Add the wine and bring to the boil, stirring continuously. Add the tomato sauce and lemon rind. Bring to the boil, then reduce the heat and simmer for 10 minutes.

3 Add the fish and prawns; cook over low heat for about 3 minutes, or until the prawns are red and the fish tender and easily flaked with a fork. Season to taste, remove the lemon rind and serve immediately.

NUTRITION PER SERVE
Protein 43 g; Fat 22 g; Carbohydrate 22 g; Dietary Fibre 4 g; Cholesterol 150 mg; 1995 kJ (477 cal)

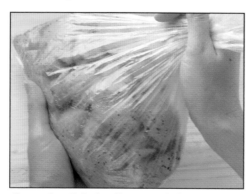

Coat the fish in flour and Cajun spice mix by putting in a bag and shaking.

Cook the fish in the oil and butter until browned on all sides.

When the fish is tender it should be easy to flake with a fork.

Use the prawn shells and trimmings to make a good base stock.

Use a slotted spoon to lift the sausage from the oil in the pan.

Add the canned tomatoes and their juice to the pan with the herbs.

After 25 minutes the rice should have absorbed most of the liquid.

SEAFOOD JAMBALAYA

Preparation time: 20 minutes
Total cooking time: 1 hour 10 minutes
Serves 6

1 kg raw king prawns
1 small onion, chopped
1 stick celery, chopped
1 cup dry white wine
1/4 cup vegetable oil
200 g spicy sausage, chopped
1 medium onion, chopped
1 medium red capsicum,
    chopped
1 stick celery, chopped
425 g can crushed tomatoes
1/2 teaspoon cayenne pepper
1/2 teaspoon cracked
    black pepper
1/4 teaspoon dried thyme
1/4 teaspoon dried oregano
2 cups long-grain rice

1 Shell the prawns, remove the large back veins and set the prawns aside. Put the trimmings in a pan with the small onion, celery, wine and 1 litre of water. Bring to the boil, then reduce the heat and simmer for 20 minutes. Strain, reserving the stock.

2 Heat the oil in a large heavy-based pan and cook the sausage for 5 minutes, until browned. Remove from the pan and set aside.

3 Add the onion, capsicum and celery to the pan and cook, stirring often, for 5 minutes. Add the tomatoes, pepper and herbs, bring to the boil and then reduce the heat to simmer, covered, for 10 minutes.

4 Return the sausage to the pan and add the rice and prawn stock. Bring back to the boil, reduce the heat and simmer, covered, for 25 minutes, until almost all the liquid has been absorbed and the rice is tender. Add the prawns, cover and cook for 5 minutes. Serve immediately.

NUTRITION PER SERVE
Protein 45 g; Fat 20 g; Carbohydrate 60 g;
Dietary Fibre 4 g; Cholesterol 265 mg;
2565 kJ (612 cal)

Vegetable Stews

CASSEROLE OF AUTUMN VEGETABLES

Preparation time: 25 minutes
Total cooking time: 30 minutes
Serves 4–6

185 g (6 oz) frozen broad
beans, thawed
150 g (5 oz) pickling onions
50 g (1³/4 oz) butter
2 teaspoons olive oil
400 g (13 oz) small parsnips
150 g (5 oz) Jerusalem
artichokes
2 tablespoons plain flour
2¹/3 cups (600 ml/20 fl oz)
chicken stock
300 ml (10 fl oz) cream
2 teaspoons grated lemon rind
1 teaspoon grated orange rind
400 g (13 oz) baby carrots,
trimmed
500 g (1 lb) baby turnips,
trimmed

1 Peel and discard the tough outer skin of the broad beans. Carefully peel the onions, leaving the flat root end attached, then cut a cross through the root end of each onion.
2 Heat the butter and oil in a large, heavy-based pan until foamy. Add the onions and cook for 7 minutes over low-medium heat, turning often to colour evenly.
3 While the onions are browning, peel the parsnips and artichokes and cut into bite-sized pieces. Add to the pan and toss well. Scatter with the flour, toss to coat and cook for 2 minutes.
4 Stir in the stock, cream and rinds. Bring to the boil, stirring, then reduce the heat and simmer for 7 minutes, or until the vegetables are half-cooked.
5 Add the carrots and turnips; toss well. Cover and cook for 4–5 minutes, or until the vegetables are just tender. Season well with salt and freshly ground pepper, stir in the broad beans to heat through, and serve.

NUTRITION PER SERVE (6)
Protein 7 g; Fat 30 g; Carbohydrate 25 g; Dietary Fibre 10 g; Cholesterol 90 mg; 1665 kJ (400 cal)

COOK'S FILE

Notes: If baby vegetables are not available, choose small vegetables and cook them for a few minutes longer.
● Fresh broad beans can be used. Add them with the carrots and turnips.
● Jerusalem artichokes are not related to globe artichokes, but come from the same family as the sunflower.

Skin the broad beans and cut a cross through the root end of the peeled onions.

Peel the small parsnips and Jerusalem artichokes and cut into bite-sized pieces.

TOMATO AND POTATO STEW

Preparation time: 30 minutes
Total cooking time: 1 hour 15 minutes
Serves 6

1/4 cup (60 ml/2 fl oz) olive oil
2 red capsicums, chopped
2 green capsicums, chopped
3 onions, thinly sliced
4 cloves garlic, crushed
2 x 400 g (13 oz) cans chopped
    tomatoes
3–4 sprigs of thyme, and extra
    to garnish
2 bay leaves
2 teaspoons caster sugar
1.2 kg (2 lb 7 oz) potatoes, cut
    into chunks
1 cup (125 g/4 oz) black olives,
    pitted
small block of Parmesan, for
    shaving

1 Heat the oil in a large, heavy-based pan. When the oil is hot, cook the capsicum, onion and garlic over medium heat for 10 minutes, or until softened. Add the chopped tomatoes, 1/2 cup (125 ml/4 fl oz) water, thyme sprigs, bay leaves and sugar. Season to taste and leave to simmer gently for 15 minutes.

2 Add the potato chunks, cover and cook very gently for 50–60 minutes, or until tender. Stir in the olives.

3 Using a vegetable peeler, carefully shave thin slivers from the Parmesan block, arrange over the stew and garnish with a sprig of thyme.

NUTRITION PER SERVE
Protein 10 g; Fat 12 g; Carbohydrate 40 g;
Dietary Fibre 9 g; Cholesterol 3 mg;
1330 kJ (320 cal)

When the oil in the pan is hot, fry the capsicum, onion and garlic until soft.

Add the potato chunks to the tomato sauce mixture.

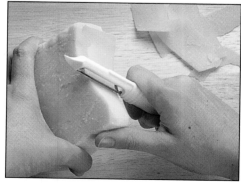

Using a vegetable peeler, carefully shave thin slivers from the Parmesan block.

LENTIL BHUJIA STEW

Preparation time: 30 minutes +
  overnight soaking + 30 minutes
  refrigeration
Total cooking time: 1 hour 10 minutes
Serves 4–6

2 cups (370 g/12 oz) green
    or brown lentils
1 large onion, grated
1 large potato, grated
1 teaspoon ground cumin
1 teaspoon ground coriander
1 teaspoon ground turmeric
3/4 cup (90 g/3 oz) plain flour
oil, for shallow-frying
2 cloves garlic, crushed
1 tablespoon grated fresh
    ginger
1 cup (250 ml/8 fl oz) tomato
    purée
2 cups (500 ml/16 fl oz)
    vegetable stock
1 cup (250 ml/8 fl oz) cream
200 g (6½ oz) green beans,
    topped, tailed and cut in half
2 carrots, sliced
2 hard-boiled eggs, chopped
sprig of rosemary, to garnish

1 Soak the lentils overnight in cold water. Drain well. Squeeze the excess moisture from the lentils, onion and potato using a tea towel. Place them in a bowl with the ground spices and flour; mix well and leave for 10 minutes. With floured hands, shape the mixture into walnut-sized balls and place on a foil-lined tray. Cover and refrigerate for 30 minutes.
2 Heat 2 cm (3/4 inch) of oil in a heavy-based pan. Cook the balls in batches over high heat until golden brown. Drain on paper towels.

3 Heat 2 tablespoons of oil in a pan; gently fry the garlic and ginger for 2 minutes. Stir in the purée, stock and cream. Bring to the boil, reduce the heat and simmer for 10 minutes. Add the beans, lentil balls and carrots. Cook, covered, for 30 minutes, stirring twice. Add the egg; cook for 10 minutes. Garnish with rosemary to serve.

NUTRITION PER SERVE (6)
Protein 23 g; Fat 30 g; Carbohydrate 45 g; Dietary Fibre 13 g; Cholesterol 125 mg; 2290 kJ (550 cal)

COOK'S FILE

Variation: Split peas can be used in this recipe in place of the lentils. Soak them in cold water overnight, then drain well before using.

Shape the lentil mixture into walnut-sized balls. Place on a foil-lined tray.

Fry the lentil balls in oil in batches over high heat, until golden brown.

Add the beans, lentil balls and carrots to the simmering sauce.

VEGETABLE STEW WITH COUSCOUS

Preparation time: 30 minutes
Total cooking time: 45 minutes
Serves 4

2 tablespoons olive oil
1 onion, sliced
2 teaspoons yellow mustard seeds
2 teaspoons ground cumin
1 teaspoon paprika
1 clove garlic, crushed
2 teaspoons grated fresh ginger
2 sticks celery, chopped
2 carrots, peeled and chopped
2 small parsnips, peeled and cubed

300 g (10 oz) pumpkin, diced
2 zucchini, halved and thickly sliced
1½ cups (375 ml/12 fl oz) vegetable stock
1 cup (185 g/6 oz) instant couscous
30 g (1 oz) butter, diced
harissa, to taste

1 Heat the oil in a large, heavy-based pan. Add the onion and cook over medium heat for 10 minutes, or until very soft and lightly golden, stirring occasionally.

2 Add the mustard seeds, cumin, paprika, garlic and ginger and stir for 1 minute. Add all the vegetables and stir to coat. Add the stock, bring to the boil, then reduce the heat and simmer, partially covered, for about 30 minutes, or until tender.

3 Place the couscous in a heatproof bowl. Add ¾ cup (185 ml/6 fl oz) of boiling water and leave to stand for 2 minutes. Add the butter, then fluff up the grains with a fork, stirring through the butter. Serve with the vegetables and a little harissa.

NUTRITION PER SERVE
Protein 7 g; Fat 17 g; Carbohydrate 40 g; Dietary Fibre 5 g; Cholesterol 20 mg; 1345 kJ (320 cal)

COOK'S FILE

Note: Harissa is a fiery relish made of ground chillies and spices. You will find it in speciality stores.

Chop the celery and peeled carrots into evenly sized pieces.

Fry the onions in the oil over medium heat until soft and golden.

Add the butter to the couscous and fluff up the grains using a fork.

CHILLI BEANS

Preparation time: 45 minutes +
overnight soaking
Total cooking time: 1 hour 35 minutes
Serves 4–6

1/2 cup (110 g/3¹/2 oz) dried
   black beans
1/2 cup (110 g/3¹/2 oz) dried
   pinto beans
1/2 cup (110 g/3¹/2 oz) dried
   chickpeas
2 small red chillies
1 small green chilli
1 tablespoon olive oil
1 onion, sliced
4 cloves garlic, finely chopped
4 cm (1¹/2 inch) piece fresh
   ginger, finely chopped
1/4 teaspoon chilli powder
2 teaspoons ground cumin
2 teaspoons ground coriander
1 litre vegetable stock
440 g (14 oz) can chopped
   tomatoes
1 small red capsicum, diced
1 small yellow capsicum, diced
1/4 cup (7 g/¹/4 oz) chopped
   coriander leaves
1/4 cup (60 ml/2 fl oz) lime juice

1 Cover the beans and chickpeas in boiling water and soak overnight. Drain and rinse well.
2 Discard the seeds and membranes from the chillies. Chop finely; set aside.

3 Heat the oil in a large pan. Cook the onion over low heat for 5 minutes, or until soft and transparent. Add the garlic, ginger, chillies, ground spices, stock, beans and chickpeas. Bring to the boil, reduce the heat, cover and simmer for 1 hour. (There should be just enough liquid to coat the beans.)
4 Add the tomatoes and the red and yellow capsicums and simmer gently for 30 minutes, or until the capsicum and beans are tender. Stir in the coriander leaves and lime juice. Season to taste with salt and freshly cracked pepper and serve.

NUTRITION PER SERVE (6)
Protein 10 g; Fat 5 g; Carbohydrate 20 g; Dietary Fibre 9 g; Cholesterol 0 mg; 711 kJ (170 cal)

Cover the dried beans and chickpeas with boiling water and leave to soak overnight.

Remove the seeds and membranes from the red and green chillies.

Add the drained beans and chickpeas to the spiced stock mixture.

CASSEROLE OF CURRIED VEGETABLES

Preparation time: 25 minutes
Total cooking time: 1 hour 25 minutes
Serves 4–6

1 tablespoon vegetable oil
1 leek, thickly sliced
2–3 cloves garlic, crushed
1 stick celery, thickly sliced
1 large carrot
1 large parsnip
1 large potato
1 medium swede or turnip
500 g (1 lb) sweet potato
500 g (1 lb) pumpkin
280 g (9 oz) can curried cooking
    sauce (see Notes)
400 ml (13 fl oz) coconut milk
1 cup (155 g/5 oz) shelled fresh
    green peas
1/2 cup (15 g/1/2 oz) chopped
    coriander leaves

1 Preheat the oven to moderate 180°C (350°F/Gas 4). Heat the oil in a large flameproof casserole dish. Cook the leek, garlic and celery over medium heat for 2–3 minutes, or until tender. Remove the pan from the heat.
2 Peel the root vegetables and cut into 5 cm (2 inch) pieces. Add them to the dish, place over medium heat and stir well to combine. Stir in the curry sauce and coconut milk and cook, stirring, for 2–3 minutes.
3 Cover and bake for about 1¼ hours, or until the vegetables are tender, stirring gently once or twice.
4 Meanwhile, cook the peas in boiling water until just tender. Drain, refresh under cold water and stir into the casserole with the coriander leaves. Serve immediately.

NUTRITION PER SERVE (6)
Protein 8 g; Fat 25 g; Carbohydrate 35 g;
Dietary Fibre 9 g; Cholesterol 4 mg;
1540 kJ (370 cal)

COOK'S FILE

Notes: Curried cooking sauces are not to be confused with concentrated curry pastes. They are available in many brands and flavours, ranging from mild to hot. Choose one to suit your taste.
● If fresh peas are not available, frozen peas can be substituted.

In a flameproof casserole dish, fry the leek, garlic and celery until tender.

Peel the root vegetables and cut them into 5 cm (2 inch) pieces.

POLENTA WITH SPICY VEGETABLES

Preparation time: 30 minutes
Total cooking time: 1 hour 10 minutes
Serves 4

1 tablespoon olive oil
1 large onion, sliced
4 cloves garlic, finely chopped
1/4 teaspoon chilli powder
2 teaspoons ground cumin
2 teaspoons ground coriander
1/2 teaspoon ground turmeric
1/2 teaspoon ground cinnamon
2 potatoes, cubed
3 carrots, thickly sliced
1 1/2 cups (375 ml/12 fl oz)
    vegetable stock
300 g (10 oz) baby yellow
    squash, halved
3 zucchini, cut into chunks
300 g (10 oz) pumpkin, cut into
    chunks
2 tablespoons chopped parsley

Polenta
1 litre vegetable stock or water
1 2/3 cups (250 g/8 oz) fine
    polenta
100 g (3 1/2 oz) butter, chopped
1/3 cup (35 g/1 1/4 oz) finely
    grated fresh Parmesan

1 Heat the oil in a large saucepan. Fry the onion over low heat for 5 minutes, or until soft and translucent. Add the garlic and spices and cook over medium heat for 3 minutes.
2 Add the potato, carrot and stock. Bring to the boil, reduce the heat, then cover and simmer for 10 minutes.
3 Add the squash and zucchini. Cover partially and simmer for 15 minutes. Add the pumpkin; cook for 10 minutes

more, or until the vegetables are soft and the mixture is thick and gravy-like. Season well with salt and freshly cracked pepper. Remove from the heat, cover and keep warm.
4 To make the polenta, bring the stock to the boil. Add the polenta in a thin stream, stirring constantly with a wooden spoon. Simmer gently for 20 minutes, stirring constantly so it doesn't stick. When thick, add the

butter and Parmesan and mix until melted. Season well and serve at once.
5 Stir the parsley into the vegetables. Spoon the polenta onto serving plates, swirling it into nests with a hole in the centre. Spoon in the spicy vegetables and serve immediately.

NUTRITION PER SERVE
Protein 15 g; Fat 30 g; Carbohydrate 65 g; Dietary Fibre 9.5 g; Cholesterol 72 mg; 2485 kJ (595 cal)

Add the pumpkin to the partially cooked vegetable mixture.

Simmer the polenta gently for 20 minutes, stirring constantly until thick.

When the polenta has thickened, add the butter and Parmesan. Stir until melted.

VEGETARIAN CHILLI

Preparation time: 15 minutes
Total cooking time: 40 minutes
Serves 6–8

3/4 cup burghul (cracked wheat)
2 tablespoons olive oil
1 large onion, finely chopped
2 cloves garlic, crushed
1 teaspoon chilli powder
2 teaspoons ground cumin
1 teaspoon cayenne pepper
1/2 teaspoon ground cinnamon
2 x 400 g cans crushed tomatoes

3 cups vegetable stock
440 g can red kidney beans,
 rinsed and drained
2 x 300 g cans chickpeas,
 rinsed and drained
310 g can corn kernels, drained
2 tablespoons tomato paste
corn chips and sour cream

1 Soak the burghul with 1 cup of hot water for 10 minutes. Heat the oil in a large heavy-based pan and cook the onion for 10 minutes, stirring often, until soft and golden.
2 Add the garlic, chilli powder, cumin, cayenne and cinnamon and

cook, stirring, for a further minute.
3 Add the tomatoes, stock and burghul. Bring to the boil and simmer for 10 minutes. Stir in the beans, chickpeas, corn and tomato paste and simmer for 20 minutes, stirring often. Serve with corn chips and sour cream.

NUTRITION PER SERVE (8)
Protein 7 g; Fat 10 g; Carbohydrate 18 g; Dietary Fibre 7 g; Cholesterol 8 mg; 780 kJ (185 cal)

COOK'S FILE

Storage time: Chilli will keep for up to 3 days in the refrigerator (and can be frozen for up to 1 month).

Stir the garlic and spices into the pan with the onion and cook for a minute.

Add the crushed tomatoes, stock and burghul to the pan.

Stir in the beans, chickpeas, corn kernels and tomato paste.

PEPPERED VEGETABLE HOTPOT

Preparation time: 30 minutes
Total cooking time: 1 hour 5 minutes
Serves 8–10

2 tablespoons olive oil
2 onions, chopped
2 leeks, washed and chopped
2 cloves garlic, crushed
6 cups chicken stock
2 tablespoons chopped fresh
    rosemary
1–2 teaspoon green peppercorns

4 large potatoes, peeled and
    cubed
2 large turnips, cubed
200 g broccoli, cut into
    small florets
200 g cauliflower, cut into
    small florets
1 cup fresh or frozen peas

1 Heat the oil in a large heavy-based pan and cook the onion and leek over medium heat for 10 minutes, or until they are tender.
2 Add the garlic and cook for 1 minute further, then add the stock, rosemary, peppercorns and potato to the pan. Bring to the boil and then reduce the heat, cover and leave to simmer for 30 minutes. Add the pieces of turnip and allow to simmer for a further 15 minutes.
3 Add the broccoli, cauliflower and peas and simmer, uncovered, for a further 5 minutes. Season to taste.

NUTRITION PER SERVE (10)
Protein 5 g; Fat 4 g; Carbohydrate 14 g; Dietary Fibre 5 g; Cholesterol 0 mg; 465 kJ (110 cal)

COOK'S FILE

Hint: Serve as a main course with pesto and crusty bread.

Wash the turnips well and roughly chop into large cubes.

Add the stock, rosemary, peppercorns and potato to the pan.

Add the broccoli, cauliflower and peas for the last 5 minutes of cooking.

MEDITERRANEAN VEGETABLE POT

Preparation time: 20 minutes
Total cooking time: 40 minutes
Serves 4

1/4 **cup olive oil**
1 onion, chopped
2 cloves garlic, crushed
1 green capsicum, chopped
1 red capsicum, chopped
3 zucchini, sliced
3 slender eggplant, sliced

2 cups long-grain rice
100 g button mushrooms, sliced
3 cups chicken stock
1 cup white wine
400 g can crushed tomatoes
2 tablespoons tomato paste
150 g feta cheese

1 Heat the oil in a large heavy-based pan and cook the onion over medium heat for about 10 minutes until very soft but not browned. Add the garlic and cook for a further minute.

2 Add the green and red capsicums and cook, stirring, for 3 minutes. Add the zucchini and eggplant and stir-fry for a further 5 minutes. Add the rice and stir-fry for 2 minutes.

3 Add the mushrooms, stock, wine, undrained crushed tomatoes and tomato paste. Stir to combine. Bring to the boil, reduce the heat, cover and simmer for 20 minutes. The rice should be tender and have absorbed most of the liquid. Serve immediately, topped with crumbled feta cheese.

NUTRITION PER SERVE
Protein 20 g; Fat 25 g; Carbohydrate 92 g; Dietary Fibre 9 g; Cholesterol 25 mg; 2980 kJ (710 cal)

Cook the onion until it is very soft but not browned.

Add the zucchini and eggplant to the pan and stir-fry a little longer.

Add the mushrooms, stock, wine, crushed tomatoes and tomato paste.

CHICKPEA AND VEGETABLE CURRY

Preparation time: 30 minutes
Total cooking time: 35 minutes
Serves 4

1 tablespoon oil
1 onion, chopped
1 tablespoon grated fresh ginger
3 cloves garlic, crushed
1/2 teaspoon fennel seeds
2 teaspoons curry powder
1 teaspoon finely chopped
    chilli, optional
400 ml coconut milk

425 g chickpeas, drained
3 medium zucchini, chopped
200 g sweet potato, chopped
150 g green beans, chopped
200 g broccoli, cut into
    small florets
1/3 cup shredded coconut

1 Heat the oil in a large heavy-based pan and cook the onion over medium heat for about 10 minutes, until soft and golden. Add the ginger, garlic, fennel seeds, curry powder and chilli (if using). Cook, stirring, for 2 minutes, until fragrant.

2 Stir in the coconut milk, chickpeas, zucchini, sweet potato, beans and broccoli and bring to the boil. Reduce the heat, cover and leave to simmer for 20 minutes, or until the vegetables are tender.

3 Preheat the oven to moderate 180°C. Spread the coconut on a large baking tray and toast in the oven for a few minutes until lightly golden. Serve over the curry as a garnish.

NUTRITION PER SERVE
Protein 15 g; Fat 30 g; Carbohydrate 30 g; Dietary Fibre 14 g; Cholesterol 0 mg; 1955 kJ (465 cal)

COOK'S FILE

Storage time: Will keep for up to 2 days in the refrigerator.

Add the ginger, garlic and spices and cook until fragrant.

Add the drained chickpeas to the pan with the other vegetables.

Spread the coconut on a baking tray and toast until lightly golden.

Vegetable Mashes

ROAST VEGETABLE MASH

Preparation time: 30 minutes
Total cooking time: 1 hour 30 minutes
Serves 4–6

2 large pontiac or sebago
    potatoes
400 g (13 oz) pumpkin
400 g (13 oz) orange sweet
    potato
2 large parsnips
1 large onion, chopped
2 tomatoes, quartered
6 cloves garlic
2 tablespoons olive oil
30 g (1 oz) butter, chopped

1 Preheat the oven to moderate 180°C (375°F/Gas 4). Peel the potatoes, pumpkin, orange sweet potato and parsnip, then cut into large pieces and place in a large baking dish with the onion, tomato and garlic. Drizzle with the oil and sprinkle with salt and freshly cracked black pepper.
2 Roast the vegetables for 1½ hours, or until soft and starting to brown, stirring every 30 minutes.
3 Transfer the vegetables to a bowl, add the butter and mash roughly with a fork. Season to taste with salt and freshly ground pepper and serve.

NUTRITION PER SERVE (6)
Protein 7.5 g; Fat 10 g; Carbohydrate 40 g; Dietary Fibre 6 g; Cholesterol 13 mg; 1170 kJ (280 cal)

Peel the potatoes, pumpkin, orange sweet potato and parsnip.

Place the cut vegetables in a large baking dish and drizzle with the oil.

Roast until the vegetables are soft and starting to brown.

Place the vegetables in a bowl, add the butter and mash roughly with a fork.

CREAMY POTATO AND PARSNIP MASH

Preparation time: 10 minutes
Total cooking time: 20 minutes
Serves 4–6

2 large potatoes
5 large parsnips
30 g (1 oz) butter
1 tablespoon milk

2 tablespoons sour cream
chopped chives, to garnish

1 Peel the potatoes and parsnips, then chop into evenly sized pieces. Cook them in a large pan of lightly salted boiling water for about 20 minutes, or until soft.
2 Drain well, then transfer to a bowl and mash with the butter, milk and sour cream until smooth and fluffy. Season generously with salt and freshly ground pepper. Sprinkle with chives and serve at once.

NUTRITION PER SERVE (6)
Protein 5 g; Fat 7 g; Carbohydrate 30 g; Dietary Fibre 5 g; Cholesterol 25 mg; 800 kJ (190 cal)

COOK'S FILE

Note: Sebago, bison, coliban, nicola, pontiac and Kind Edward are some good all-purpose potatoes that give successful results in this recipe.

Peel the potatoes and parsnips and chop them into evenly sized pieces.

Drain the vegetables well and transfer to a large bowl.

Add the butter, milk and sour cream and mash until smooth and fluffy.

WATERCRESS AND POTATO MASH

Preparation time: 20 minutes
Total cooking time: 25 minutes
Serves 4–6

1.5 kg (3 lb) sebago or pontiac potatoes
250 g (8 oz) watercress, washed and trimmed

1 clove garlic, crushed
1/2 cup (125 ml/4 fl oz) cream
60 g (2 oz) butter

1 Peel and chop the potatoes, then cook in lightly salted boiling water for 20 minutes, or until tender.
2 Blanch the watercress in boiling water for 2 minutes, then rinse with cold water to hold the colour. Chop the watercress finely and place in a pan. Warm gently over low heat.

3 Drain the potatoes, add the crushed garlic, cream and butter, then mash until smooth and creamy. Season to taste with salt and pepper.
4 Stir the warmed watercress into the mashed potato mixture. Serve at once, garnished with roughly ground cracked peppercorns.

NUTRITION PER SERVE (6)
Protein 8 g; Fat 20 g; Carbohydrate 35 g; Dietary Fibre 6 g; Cholesterol 55 mg; 1370 kJ (330 cal)

Drain the blanched watercress well, then chop finely.

Drain the potatoes, then add the garlic, cream and butter and mash until smooth.

Stir the warmed watercress through the mashed potato mixture.

ROASTED PUMPKIN AND WALNUT MASH

Preparation time: 20 minutes
Total cooking time: 1 hour
Serves 4

12 walnut halves
1.5 kg (3 lb) pumpkin
olive oil, for brushing
1/3 cup (80 ml/2¾ fl oz) cream
90 g (3 oz) butter
1 tablespoon chopped parsley

1 Preheat the oven to hot 220°C (425°F/Gas 7). Place the walnuts on a baking tray, transfer to the oven and bake for 3–5 minutes, or until the walnuts are brown. Remove from the oven and leave to cool, then chop the walnuts roughly.
2 Peel the pumpkin and chop into even-sized pieces. Place on a baking tray, brush the pumpkin with olive oil, then transfer to the oven and roast for 1 hour, or until soft in the centre.
3 Gently warm the cream in a small saucepan. Place the roasted pumpkin in a food processor and blend with the pulse button until smooth. Add the cream and salt and pepper to taste, then pulse again until well combined. Do not overprocess.
4 Melt the butter in a small pan and gently cook until nut coloured. Add the chopped parsley, then spoon the mixture over the mash. Garnish with the chopped walnuts to serve.

NUTRITION PER SERVE
Protein 10 g; Fat 35 g; Carbohydrate 25 g; Dietary Fibre 5 g; Cholesterol 85 mg; 1826 kJ (436 cal)

When the roasted walnuts have cooled, chop them roughly.

Place the peeled pumpkin pieces on a baking tray and brush with olive oil.

Blend the roasted pumpkin in a food processor until smooth. Add the cream.

YELLOW SPLIT PEA AND GARLIC MASH

Preparation time: 10 minutes +
15 minutes standing
Total cooking time: 1 hour 15 minutes
Serves 4–6

500 g (1 lb) packet dried yellow split peas
2–3 cloves garlic, crushed
1 onion, finely diced
1½ litres chicken stock
1 teaspoon salt

2 tablespoons extra virgin olive oil
2 tablespoons finely chopped parsley

1 Rinse the split peas well, then place them in a large pan with the garlic, diced onion, chicken stock and salt. Bring to the boil and skim off any froth. Reduce the heat, then cover and simmer for 1 hour without stirring, or until the split peas are of a thick, puréed consistency.
2 If the mixture is too wet, remove the lid and simmer for 10–15 minutes, or until thick.

3 Remove the pan from the heat and leave the peas to stand for 15 minutes, or until mash-like. Add the olive oil and chopped parsley and beat with a wooden spoon. Season to taste with salt and freshly ground black pepper and serve.

NUTRITION PER SERVE (6)
Protein 6 g; Fat 7 g; Carbohydrate 7 g; Dietary Fibre 4 g; Cholesterol 0 mg; 470 kJ (113 cal)

COOK'S FILE

Serving suggestion: This mash is lovely with roast chicken and warm pitta bread.

Bring the peas, garlic, onion, stock and salt to the boil, skimming off any froth.

Cover and simmer the split pea mixture until thick and of a puréed consistency.

When the peas have cooled and thickened, beat in the olive oil and parsley.

Roasted pumpkin and walnut mash (top) with Yellow split pea and garlic mash

CHAMP

Preparation time: 10 minutes
Total cooking time: 25 minutes
Serves 4–6

1 kg (2 lb) floury potatoes, such
    as sebago or pontiac
1 cup (250 ml/8 fl oz) milk
6 spring onions, finely chopped
60 g (2 oz) butter

1 Peel the potatoes, then chop them into evenly sized pieces. Cook the potatoes in a pan of lightly salted boiling water for about 20 minutes, or until tender. Drain and mash well.

2 Meanwhile, pour the milk into a saucepan. Add two-thirds of the finely chopped spring onions and poach them over low heat for 15 minutes. Strain the milk, discarding the spring onions, and whip it into the mashed potato until creamy.

3 Melt the butter in a small pan over low heat. Add the remaining spring onions and gently cook them for about 4 minutes, or until softened.

4 Drizzle the melted butter over the mashed potato, spoon the softened spring onion over the top and serve immediately.

NUTRITION PER SERVE (6)
Protein 6 g; Fat 10 g; Carbohydrate 25 g;
Dietary Fibre 3 g; Cholesterol 30 mg;
890 kJ (215 cal)

Cook the potatoes for about 20 minutes, or until tender.

Strain the milk into the mashed potato, discarding the poached spring onions.

Add the remaining spring onions to the melted butter and cook until softened.

ORANGE SWEET POTATO CRUMBLE

Preparation time: 25 minutes
Total cooking time: 40 minutes
Serves 4–6

1 kg (2 lb) orange sweet
   potato
50 g (1³/₄ oz) butter
¹/₃ cup (80 ml/2³/₄ fl oz) milk
   or cream
¹/₄ teaspoon ground cinnamon

Crumble Topping
480 g (15 oz) loaf sourdough
   bread
¹/₂ cup (55 g/2 oz) freshly
   grated Parmesan
1 teaspoon dried thyme

1 Preheat the oven to moderate 180°C (350°F/Gas 4). Peel the orange sweet potato, cut it into chunks, then cook in lightly salted boiling water for about 15 minutes, or until tender. Drain well and return to the saucepan.
2 Mash with a potato masher, adding the butter, milk and cinnamon. Season to taste with salt and freshly ground pepper, then spoon into a shallow casserole dish and smooth the top.
3 To make the crumble topping, remove the crusts from the bread. Break the bread into smaller pieces and finely chop in a food processor. Mix in the Parmesan and thyme, then scatter over the mash and bake for 20 minutes, or until the crumble is golden and crispy. Serve immediately.

NUTRITION PER SERVE (6)
Protein 20 g; Fat 20 g; Carbohydrate 105 g; Dietary Fibre 8 g; Cholesterol 50 mg; 2900 kJ (690 cal)

Peel the orange sweet potato and cut into evenly sized chunks.

Spread the mashed potato mixture into a shallow casserole dish.

Sprinkle the crumble topping over the mixture and bake until golden and crisp.

PUMPKIN AND WHITE BEAN PUREE

Preparation time: 25 minutes
Total cooking time: 1 hour 20 minutes
Serves 4

1 kg (2 lb) pumpkin
1 tablespoon olive oil
1 small onion, chopped
1–2 cloves garlic, chopped
1 stick celery, chopped
1 carrot, chopped
300 g (10 oz) can butter beans,
    drained and rinsed
1/3 cup (35 g/1¼ oz) freshly
    grated Parmesan

1 Preheat the oven to moderate 180°C (350°F/Gas 4). Peel the pumpkin, chop into evenly sized pieces and set aside. Heat the oil in a large flameproof dish on the stove top. Add the onion, garlic, celery and carrot and cook, stirring often, for about 5 minutes, or until the vegetables are softened but not browned. Add the pumpkin and stir thoroughly.

2 Cover the dish with baking paper and bake in the oven for 45 minutes, or until the vegetables are cooked but not browned, stirring the mixture about 3 times during cooking. Allow the vegetables to cool slightly, then transfer to a food processor. Add the drained beans and half the Parmesan and blend to a purée.

3 Spoon the purée into 4 oiled 1-cup (250 ml/8 fl oz) ovenproof ramekins. Smooth the surface and sprinkle with the remaining Parmesan. Bake for about 30 minutes, or until the purée is hot, bubbling and browned.

NUTRITION PER SERVE
Protein 10 g; Fat 9 g; Carbohydrate 20 g; Dietary Fibre 5 g; Cholesterol 8 mg; 825 kJ (200 cal)

COOK'S FILE

Note: Dried beans can be used in this recipe. Soak them in a large bowl of water overnight, drain well, then boil in a large pot of water for 1 hour, or until tender. Drain well. You will need to cook about ½ cup (100 g/3½ oz) of dried beans for this recipe.

Add the pumpkin pieces to the softened vegetables and cover with baking paper.

Blend the baked vegetables, drained beans and half the Parmesan in a food processor.

Sprinkle the ramekins with the remaining Parmesan and bake for 30 minutes.

CREAMY PARSNIP MASH

Preparation time: 10 minutes
Total cooking time: 15 minutes
Serves 4

1 kg (2 lb) parsnips
20 g (¾ oz) butter
2 tablespoons cream

1/4 teaspoon ground nutmeg
1 tablespoon finely chopped
    parsley

1 Peel the parsnips, chop into evenly sized pieces and cook in boiling salted water for 15–20 minutes, or until tender. Drain thoroughly.

2 Mash the parsnips well using a potato masher. Using a wooden spoon, gradually beat in the butter, cream,

nutmeg, and salt and pepper to taste. Sprinkle with parsley to serve.

NUTRITION PER SERVE
Protein 5 g; Fat 9 g; Carbohydrate 25 g; Dietary Fibre 7 g; Cholesterol 25 mg; 840 kJ (200 cal)

COOK'S FILE

Note: You could use a food processor to mash the parsnip and to blend in the remaining ingredients.

Peel the parsnips and chop them into evenly sized pieces.

Drain the cooked parsnips and mash them using a potato masher.

Gradually beat in the butter, cream, nutmeg, and salt and pepper to taste.

Pumpkin and white bean purée (top) with Creamy parsnip mash

CREAMY MUSHROOM AND POTATO BAKE

Preparation time: 25 minutes
Total cooking time: 50 minutes
Serves 4–6

1 kg (2 lb) potatoes
1 tablespoon cream
20 g (³⁄₄ oz) butter
1 egg yolk
¹⁄₄ teaspoon nutmeg

Mushroom Filling
40 g (1¹⁄₄ oz) butter
125 g (4 oz) mushrooms, finely chopped
2 spring onions, finely chopped
50 g (1³⁄₄ oz) ham, finely chopped
60 g (2 oz) Gruyère cheese, grated
1 cup (90 g/3 oz) fresh breadcrumbs

1 Peel the potatoes and cut them into evenly sized pieces. Cook in boiling salted water for about 15 minutes, or until tender. Drain the potatoes, then mash thoroughly. While the potatoes are still hot, gradually beat in the cream, butter, egg yolk and nutmeg. Season to taste with salt and freshly ground black pepper and set aside.
2 To make the mushroom filling, melt half the butter in a pan and cook the mushrooms and spring onions for 2–3 minutes, or until softened. Add the ham and black pepper to taste. Stir well and set aside.
3 Preheat the oven to hot 200°C (400°F/Gas 6). Divide the mashed potato into 2 portions. Spread the first portion evenly into a well-greased 23 cm (9 inch) round ovenproof pie

dish. Spread the mushroom filling over the top, sprinkle with the grated cheese, then spread the remaining mashed potato over the top.
4 Melt the remaining butter and stir it through the breadcrumbs, mixing well. Spread the breadcrumbs evenly over the mashed potato, then bake for 30 minutes, or until lightly browned. Serve at once.

NUTRITION PER SERVE (6)
Protein 10 g; Fat 15 g; Carbohydrate 35 g; Dietary Fibre 4 g; Cholesterol 75 mg; 1315 kJ (315 cal)

Stir the cream, butter, egg yolk and nutmeg into the hot mashed potato.

Fry the mushrooms and spring onions in half the melted butter until soft.

Sprinkle the grated cheese over the mushroom filling.

SWEDE AND ORANGE MASH

Preparation time: 10 minutes
Total cooking time: 20 minutes
Serves 4

1 kg (2 lb) swedes
45 g (1½ oz) butter, chopped
1 teaspoon finely grated orange rind
⅓ cup (80 ml/2¾ fl oz) orange juice
2 teaspoons honey
ground cinnamon, for sprinkling

1 Peel the swedes to remove the thick skin. Chop into evenly sized pieces and cook in lightly salted boiling water until tender. Drain well.

2 While the swedes are still hot, mash them with the butter, orange rind, orange juice and honey. Season to taste with salt and freshly ground pepper. Sprinkle with cinnamon and serve immediately.

NUTRITION PER SERVE
Protein 4 g; Fat 9 g; Carbohydrate 14 g; Dietary Fibre 7 g; Cholesterol 30 mg; 640 kJ (150 cal)

COOK'S FILE

Notes: When grating oranges, avoid the white pith as it has a bitter taste.

• Swedes are often confused with turnips. Turnips are white or pinky white and are usually sold with the green stems attached; swedes are generally bigger with a more yellow flesh. If the swedes are young, you will only need to peel them thinly. Older swedes develop a hard woody stem, best removed by peeling thickly.

Serving suggestion: This mash is lovely with pork, chicken or lamb.

Using a vegetable peeler, peel the swedes to remove the thick skin.

Cook the swedes in boiling water until tender and drain well.

While the swedes are still hot, mash them with the butter, rind, juice and honey.

POTATO AND ZUCCHINI MASH WITH PARMESAN

Preparation time: 10 minutes
Total cooking time: 20 minutes
Serves 4

200 g (6½ oz) zucchini
500 g (1 lb) potatoes (see Note)
30 g (1 oz) butter
1 clove garlic, crushed
¼ cup (60 ml/2 fl oz) cream
¼ cup (25 g/¾ oz) freshly grated Parmesan

1 Grate the zucchini finely, then squeeze the flesh to remove as much moisture as possible. Set aside.
2 Peel the potatoes and chop them into evenly sized pieces, then cook in lightly salted boiling water for about 20 minutes, or until tender.
3 Drain the potatoes thoroughly, then return them to the pan over low heat. Add the butter, garlic and cream and mash until fluffy.
4 Add the grated zucchini and stir well with a wooden spoon until the zucchini has heated through. Remove the pan from the heat, then stir in the grated Parmesan and season to taste with salt and freshly ground black pepper.

NUTRITION PER SERVE
Protein 6.5 g; Fat 15 g; Carbohydrate 20 g; Dietary Fibre 3 g; Cholesterol 50 mg; 970 kJ (230 cal)

COOK'S FILE

Note: Floury potatoes are generally good for mashing. Pontiac and sebago are good all-purpose potatoes that can be relied upon to give good results.

Squeeze the finely grated zucchini to remove as much moisture as possible.

Add the butter, garlic and cream to the potatoes and mash until fluffy.

Stir the grated zucchini into the potato mixture until heated through.

Peel the potatoes using a vegetable peeler and chop into evenly sized pieces.

Roll the potato balls in the egg, then the crushed noodles.

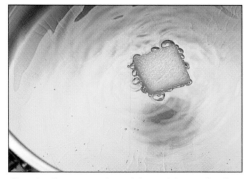

Gently drop a cube of bread into the hot oil to test the temperature.

Deep-fry the thistles in small batches for 2 minutes, or until crisp and golden.

POTATO THISTLES

Preparation time: 25 minutes
Total cooking time: 25 minutes
Makes 30

Thistles
800 g (1 lb 10 oz) potatoes
¼ cup (25 g/¾ oz) freshly grated Parmesan
2 tablespoons cream
20 g (¾ oz) butter
1 egg yolk
good pinch of ground nutmeg

Noodle Coating
90 g (3 oz) thin vermicelli noodles
⅓ cup (40 g/1¼ oz) plain flour
1 egg, beaten with 2 teaspoons water
oil, for deep-frying

1 To make the thistles, peel the potatoes and chop into evenly sized pieces. Cook in lightly salted boiling water for 15 minutes, or until tender. Drain the potatoes, then mash them thoroughly. While still hot, beat in the remaining thistle ingredients. Leave to cool, then roll the mixture into small, evenly sized balls.

2 To make the noodle coating, crush the noodles finely, mix them with the flour and then spread them on a tray. Roll the potato balls in the beaten egg, then the crushed noodles.

3 Heat 5 cm (2 inches) of oil in a large, deep pan. Drop a 1 cm (½ inch) cube of bread into the oil: if it turns golden brown in 20 seconds, the oil is ready. Cook the thistles a few at a time for 2 minutes, or until crisp and golden—do not overcook, or they will burst. Drain on paper towels and serve hot.

NUTRITION PER THISTLE
Protein 2 g; Fat 4 g; Carbohydrate 7 g; Dietary Fibre 0 g; Cholesterol 15 mg; 280 kJ (70 cal)

Mashed Potato Magic

Mashed potato is a widely loved comfort food, and there are probably as many versions of this fluffy favourite as there are cooks. What follows is a simple recipe for a classic potato mash, and a handful of ways to stir in a dash of gourmet flavour and bring your meal to life. Bon appetit!

CREAMY MASHED POTATO

Peel 800 g (1 lb 10 oz) potatoes, cut into evenly sized pieces and place in a large pan of lightly salted cold water. Bring to the boil, reduce the heat and simmer until just tender. Drain well, return to the pan and stir over low heat until the liquid evaporates. Mash until smooth, or push through a sieve to remove any lumps. Heat $1/3$ cup (80 ml/$2^3/4$ fl oz) milk and 45 g ($1^1/2$ oz) chopped butter in a pan until the butter melts, then beat into the potato with a wooden spoon. Stir in salt and freshly ground pepper to taste, any other flavourings (see below) and serve at once. Serves 4.

NUTRITION PER SERVE
Protein 6 g; Fat 10 g; Carbohydrate 30 g; Dietary Fibre 3 g; Cholesterol 30 mg; 945 kJ (225 cal)

GOUDA & CARAWAY MASH

Mix together $1/4$ teaspoon caraway seeds, 100 g ($3^1/2$ oz) grated Gouda cheese, 1 tablespoon chopped fresh parsley and 2 tablespoons milk. Stir into the creamy mashed potato and sprinkle with extra caraway seeds. Serves 4.

NUTRITION PER SERVE
Protein 12 g; Fat 18 g; Carbohydrate 30 g; Dietary Fibre 3 g; Cholesterol 30 mg; 1370 kJ (330 cal)

PANCETTA & GARLIC POTATO

Thinly slice 2 garlic cloves and lightly brown in 30 g (1 oz) butter. Stir into the creamy mashed potato with 2 tablespoons chopped fresh garlic chives and 2 tablespoons sour cream. Top with crisp strips of pancetta. Serves 4.

NUTRITION PER SERVE
Protein 6 g; Fat 20 g; Carbohydrate 30 g; Dietary Fibre 3.5 g; Cholesterol 64 mg; 1337 kJ (320 cal)

PESTO POTATO

Swirl 2–3 tablespoons of pesto (bought or homemade) through the creamy mashed potato. Top with toasted pine nuts and flakes of Parmesan. Serves 4.

NUTRITION PER SERVE
Protein 8 g; Fat 15 g; Carbohydrate 30 g; Dietary Fibre 3.5 g; Cholesterol 37 mg; 1205 kJ (290 cal)

SWEET POTATO & ROASTED CORN

GOUDA & CARAWAY

LEEK & BACON

LEEK & BACON MASH

Finely chop a small leek and a bacon rasher and gently fry in 30 g (1 oz) butter until the leek is soft. Fold into the creamy mashed potato with 2 tablespoons plain yoghurt and a finely chopped spring onion and sprinkle with sliced spring onion. Serves 4.

NUTRITION PER SERVE
Protein 8 g; Fat 17 g; Carbohydrate 30 g; Dietary Fibre 4 g; Cholesterol 57 mg; 1276 kJ (305 cal)

MUSHROOM MASH

Gently fry 150 g (5 oz) finely sliced button mushrooms in 45 g (1½ oz) butter until soft and lightly browned. Stir 2 teaspoons wholegrain mustard into the creamy mashed potato, fold in the mushrooms and add a little extra milk if the mixture is too thick. Garnish with sage. Serves 4.

NUTRITION PER SERVE
Protein 7 g; Fat 20 g; Carbohydrate 30 g; Dietary Fibre 4 g; Cholesterol 60 mg; 1325 kJ (317 cal)

ROASTED CAPSICUM & CUMIN POTATO

Quarter a red capsicum, remove the seeds and membrane and grill until the skin blisters and blackens. Peel away the skin, cut the capsicum into thin strips, then fold through the creamy mashed potato with 1–2 tablespoons ricotta cheese and ¼–½ teaspoon ground cumin. Sprinkle with cumin seeds. Serves 4.

NUTRITION PER SERVE
Protein 7 g; Fat 10 g; Carbohydrate 30 g; Dietary Fibre 3 g; Cholesterol 40 mg; 1020 kJ (245 cal)

SWEET POTATO & ROASTED CORN MASH

Instead of the potato, cook and mash 800 g (1 lb 10 oz) orange sweet potato in the creamy mashed potato recipe. Cook a cob of corn in boiling water for 5 minutes, drain and refresh in cold water, then chargrill in a lightly oiled pan until well browned all over. Slice the kernels off the cob and mix into the orange sweet potato with 4 finely chopped spring onions. Sprinkle with diced crispy bacon. Serves 4.

NUTRITION PER SERVE
Protein 7 g; Fat 1 g; Carbohydrate 40 g; Dietary Fibre 5 g; Cholesterol 5 mg; 800 kJ (190 cal)

MUSHROOM MASH

PANCETTA & GARLIC

PESTO POTATO

ROASTED CAPSICUM & CUMIN POTATO

CREAMY MASHED POTATO

ORANGE SWEET POTATO MASH WITH CORIANDER

Preparation time: 15 minutes
Total cooking time: 20 minutes
Serves 4

750 g (1¹/₂ lb) orange sweet
   potato
45 g (1¹/₂ oz) butter, chopped
1 clove garlic, crushed
2 teaspoons grated fresh ginger

Peel the sweet potato, and cut into evenly sized pieces.

1¹/₂ tablespoons chopped
   coriander
2 teaspoons soy sauce
sprigs of coriander, to garnish

1 Peel the sweet potato, chop into evenly sized pieces, then cook in a pot of lightly salted boiling water for 10–15 minutes, or until tender. Drain.
2 Melt the butter in a small pan and add the garlic and ginger. Cook over low heat, stirring, for 1 minute.
3 Mash the hot sweet potato until almost smooth. Stir through the garlic

Fry the garlic and ginger in the melted butter over low heat.

mixture, chopped coriander and soy sauce. Garnish with coriander sprigs and serve immediately.

NUTRITION PER SERVE
Protein 3 g; Fat 10 g; Carbohydrate 30 g; Dietary Fibre 4 g; Cholesterol 30 mg; 935 kJ (220 cal)

COOK'S FILE

Serving suggestion: This mash is lovely with pork, chicken, beef or lamb.
Note: Orange sweet potato is sweeter than regular potatoes, with a texture between a potato and a pumpkin.

Mash the hot sweet potato and stir in the garlic mixture, coriander and soy sauce.

CELERIAC, POTATO AND ROASTED GARLIC MASH

Preparation time: 20 minutes
Total cooking time: 45 minutes
Serves 4–6

juice of 1 lemon
1 kg (2 lb) celeriac
500 g (1 lb) sebago or pontiac
   potatoes, peeled and chopped
4 fat cloves garlic, unpeeled
50 g (1³/₄ oz) butter
2 tablespoons cream

Add the lemon juice to a large bowl of water. Add the peeled, chopped celeriac.

Orange sweet potato mash with coriander (top) and Celeriac, potato and roasted garlic mash

1 Preheat the oven to hot 200°C (400°F/ Gas 6). Add the lemon juice to a large bowl of water. Peel and chop the celeriac, placing it in the lemon-water to prevent browning.
2 Cook the celeriac and potatoes in separate pans of lightly salted boiling water. Cook the potatoes for about 15 minutes, or until tender; cook the celeriac for 25 minutes, or until tender. Drain them both well.
3 Meanwhile, place the unpeeled garlic on a baking tray and bake in the oven for 20 minutes, or until softened. Allow to cool a little, then peel away the skins.

Remove the skins from the cooled cloves of roasted garlic.

4 While the drained potato is still hot, mash it with the butter and cream using a potato masher—do not use a food processor, or the mixture will become gluggy.
5 Put the drained celeriac and the roasted garlic into a food processor and process until smooth, then beat the celeriac mixture into the potato mixture with a wooden spoon. Season to taste with salt and freshly ground black pepper and serve hot.

NUTRITION PER SERVE (6)
Protein 5 g; Fat 10 g; Carbohydrate 20 g; Dietary Fibre 9 g; Cholesterol 30 mg; 815 kJ (195 cal)

Beat the celeriac and garlic mixture into the mashed potato.

CAULIFLOWER AND FENNEL PUREE

Preparation time: 10 minutes
Total cooking time: 25 minutes
Serves 6

1 medium fennel bulb (see Note)
1 large cauliflower, trimmed
90 g (3 oz) butter
1 tablespoon cider vinegar or
    white wine vinegar
1 teaspoon salt
1/4 teaspoon sugar

1 Reserving the fronds, trim the fennel and finely chop the bulb and thin green stems. Set the stems aside. Cut the cauliflower into florets.

2 In a large pan, melt two-thirds of the butter and gently fry the chopped fennel bulb for 5 minutes, stirring occasionally. Add the cauliflower, toss to coat and cook for 1–2 minutes, then add enough water to just cover.

3 Add the vinegar, salt and sugar and bring to the boil. Reduce the heat and simmer for 15 minutes, or until the cauliflower is very tender. Drain thoroughly, then transfer to a food processor and blend to a smooth purée. Stir in the rest of the butter and the chopped fennel stems. Season to taste and garnish with fennel fronds.

NUTRITION PER SERVE
Protein 6 g; Fat 15 g; Carbohydrate 7 g; Dietary Fibre 6 g; Cholesterol 40 mg; 2015 kJ (480 cal)

COOK'S FILE

Note: Fennel bulbs are usually sold already trimmed but, if possible, buy an untrimmed bulb for this recipe, so you can use the stalks to add flavour, and the fronds to garnish.

Trim the fennel, reserving the fronds and thin green stems. Chop the bulb finely.

Add the cauliflower florets to the fennel and add enough water to just cover.

Stir the remaining butter and finely chopped fennel stems into the purée.

CREAMY CORN AND POTATO MASH

Preparation time: 15 minutes
Cooking time: 15 minutes
Serves 4

6 fresh corn cobs
1 large pontiac potato (about 200 g/6¹/₂ oz), peeled and chopped
40 g (1¹/₄ oz) butter
1 onion, chopped
2 tablespoons cream

1 Remove the husks and silks from the corn. Cook the corn cobs in a large pan of lightly salted boiling water for about 5 minutes, then drain and allow to cool.

2 Cook the potato in a separate pan of lightly salted boiling water until tender, then drain well and mash.

3 Melt the butter in a small pan over low heat. Add the onion and cook, stirring, for about 5–10 minutes, or until very soft but not browned.

4 Cut the kernels from the corn with a sharp knife, then blend them with the cooked onion in a food processor until smooth, adding salt and freshly cracked black pepper to taste. Stir in the mashed potato and cream, and season again with salt to taste.

NUTRITION PER SERVE
Protein 10 g; Fat 15 g; Carbohydrate 60 g; Dietary Fibre 9.5 g; Cholesterol 40 mg; 1760 kJ (420 cal)

COOK'S FILE

Note: When removing cobs of corn from their husks, wipe around the cob using a damp cloth: this will help remove the silks that persistently cling to the corn kernels.

Remove the husks and silks from the cobs of corn.

Using a sharp knife, cut the kernels from the cooled corn.

Stir the mashed potato and cream into the puréed corn mixture.

JERUSALEM ARTICHOKE PUREE

Preparation time: 20 minutes
Total cooking time: 12 minutes
Serve 4–6

rind and juice from 1 lemon
1 kg (2 lb) Jerusalem artichokes
20 g (³/₄ oz) butter
2 tablespoons olive oil

1 Add half the lemon juice to a large bowl of water. Peel and slice the artichokes, placing them in the lemon-water as you work to prevent them discolouring. Cook them in a large pot of boiling salted water for 12 minutes, or until tender. Drain well.
2 In a food processor, purée the artichokes, butter, 1 tablespoon of the reserved lemon juice and 1 teaspoon of the lemon rind, adding more juice and rind to taste. With the motor still running, gradually pour in the oil, mixing until it is incorporated. Season to taste and serve hot.

NUTRITION PER SERVE (6)
Protein 4 g; Fat 9 g; Carbohydrate 6 g; Dietary Fibre 5 g; Cholesterol 9 mg; 515 kJ (125 cal)

COOK'S FILE

Note: Jerusalem artichokes have a white, sweet, nutty flesh. Buy tubers that look firm and fresh.

Peel and slice the artichokes, placing them in the lemon-water to stop browning.

In a food processor, purée the artichokes, butter, and some rind and lemon juice.

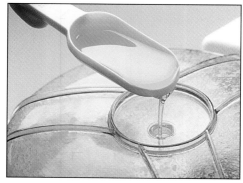

With the motor still running, gradually add the oil and process until incorporated.

CUMIN, MAPLE AND ORANGE SWEET POTATO MASH

Preparation time: 30 minutes
Total cooking time: 15 minutes
Serves 4

750 g (1½ lb) floury potatoes, such as pontiac or spunta
850 g (1 lb 12 oz) orange sweet potato
70 g (2¼ oz) butter
1 onion, very finely chopped
2 teaspoons ground cumin
1 teaspoon ground coriander
1–2 tablespoons maple syrup
⅓ cup (80 ml/2¾ fl oz) cream or milk

1 Peel and chop the potatoes and orange sweet potatoes, then cook them in separate pans of lightly salted boiling water until very tender.
2 While the potato and sweet potato are cooking, melt 40 g (1¼ oz) of the butter in a small frying pan. When the butter is foaming, add the onion and cook over medium heat for 3–4 minutes, or until soft and lightly golden. Stir in the cumin and coriander and cook for 1 minute. Add 1 tablespoon of maple syrup, and half the cream or milk; simmer for about 1 minute. Remove from the heat.
3 Drain the potato and sweet potato and mash separately until smooth and creamy, seasoning to taste. Add the remaining butter and the cream or milk to the potato, beating until creamy. Add the onion mixture to the sweet potato, adding more maple syrup to taste, and beating until smooth.
4 Using a large metal spoon, carefully fold the potato mash with the sweet potato mash, being careful not to overmix—the colours should be quite separate for a marbled effect.

NUTRITION PER SERVE
Protein 9 g; Fat 25 g; Carbohydrate 70 g; Dietary Fibre 8 g; Cholesterol 70 mg; 2245 kJ (535 cal)

Peel the potatoes and orange sweet potatoes. Chop into evenly sized pieces.

Add some maple syrup and half the cream or milk to the fried onion and spices.

Gently fold the potato and orange sweet potato mashes together.

CREAMY POLENTA WITH PARMESAN, PAPRIKA AND GARLIC

Preparation time: 10 minutes
Total cooking time: 10 minutes
Serves 4

1 teaspoon salt
2 cloves garlic, crushed
1 cup (150 g/5 oz) instant polenta
1/2 cup (125 ml/4 fl oz) cream
40 g (1 1/4 oz) butter, chopped
1/3 cup (35 g/1 1/4 oz) freshly
    grated Parmesan
1/4 teaspoon paprika, and extra
    to garnish
Parmesan shavings, to garnish

1 In a large, heavy-based pan, bring 3 1/2 cups (875 ml/28 fl oz) water to the boil. Add the salt and garlic. Stir in the polenta with a wooden spoon, breaking up any lumps. Cook over medium heat for 4–5 minutes, or until smooth, stirring often.

2 Add half the cream and cook for 2–3 minutes, or until the polenta is thick and comes away from the pan. Stir in the butter. Remove from the heat and stir in the Parmesan, paprika and remaining cream. Transfer to a warm serving bowl and sprinkle with paprika. Garnish with Parmesan shavings and serve at once.

NUTRITION PER SERVE
Protein 7 g; Fat 25 g; Carbohydrate 30 g; Dietary Fibre 1 g; Cholesterol 80 mg; 1510 kJ (360 cal)

COOK'S FILE

Notes: Polenta must be served hot to keep its creamy, light consistency.
● Use a vegetable peeler to peel cheese shavings from a block of Parmesan.

Pour the polenta into the boiling water, stirring well with a wooden spoon.

Add half the cream to the polenta and cook for 2–3 minutes, or until thick.

Stir in the Parmesan, paprika and the rest of the cream.

POTATO AND GARLIC MASH WITH FRESH TOMATO RELISH

Preparation time: 40 minutes
Total cooking time: 25 minutes
Serves 4

1.5 kg (3 lb) floury potatoes
50 g (1³/₄ oz) butter
3 cloves garlic, crushed
¹/₄ cup (60 ml/2 fl oz) cream

Fresh Tomato Relish
2 tablespoons olive oil
1 onion, finely chopped
2 cloves garlic, crushed
2 teaspoons ground cumin
2 teaspoons ground coriander
3 ripe tomatoes, chopped
2 teaspoons soft brown sugar
¹/₄ cup (30 g/1 oz) sultanas or raisins
1 teaspoon balsamic vinegar
1 tablespoon chopped oregano
1 tablespoon chopped lemon thyme
1 tablespoon chopped parsley

1 Peel the potatoes and cut into evenly sized pieces. Cook in lightly salted boiling water until tender.

2 While the potatoes are cooking, make the fresh tomato relish. Heat the oil in a heavy-based pan, add the onion, garlic, cumin and coriander and stir over medium heat for 2–3 minutes, or until the onion softens. Add the tomatoes and cook for 5–10 minutes. Stir in the sugar, sultanas and vinegar and simmer for 5 minutes. Stir in the herbs and keep the relish warm.

3 Drain the potatoes well. Add the butter, garlic and cream and mash until smooth and creamy. Season with salt and freshly ground pepper. Serve topped with the tomato relish and sprinkle with fresh herbs.

NUTRITION PER SERVE
Protein 10 g; Fat 30 g; Carbohydrate 60 g; Dietary Fibre 8 g; Cholesterol 50 mg; 2205 kJ (530 cal)

Fry the onion, garlic and spices in the hot oil until the onion softens.

Add the sugar, sultanas and vinegar and simmer for 5 minutes.

Mash the potatoes, butter, garlic and cream until smooth and creamy.

COLCANNON

Preparation: 15 minutes
Cooking time: 15–20 minutes
Serves 4

800 g (1 lb 10 oz) floury
    potatoes
90 g (3 oz) butter, chopped
3 cups (225 g/7 oz) finely
    shredded green cabbage
8 spring onions, finely
    chopped
2/3 cup (170 ml/5½ fl oz) milk

pinch of ground nutmeg
chopped parsley, to garnish

1 Peel the potatoes and cut them into evenly sized pieces. Cook them in lightly salted boiling water for about 15 minutes, or until tender. Drain the potatoes, return them to the pan and stir over low heat until all the moisture has evaporated, then mash well.
2 Melt a third of the butter in a frying pan, add the shredded cabbage and stir-fry over high heat until softened and lightly browned. Stir in the chopped spring onions.

3 Add the remaining butter and milk to the mashed potato. Stir the cabbage mixture into the potato with the nutmeg, and salt and freshly ground pepper to taste. Sprinkle with chopped parsley to serve.

NUTRITION PER SERVE
Protein 8 g; Fat 20 g; Carbohydrate 30 g; Dietary Fibre 6 g; Cholesterol 60 mg; 1412 kJ (340 cal)

COOK'S FILE

Note: King Edward, russet and spunta are some floury potatoes. You could also use pontiac or sebago.

Stir the drained potatoes over medium heat until the moisture has evaporated.

Fry the cabbage in a third of the butter until softened. Stir in the spring onions.

Add the remaining butter and milk to the mashed potato.

CARROT AND TURNIP MASH WITH GOLDEN APPLES

Preparation time: 30 minutes
Total cooking time: 15–20 minutes
Serves 4

3 large carrots
3 large turnips or swedes
1 green apple
1 red apple
60 g (2 oz) butter
2 teaspoons soft brown sugar
1 tablespoon golden syrup
1 teaspoon Dijon mustard
1 teaspoon mixed spice
finely chopped chives, to serve

1 Peel and chop the carrots and turnips and cook in lightly salted boiling water until very tender.
2 Meanwhile, core the apples with an apple corer, leaving the skin on, and cut into 1 cm (1/2 inch) slices.
3 Melt two-thirds of the butter in a large non-stick frying pan. Add the sugar, syrup, mustard and mixed spice. Stir over medium heat until the sugar starts to dissolve, then add the apple slices in a single layer. Simmer gently for 8–10 minutes over medium-low heat until the apples are tender, golden yet still firm, carefully turning once or twice during cooking.
4 Drain the turnips and carrots. Add the remaining butter and some salt and pepper and mash until smooth. Serve with the apple slices, sprinkled with chives and cracked pepper.

NUTRITION PER SERVE
Protein 3 g; Fat 12 g; Carbohydrate 25 g; Dietary Fibre 7 g; Cholesterol 40 mg; 920 kJ (220 cal)

Leaving the skin on, core the apples using an apple corer, then cut into slices.

In a single layer, add the apple slices to the spiced sugar syrup.

Season the turnips and carrot, then mash with the remaining butter until smooth.

Breads

ROSEMARY BREAD TRIOS

Preparation time: 40 minutes
+ 1 hour 40 minutes rising
Total cooking time: 15 minutes
Makes 10 trios

7 g (¼ oz) sachet dried yeast
1 teaspoon caster sugar
4 cups (500 g/1 lb) plain flour
1 tablespoon caster sugar, extra
1 teaspoon salt
1 cup (250 ml/8 fl oz) warm
   milk
¼ cup (60 ml/2 fl oz) vegetable
   oil
10 small sprigs of rosemary
1 egg yolk
sea salt flakes, to sprinkle

1 Combine the yeast, caster sugar and ½ cup (125 ml/4 fl oz) of warm water in a small bowl. Cover and set aside in a warm place for 10 minutes, or until frothy.
2 Sift the flour into a large bowl and stir in the extra caster sugar and salt. Make a well in the centre and pour in the warm milk, oil and frothy yeast. Mix to a soft dough, gather into a ball then turn out onto a lightly floured surface and knead for 10 minutes, or until smooth and elastic. Add a little extra flour if the dough becomes too sticky. Place in a large, oiled bowl, cover loosely with greased plastic wrap and leave in a warm place for 1 hour, or until doubled in size.
3 Punch down the dough by giving it one firm blow with your fist to expel the air, then turn out onto a lightly floured surface and knead for 1 minute. Lightly grease 2 large baking trays. Divide the dough into 10 pieces. Form each piece into three balls—keeping the remaining pieces covered—and place close together on the prepared baking tray; add a sprig of rosemary onto the centre of each trio. Repeat with the remaining pieces of dough, and lay each set separately on the baking tray.
4 Cover the trios with a damp tea towel and set aside for 20 minutes, or until well risen. Preheat the oven to moderate 180°C (350°F/Gas 4). Brush the trios lightly with the combined egg yolk and 1 teaspoon of water and sprinkle with the sea salt flakes. Bake for 15 minutes, or until golden brown. Allow to cool on a wire rack and replace the rosemary sprigs with fresh ones, if you want.

NUTRITION PER TRIO
Protein 7 g; Fat 8 g; Carbohydrate 40 g; Dietary Fibre 2 g; Cholesterol 20 mg; 1080 kJ (260 cal)

COOK'S FILE

Note: Dried yeast generally comes in a box containing 7 g sachets and is available from supermarkets. Fresh yeast is interchangeable—use 15 g of fresh yeast for 7 g dried.

Knead the dough on a lightly floured surface until smooth and elastic.

Arrange the 3 balls together on a lightly greased baking tray.

MINI WHOLEMEAL LOAVES

Preparation time: 40 minutes
+ 2 hours rising
Total cooking time: 45 minutes
Serves 8

15 g (1/2 oz) fresh yeast
    (or 7 g/1/4 oz dried yeast)
1 tablespoon caster sugar
1/2 cup (125 ml/4 fl oz) warm
    milk
4 cups (600 g /11/4 lb) whole-
    meal plain flour
1 teaspoon salt
1/4 cup (60 ml/2 fl oz) oil
1 egg, lightly beaten

1 Grease four 13 x 61/2 x 5 cm (5 x 23/4 x 2 inch) baking tins. Mix the yeast, sugar and milk in a small bowl. Cover and set aside in a warm place until frothy.

2 Combine the flour and salt in a large bowl. Make a well in the centre and pour the oil, 1 cup (250 ml/8 fl oz) of warm water and the frothy yeast into the well. Mix to a soft dough and gather into a ball; turn out onto a floured surface and knead for 10 minutes. Add a little extra flour if the dough is too sticky. Put in a large oiled bowl, cover loosely with greased plastic wrap and leave in a warm place for 1 hour, or until well risen.

3 Punch down the dough, turn out onto a floured surface and knead for 1 minute, or until smooth. Divide into four; knead into shape and put in the tins. Cover with a damp tea towel and leave in a warm place for 45 minutes, or until risen. Preheat the oven to hot 210°C (415°F/Gas 6–7).

4 Brush the loaf tops with the beaten egg. Bake for 10 minutes, reduce the temperature to moderate 180°C (350°F/Gas 4) and bake for a further 30–35 minutes, or until the base sounds hollow when tapped. Cover with foil if the tops become too brown.

NUTRITION PER SERVE
Protein 10 g; Fat 10 g; Carbohydrate 40 g; Dietary Fibre 9 g; Cholesterol 25 mg; 1270 kJ (305 cal)

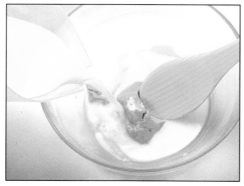

Mix the fresh yeast, sugar and milk in a small bowl until smooth.

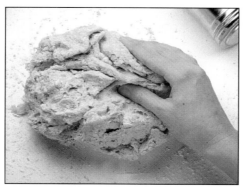

Gather into a ball and turn out onto a lightly floured surface.

Shape the dough into small loaves and place in the greased baking tins.

PARMESAN AND PROSCIUTTO LOAF

Preparation time: 30 minutes
  + 2 hours rising
Total cooking time: 25 minutes
Serves 6

7 g (¹/₄ oz) dried yeast
1 teaspoon caster sugar
¹/₂ cup (125 ml/4 fl oz) warm
  milk
2 cups (250 g/8 oz) plain flour
1 teaspoon salt
1 egg, lightly beaten
30 g (1 oz) butter, melted and
  cooled slightly
1 tablespoon milk, extra

60 g (2 oz) sliced prosciutto,
  finely chopped
¹/₂ cup (35 g/1¹/₄ oz) grated
  Parmesan

1 Grease a baking tray. Mix the yeast, sugar and milk in a bowl. Cover and set aside in a warm place for 10 minutes, or until frothy.
2 Mix the flour and salt in a bowl. Make a well in the centre and add the egg, butter and frothy yeast. Mix to a soft dough and gather into a ball; turn out onto a floured surface and knead for 8 minutes, or until elastic.
3 Put in an oiled bowl, cover loosely with greased plastic wrap and leave in a warm place for 1¹/₄ hours, or until doubled in size.

4 Punch down the dough, turn out onto a floured surface and knead for 30 seconds, or until smooth. Roll out to a rectangle, 30 x 20 cm (12 x 8 inches), and brush with some extra milk. Sprinkle with the prosciutto and Parmesan, leaving a border. Roll lengthways into a log shape.
5 Lay on the baking tray and brush with the remaining milk. Using a sharp knife, slash the loaf diagonally at intervals. Leave to rise in a warm place for 30 minutes. Preheat the oven to hot 220°C (425°F/Gas 7). Bake the loaf for 25 minutes, or until golden.

NUTRITION PER SERVE
Protein 10 g; Fat 9 g; Carbohydrate 30 g; Dietary Fibre 2 g; Cholesterol 60 mg; 1060 kJ (250 cal)

Sprinkle the prosciutto and Parmesan on the dough, leaving a clear border.

Roll up the dough tightly lengthways into a log shape.

Using a sharp knife, slash the loaf diagonally at intervals.

CHILLI, CORN AND RED CAPSICUM MUFFINS

Preparation time: 15 minutes
Total cooking time: 25 minutes
Makes 12 muffins

1 cup (125 g/4 oz) plain flour
1/4 teaspoon salt
1 tablespoon baking powder
1 cup (150 g/5 oz) polenta
1 tablespoon soft brown sugar
1 egg
1/4 cup (60 ml/2 fl oz) corn oil

2/3 cup (170 ml/5 1/2 fl oz) milk
   or buttermilk
1 red chilli, finely chopped
1 small red capsicum, finely
   chopped
2 tablespoons chopped basil
   leaves
420 g (13 1/3 oz) can corn
   kernels, drained

1 Grease twelve 1/2-cup (125 ml/ 4 fl oz) capacity muffin tins. Preheat the oven to moderately hot 200°C (400°F/Gas 6). Sift the flour, salt and baking powder into a bowl and mix in the polenta and sugar. Beat together the egg, oil and milk and add to the dry ingredients. Stir until just moistened, but do not overmix. Add the chilli, capsicum, basil and corn and mix briefly.

2 Spoon the mixture into the muffin tins. Bake for 25 minutes, or until the muffins are well risen. Leave for a few minutes, before turning out onto a wire rack to cool.

NUTRITION PER MUFFIN
Protein 4 g; Fat 6 g; Carbohydrate 25 g; Dietary Fibre 2 g; Cholesterol 20 mg; 730 kJ (175 cal)

Stir the brown sugar and polenta into the sifted flour mixture.

Mix the chilli, capsicum, basil and corn briefly into the flour mixture.

Spoon the mixture into the greased muffin tins.

FOUGASSE

Preparation time: 20 minutes
   + 1 hour 30 minutes rising
Total cooking time: 35 minutes
Serves 4–6

7 g (1/4 oz) dried yeast
1 teaspoon sugar
3 cups (375 g/12 oz) plain
   flour
1 cup (150 g/5 oz) wholemeal
   plain flour
2 teaspoons salt

1 Mix the yeast, sugar and 1/2 cup (125 ml/4 fl oz) of warm water in a bowl. Cover and set aside in a warm place for 10 minutes, or until foamy.

2 Sift the flours and salt, return the husks and make a well in the centre. Pour in 1 cup (250 ml/8 fl oz) of extra warm water and the foamy yeast. Mix to a soft dough and gather into a ball. Turn out onto a floured surface and knead for 10 minutes, or until smooth.

3 Place in a large, lightly oiled bowl, cover loosely with greased plastic wrap and leave in a warm place for 1 hour, or until doubled in size.

4 Punch down the dough and knead for 1 minute. Press into a large, oval shape 2 cm (3/4 inch) thick and make several cuts on either side. Lay on a large, floured baking tray, cover with greased plastic wrap and leave to rise for 20 minutes. Preheat the oven to hot 210°C (415°F/Gas 6–7).

5 Bake for 35 minutes, or until crisp. After 15 minutes, spray with water to make the crust crispy.

NUTRITION PER SERVE (6)
Protein 10 g; Fat 1 g; Carbohydrate 70 g; Dietary Fibre 6 g; Cholesterol 0 mg; 1415 kJ (340 cal)

Leave the yeast mixture in a warm place until well risen and foamy.

Punch down the dough and knead on a floured surface until smooth.

Using a sharp knife, make several slashes on either side of the bread.

**Chilli, corn and red capsicum muffins (top)
with Fougasse**

WHITE DINNER ROLLS

Preparation time: 15 minutes
  + 1 hour 30 minutes rising
Total cooking time: 20 minutes
Makes 12 rolls

1 teaspoon dried yeast
½ teaspoon caster sugar
2 cups (250 g/8 oz) plain flour
½ teaspoon salt
1 tablespoon dried whole milk
    powder
2 teaspoons caster sugar, extra
1½ tablespoons oil
1 tablespoon milk
poppy seeds, sesame seeds,
    caraway seeds, sea salt
    flakes or plain flour,
    to decorate

1 Combine the yeast, sugar and ¼ cup (60 ml/2 fl oz) of warm water in a bowl. Cover and set aside in a warm place for 10 minutes, or until frothy.
2 Mix the flour, salt, milk powder and extra sugar in a bowl. Make a well in the centre, and pour in the oil, ½ cup (125 ml/4 fl oz) of warm water and the frothy yeast. Mix to a soft dough and knead for 10 minutes, or until smooth and elastic. Add a little extra flour if needed.
3 Place in a lightly oiled bowl, cover loosely with greased plastic wrap and leave in a warm place for 1 hour, or until doubled in size.
4 Punch down, knead for 1 minute and divide into twelve. To shape into spirals, roll each portion into a 30 cm (12 inch) rope, coil tightly and tuck under the end to seal. To shape into knots, tie each rope; or shape into ovals and leave plain or slash diagonally.
5 Place apart on lightly greased trays

and cover loosely with a damp tea towel. Leave to rise for 20 minutes. Preheat the oven to moderate 180°C (350°F/Gas 4). Brush with the milk and then sprinkle with your choice of seeds, sea salt flakes or plain flour topping. Bake for 15–20 minutes, or until browned.

NUTRITION PER ROLL
Protein 3 g; Fat 1 g; Carbohydrate 15 g; Dietary Fibre 1 g; Cholesterol 1 mg; 335 kJ (100 cal)

Pour in the oil, warm water and frothy yeast and mix in with a flat-bladed knife.

To make the spirals, coil up the long rope and tuck the end under.

Cover the rolls with a damp tea towel and leave to rise in a warm place.

PUMPKIN DAMPER

Preparation time: 25 minutes
Total cooking time: 25 minutes
Serves 8

1 cup (125 g/4 oz) self-raising
    flour
1½ cups (225 g/7¼ oz)
    wholemeal self-raising flour
1 teaspoon baking powder
1 teaspoon salt
3 tablespoons grated Parmesan
1 egg, lightly beaten
2 teaspoons tomato paste

1 cup (250 g/8 oz) mashed
    pumpkin, well-drained
    (see Note)
3 tablespoons chopped basil
30 g (1 oz) butter, melted
3 tablespoons milk
2 tablespoons pepitas
    (pumpkin seeds)

1 Preheat the oven to hot 210°C (415°F/Gas 6–7). Grease 1 baking tray. Sift the flours, baking powder and salt into a bowl and return the husks. Add the Parmesan and mix in the egg, tomato paste, pumpkin, basil, butter and milk. Mix to a soft dough.

2 Turn out onto a floured surface and knead until smooth. Flatten out to a circle 20 cm (8 inches) in diameter.
3 Place on the baking tray. Using a sharp knife, mark into 8 portions. Brush with water and sprinkle with the pepitas. Bake for 25 minutes, or until cooked through.

NUTRITION PER SERVE
Protein 8 g; Fat 7 g; Carbohydrate 30 g; Dietary Fibre 4 g; Cholesterol 40 mg; 870 kJ (205 cal)

COOK'S FILE

Note: You will need 400 g (13 oz) of unpeeled raw pumpkin.

Mix together the mashed pumpkin, egg, tomato paste, basil, butter and milk.

Cut through the mixture with a flat-bladed knife until it forms a soft dough.

Using a sharp knife, make deep cuts to form 8 portions.

SAVOURY SCROLL

Preparation time: 35 minutes
Total cooking time: 35 minutes
Serves 6

1 cup (125 g/4 oz) grated
   Cheddar
¼ cup (25 g/¾ oz) grated
   Parmesan
1 onion, chopped
1 red capsicum, chopped
100 g (3¼ oz) pancetta,
   chopped
¼ cup (15 g/½ oz) chopped
   parsley
3 cups (375 g/12 oz) self-raising
   flour
1 teaspoon salt
60 g (2 oz) butter, cubed
1¼ cups (315 ml/10 fl oz)
   buttermilk
2 tablespoons olive oil

1 Grease 1 baking tray. Preheat the oven to moderately hot 200°C (400°F/Gas 6). To make the filling, combine the Cheddar, Parmesan, onion, capsicum, pancetta and parsley. Season well with salt and pepper.

2 Sift the flour and salt into a large bowl. Add the butter and rub in with your fingertips until the mixture is crumbly. Make a well in the centre and pour in the buttermilk; mix to a soft dough and gather into a ball. Turn out onto a lightly floured surface and knead until smooth and elastic.

3 Roll out the dough to make a 50 x 25 cm (20 x 10 inch) rectangle. Sprinkle the filling over the top, leaving a 2 cm (¾ inch) border and press the filling down slightly. Roll up lengthways, enclosing the filling. Bring the ends together to form a ring and brush the ends with some water. Press to seal.

4 Place on the prepared tray, snip the outside edge of the scroll with scissors at regular intervals, so the filling is exposed. Bake for 15 minutes, reduce the temperature to moderate 180°C (350°F/Gas 4) and bake for a further 20 minutes, or until golden brown. Brush with the olive oil.

NUTRITION PER SERVE
Protein 20 g; Fat 30 g; Carbohydrate 50 g; Dietary Fibre 3 g; Cholesterol 105 mg; 2195 kJ (525 cal)

Chop the onion and capsicum into small cubes and the pancetta into small pieces.

Using your fingertips, rub the butter into the flour.

Tightly roll up the filled dough lengthways into a log shape.

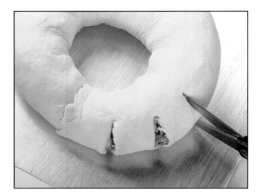

Using sharp scissors, snip the outside edge of the scroll at intervals.

ZUCCHINI AND OLIVE BREAD

Preparation time: 10 minutes
Total cooking time: 40 minutes
Serves 6–8

1 cup (135 g/4½ oz) finely
    grated zucchini
2 cups (250 g/8 oz) self-raising
    flour
1 teaspoon baking powder
1 teaspoon salt
1 teaspoon caster sugar
1 cup (125 g/4 oz) grated
    Cheddar

2 tablespoons chopped chives
12 pitted black olives, sliced
2 eggs
1 cup (250 ml/8 fl oz) milk
3 tablespoons olive oil

1 Preheat the oven to moderately hot 200°C (400°F/Gas 6). Generously grease one 20 x 10 cm (8 x 4 inch) loaf tin.
2 Squeeze as much moisture from the zucchini as possible and set aside.
3 In a large bowl sift the flour, baking powder, salt and sugar. Add the Cheddar, chives and olives. Beat the eggs and add the milk, oil and the zucchini and combine. Make a well in

the centre of the dry ingredients and add the zucchini mixture. Stir for 30 seconds, or until well combined.
4 Pour into the prepared tin and bake for 35–40 minutes, or until a skewer inserted comes out clean. Leave to rest for 5 minutes, then turn out onto a wire rack to cool.

NUTRITION PER SERVE (8)
Protein 10 g; Fat 15 g; Carbohydrate 25 g; Dietary Fibre 2 g; Cholesterol 65 mg; 1160 kJ (280 cal)

COOK'S FILE

Hint: The best olives to use are Spanish as Kalamata olives taste a little bitter when cooked.

Generously grease the loaf tin with melted butter or oil.

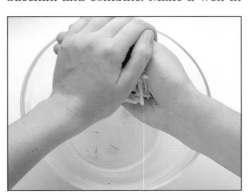

Squeeze the excess moisture from the zucchini over a bowl or the kitchen sink.

Mix in the grated Cheddar, chives and olives to the flour mixture.

RICOTTA AND DILL BUNS

Preparation time: 20 minutes
  + 1 hour 40 minutes rising
Total cooking time: 45 minutes
Makes 8 buns

7 g (¼ oz) dried yeast
1½ tablespoons caster sugar
250 g (8 oz) ricotta cheese
30 g (1 oz) butter, softened
¼ small onion, grated
¼ teaspoon bicarbonate of soda
1 egg
3¾ cups (465 g/14½ oz) plain
  flour
2 tablespoons chopped dill

1 Mix together the yeast, sugar and ¼ cup (60 ml/2 fl oz) of warm water in a bowl. Cover the bowl and set aside in a warm place for 10 minutes, or until frothy.

2 Put the ricotta, butter, onion, bicarbonate of soda and egg in a food processor with 1 teaspoon of salt and process until smooth. Add the frothy yeast and 3 cups (375 g/12 oz) of the flour. Add the remaining flour and mix to a smooth dough. Turn out the dough onto a floured surface and knead for 6–8 minutes, or until smooth. Add the dill during the last minute of kneading.

3 Put in an oiled bowl, cover loosely with greased plastic wrap and set aside for 1 hour, or until doubled in size. Lightly grease one 20 x 30 cm (8 x 12 inch) tray.

4 Punch down the dough and divide into 8 pieces. Form into rounds and lay on the tray. Make 2 slashes on each bun. Cover with a damp tea towel for 30 minutes, or until well risen.

5 Preheat the oven to moderate 180°C (350°F/Gas 4). Bake the buns for 40–45 minutes, or until golden. Check after 20 minutes and reduce the oven to warm 170°C (325°F/Gas 3) if they are too brown.

NUTRITION PER BUN
Protein 10 g; Fat 8 g; Carbohydrate 50 g; Dietary Fibre 2 g; Cholesterol 50 mg; 1250 kJ (300 cal)

Scrape down the sides of the bowl and process the ricotta mixture until smooth.

Knead the chopped dill into the dough during the last minute of kneading.

Using a sharp knife, slash the top of each bun twice.

GRISSINI

Preparation time: 40 minutes
  + 30 minutes rising
Total cooking time: 30 minutes
Makes 18 grissini

7 g (¹/4 oz) dried yeast
1 tablespoon caster sugar
²/3 cup (170 ml/5¹/2 fl oz) milk
50 g (1³/4 oz) butter
3¹/2–4 cups (500 g/1 lb) plain
    flour
1 teaspoon salt
sea salt flakes, sesame
    seeds or poppy seeds,
    to decorate

1 Grease 3 baking trays. Mix the yeast, sugar and ¹/2 cup (125 ml/ 4 fl oz) of warm water. Cover and set aside for 10 minutes, or until frothy. In a small pan, heat the milk and butter until the butter has melted.
2 Mix 3¹/2 cups (435 g/14 oz) of the flour and the salt in a bowl. Make a well in the centre and pour in the milk mixture and frothy yeast. Add enough of the remaining flour to mix to a soft dough, then turn out onto a lightly floured surface and knead for 10 minutes, or until smooth and elastic. Divide into 18 pieces.
3 Roll each piece to the thickness of a pencil and 30 cm (12 inches) in length. Place the grissini 3 cm (1¹/4 inches)

apart on the baking trays. Cover loosely with greased plastic wrap and leave for 20 minutes.
4 Preheat the oven to hot 210°C (415°F/Gas 6–7). Brush the grissini with cold water and sprinkle with the sea salt or your choice of sesame or poppy seeds. Bake for 15–20 minutes, or until golden brown. Remove from the oven and cool on a wire rack. Reduce the temperature to moderate 180°C (350°F/Gas 4). Return the grissini to the trays, and bake for a further 5–10 minutes, or until crisp.

NUTRITION PER GRISSINO
Protein 3 g; Fat 3 g; Carbohydrate 22 g; Dietary Fibre 1 g; Cholesterol 8 mg; 540 kJ (130 cal)

Heat the milk and butter in a small pan until the butter is melted.

Roll each piece out very thinly on a lightly floured surface.

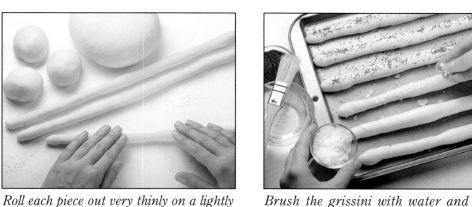

Brush the grissini with water and add some poppy seeds and sea salt flakes.

OLIVE OIL AND GARLIC GRIDDLE BREADS

Preparation time: 10 minutes
 + 20 minutes + 5 minutes resting
Total cooking time: 20 minutes
Serves 8–10

3¼ cups (400 g/13 oz) plain
  flour
½ teaspoon bicarbonate of soda
½ teaspoon salt
1 teaspoon caster sugar
125 g (4 oz) chilled butter, cut
  into cubes
½ cup (125 ml/4 fl oz)
  buttermilk

1 egg, lightly beaten
2 tablespoons olive oil
2 tablespoons chopped chives
1 clove garlic, crushed
olive oil, for cooking

1 Sift the flour, bicarbonate of soda, salt and sugar. Add the butter and rub in with your fingertips until crumbly. Make a well in the centre and add the buttermilk, egg and oil; stir until the mixture clumps together.
2 Turn out onto a floured surface and knead, gradually incorporating the chives and garlic as you work. Knead for 1 minute, or until you have a uniform, spongy dough.
3 Form into a ball, divide in half and roll out each portion on a floured surface to 7 mm (¾ inch) thick. Using a 6 cm (2½ inch) biscuit cutter, cut out circles and set aside, covered, for 10 minutes. Repeat with the other half.
4 Heat 1 tablespoon of oil in a heavy-based frying pan with a lid. To test the heat of the pan, put a piece of the dough in the pan, cover and fry on one side. Turn it over and brown the other side, uncovered. The dough is cooked when it feels light and hollow. Fry the rest of the dough in batches, adding more oil as needed.

NUTRITION PER SERVE (10)
Protein 6 g; Fat 20 g; Carbohydrate 30 g; Dietary Fibre 2 g; Cholesterol 50 mg; 1250 kJ (300 cal)

On a lightly floured surface, gradually knead in the chives and garlic.

Cut out circles using a biscuit cutter and set aside to allow them to rest.

Fry the breads in batches until browned, light and hollow.

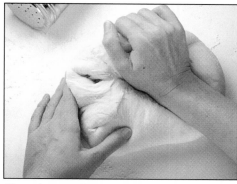

Knead on a lightly floured surface until light and elastic.

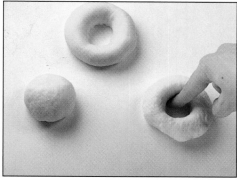

Poke your finger into the centre of each ball and make a hole.

Add the bagels to a frying pan of boiling water and boil for 1 minute only.

Sprinkle the top of each bagel with the poppy seeds.

MINI BAGELS

Preparation time: 50 minutes
+ 1 hour 25 minutes rising
Total cooking time: 30 minutes
Makes 22 bagels

15 g (¹/₂ oz) fresh yeast
   or 7 g (¹/₄ oz) dried yeast
1 tablespoon sugar
²/₃ cup (170 ml/5¹/₂ fl oz) warm
   milk
4 cups (500 g/1 lb) plain flour
1 teaspoon salt
30 g (1 oz) butter, melted
1 egg, lightly beaten
1 tablespoon poppy seeds

1 Lightly grease 3 baking trays.
Combine the yeast, sugar and milk in
a bowl. Cover and set aside in a warm
place for 10 minutes, or until frothy.
Sift the flour and salt into a large
bowl. Make a well in the centre and
add the butter, frothy yeast and
²/₃ cup (170 ml/5¹/₂ fl oz) of warm
water. Mix to a soft dough and gather
into a ball. Knead for 10 minutes, or
until elastic. Place in a lightly oiled
bowl, cover loosely with greased
plastic wrap and leave for 1 hour, or
until doubled in size.
2 Punch down the dough and knead
on a well-floured surface until smooth.
Divide into 22 pieces. Working with
1 piece at a time (keeping the others
covered with a damp tea towel) roll
into tight balls. Poke a finger through
the centre and gently enlarge the hole
until it forms a doughnut. Lay on
the baking trays, cover with the tea
towel and leave for 10–15 minutes, or
until risen.
3 Bring a large frying pan of water to
the boil. Add 3–4 bagels at a time and
cook for 1 minute. Remove with a
slotted spoon and lay on the trays.
They will be deflated at this stage.
4 Preheat the oven to moderate 200°C
(400°F/Gas 6). Brush the bagels with
the egg and sprinkle with the poppy
seeds. Bake for 25 minutes, or
until browned.

NUTRITION PER BAGEL
Protein 4 g; Fat 2 g; Carbohydrate 20 g;
Dietary Fibre 1 g; Cholesterol 15 mg;
440 kJ (105 cal)

ROASTED RED CAPSICUM BUNS

Preparation time: 40 minutes
  + 1 hour 40 minutes rising
Total cooking time: 1 hour
Makes 8 buns

2 red capsicums, cut into large
  flat pieces
7 g (1/4 oz) dried yeast
2 teaspoons sugar
4 cups (500 g/1 lb) plain
  flour
1 teaspoon salt
1 tablespoon olive oil
1 egg, lightly beaten

1 Place the capsicum skin-side-up under a hot grill, until the skins blacken. Cool in a plastic bag, then peel away the skin and cut the capsicum into cubes.

2 Combine the dried yeast, sugar and 1/2 cup (125 ml/4 fl oz) of warm water in a bowl and leave in a warm place for 10 minutes, or until frothy.

3 Sift the flour and salt into a bowl, make a well in the centre and pour in the oil, the frothy yeast and 1 1/4 cups (315 ml/10 fl oz) of warm water. Mix to a soft dough, gather into a ball and knead on a floured surface until smooth. Add a little extra flour if needed. Place in a lightly oiled bowl, cover loosely with greased plastic wrap and leave in a warm place for 1 hour, or until doubled.

4 Punch down the dough, turn out onto a floured surface and knead for 10 minutes, adding the capsicum half way through. Divide the dough into eight and form into rounds. Lay apart on a greased baking tray. Cover with a damp tea towel and leave for 30 minutes, or until well risen. Preheat the oven to moderate 180°C (350°F/ Gas 4). Brush the buns with beaten egg. Bake for 40–45 minutes, or until the base sounds hollow when tapped.

NUTRITION PER BUN
Protein 9 g; Fat 4 g; Carbohydrate 50 g; Dietary Fibre 3 g; Cholesterol 20 mg; 1125 kJ (270 cal)

Sift the flour and salt together into a large bowl.

On a lightly floured surface, knead the dough until smooth.

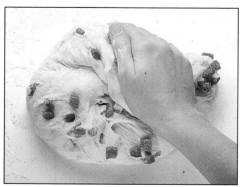

On a well-floured surface, knead in the capsicum.

WALNUT BREAD

Preparation time: 20 minutes
  + 1 hour 40 minutes rising
Total cooking time: 40 minutes
Serves 8–10

1¹/2 cups (185 g/6 oz) chopped
    walnuts
7 g (¹/4 oz) dried yeast
1 teaspoon sugar
2 cups (250 g/8 oz) plain flour
1 cup (150 g/5 oz) wholemeal
    plain flour
1 cup (100 g/3¹/2 oz) rye flour
1 teaspoon salt
1 tablespoon plain flour, extra

1 Lay the walnuts on a baking tray and bake in a moderate 180°C (350°F/Gas 4) oven for 5 minutes, or until lightly toasted. Set aside to cool.
2 Mix the yeast, sugar and ¹/2 cup (125 ml/4 fl oz) of warm water in a bowl. Cover and set aside in a warm place for 10 minutes, or until frothy.
3 Combine the flours, salt and walnuts in a large bowl. Make a well in the centre and pour in another 1 cup (250 ml/8 fl oz) of warm water and the frothy yeast. Mix with a flat-bladed knife to a soft dough and gather into a ball. Turn out onto a lightly floured surface and knead for 10 minutes, or until smooth and elastic.

4 Place into a large, lightly oiled bowl, cover loosely with greased plastic wrap and leave for 1 hour, or until slightly risen.
5 Knead for 1 minute. Divide in half and form into 2 rounds 2.5 cm (1 inch) thick. Lay on a floured baking tray and cover with a damp tea towel. Set aside in a warm place for 30 minutes.
6 Sprinkle the top of the loaves with the extra flour by hand or with a sifter. Using a sharp knife, slash the dough diagonally. Bake for 35 minutes, or until crusty and brown.

NUTRITION PER SERVE (10)
Protein 10 g; Fat 10 g; Carbohydrate 40 g; Dietary Fibre 6 g; Cholesterol 0 mg; 1280 kJ (305 cal)

Bake the chopped walnuts on a baking tray until lightly toasted.

Shape each half into a round and place on a lightly floured baking tray.

Sprinkle the loaves with the extra flour by hand or use a sifter.

ONION BUNS

Preparation time: 25 minutes
+ 1 hour 40 minutes rising
Total cooking time: 35 minutes
Makes 12 buns

7 g (¼ oz) dried yeast
1 teaspoon sugar
1 tablespoon olive oil
2 onions, finely chopped
4 cups (500 g/1 lb) plain flour
2 teaspoons salt
1 egg, lightly beaten
1 tablespoon sesame seeds

1 Mix the yeast, sugar and ½ cup (125 ml/4 fl oz) of warm water in a bowl. Cover and set aside in a warm place for 10 minutes, or until frothy. Heat the oil in a frying pan and cook the onion until golden.

2 Sift the flour and salt into a bowl. Stir in the onion and make a well in the centre. Pour in 1 cup (250 ml/8 fl oz) of warm water and the yeast. Mix to a soft dough and knead for 10 minutes, or until smooth. Put in an oiled bowl, cover with greased plastic wrap and leave for 1 hour, or until doubled. Grease twelve ½ cup (125 ml/4 fl oz) capacity muffin tins.

3 Punch down the dough, turn out onto a lightly floured surface and knead for 1 minute. Divide the dough into 12 portions and shape each portion into a ball. Place in the tin, cover with a damp tea towel and set aside in a warm place for 30 minutes, or until well risen. Preheat the oven to moderate 180°C (350°F/Gas 4). Brush the buns with the egg and sprinkle with sesame seeds. Bake for 30 minutes, or until crusty.

NUTRITION PER BUN
Protein 6 g; Fat 3 g; Carbohydrate 30 g; Dietary Fibre 2 g; Cholesterol 15 mg; 750 kJ (180 cal)

Cook the finely chopped onion until golden brown.

Place the balls into the large, greased muffin tins.

Brush the buns with the egg and sprinkle with the sesame seeds.

SUNFLOWER BREAD

Preparation time: 10 minutes
Total cooking time: 45 minutes
Serves 6–8

1¼ cups (155 g/5 oz) self-raising flour
1 tablespoon caster sugar
2 teaspoons baking powder
1 teaspoon salt
¾ cup (110 g/3½ oz) fine polenta

½ cup (60 g/2 oz) grated Cheddar
2 tablespoons chopped flat-leaf parsley
1 teaspoon dried oregano
2 eggs
1 cup (250 ml/8 fl oz) milk
⅓ cup (80 ml/2¾ fl oz) sunflower oil
2 tablespoons sunflower seeds

1 Preheat the oven to moderate 180°C (350°F/Gas 4). Grease one 20 x 10 cm (8 x 4 inch) loaf tin and line the base with baking paper.

2 Sift the flour, sugar, baking powder and salt into a large bowl. Add the polenta, Cheddar, parsley and oregano. Combine the eggs, milk and oil and pour onto the dry ingredients. Stir until combined.

3 Pour into the tin and sprinkle with the sunflower seeds. Bake for 45 minutes, or until a skewer inserted into the centre comes out clean.

NUTRITION PER SERVE (8)
Protein 8 g; Fat 15 g; Carbohydrate 30 g; Dietary Fibre 1 g; Cholesterol 60 mg; 1215 kJ (290 cal)

Line the base of the greased tin with baking paper.

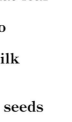
Add the polenta, Cheddar, parsley and oregano to the bowl and mix.

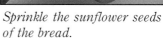
Sprinkle the sunflower seeds over the top of the bread.

Onion buns (top) with Sunflower bread

BAKED BUTTERMILK CRISPBREADS

Preparation time: 15 minutes
  + 40 minutes resting
Total cooking time: 1 hour
Makes 12 crispbreads

1 onion, thinly sliced into rings
3¹/2 teaspoons salt
2²/3 cups (335 g/11 oz) plain
    flour
¹/2 teaspoon bicarbonate of soda
20 g (¹/2 oz) cold butter, cubed
²/3 cup (170 ml/5¹/2 fl oz)
    buttermilk
4 spring onions, sliced
1 tablespoon finely chopped
    oregano or marjoram
80 g (2³/4 oz) butter, melted

1 Put the onion in a colander and sit the colander in a bowl. Sprinkle with 3 teaspoons of the salt. Set aside for 20 minutes, rinse and squeeze dry.

2 Place 2 cups (250 g/8 oz) of the flour, the remaining salt, bicarbonate of soda and butter into a food processor. Blend until crumbly. With the motor running, pour in the buttermilk. Stop processing when the mixture begins to clump together.

3 Transfer to a lightly floured surface and gradually knead in the remaining flour, onion rings, spring onion and oregano or marjoram. You may need a little extra flour. Knead until the dough is almost smooth. Cover with plastic wrap and set aside to rest for 20 minutes.

4 Preheat the oven to moderately hot 200°C (400°F/Gas 6). Divide the dough into 12 portions and working with 1 piece at a time, leave the rest covered. Roll these out thinly on a lightly floured surface to form a circle, about 14 cm (5¹/2 inches) in diameter.

5 Brush 1 side of each bread with the melted butter and lay on a baking tray, buttered-side-down. Brush with butter. You should fit 3 crispbreads on each tray. Bake for 8–10 minutes, turn over and bake for another 5 minutes, or until golden brown. Repeat with the remaining dough.

NUTRITION PER CRISPBREAD
Protein 4 g; Fat 10 g; Carbohydrate 20 g; Dietary Fibre 1 g; Cholesterol 25 mg; 675 kJ (160 cal)

Sprinkle the sliced onion with salt and sit the colander over a bowl to drain.

Process the dough until the mixture clumps around the blade.

Brush the rolled breads with the melted butter.

Using tongs, turn the browned crispbreads over and bake the other side.

TOMATO HERB ROLLS

Preparation time: 30 minutes
+ 1 hour 35 minutes rising
Total cooking time: 35 minutes
Makes 12 rolls

7 g (¼ oz) dried yeast
1 teaspoon sugar
4 cups (500 g/l lb) plain flour
1 teaspoon salt
2 cloves garlic, finely chopped
½ cup (75 g/2½ oz) sun-dried
   tomatoes, finely chopped
1 tablespoon chopped oregano
1 tablespoon chopped marjoram

1 tablespoon chopped thyme
2 tablespoons chopped flat-leaf
   parsley
30 g (1 oz) butter, melted
½ cup (125 ml/4 fl oz) milk,
   plus extra, to glaze

1 Mix the yeast, sugar and ½ cup (125 ml/4 fl oz) of warm water in a bowl. Set aside for 10 minutes, or until frothy. Sift the flour and salt into a bowl and make a well in the centre.
2 Mix in the garlic, sun-dried tomato and herbs. Pour in the melted butter, frothy yeast and milk and mix to a soft dough. Knead on a lightly floured surface for 10 minutes, or until

smooth. Cover loosely with greased plastic wrap and leave for 45 minutes, or until well risen.
3 Punch down and knead for 5 minutes. Divide into twelve and roll into balls. Lay apart on a greased baking tray. Leave for 30 minutes, or until well risen. Preheat the oven to hot 210°C (415°F/Gas 6–7). Brush the rolls with milk and bake for 10 minutes. Reduce the oven to 180°C (350°F/Gas 4) and bake for 20–25 minutes, or until golden.

NUTRITION PER ROLL
Protein 5 g; Fat 3 g; Carbohydrate 30 g; Dietary Fibre 2 g; Cholesterol 8 mg; 730 kJ (175 cal)

Add the garlic, sun-dried tomato and herbs to the flour mixture.

Using a sharp floured knife, divide the dough into 12 equal portions.

The rolls are cooked when the bases sound hollow when tapped.

CHEESE AND HERB PULL-APART LOAF

Preparation time: 25 minutes
+ 1 hour 40 minutes rising
Total cooking time: 30 minutes
Serves 6–8

7 g (¼ oz) dried yeast
1 teaspoon sugar
4 cups (500 g/1 lb) plain flour
1½ teaspoons salt
2 tablespoons chopped parsley
2 tablespoons chopped chives
1 tablespoon chopped thyme
60 g (2 oz) Cheddar, grated
milk, to glaze

1 Combine the yeast, sugar and ½ cup (125 ml/4 fl oz) of warm water in a small bowl. Cover and set aside in a warm place for 10 minutes, or until frothy.

2 Sift the flour and salt into a bowl. Make a well in the centre and pour in 1 cup (250 ml/8 fl oz) warm water and the frothy yeast. Mix to a soft dough. Knead on a lightly floured surface for 10 minutes, or until smooth. Put the dough in an oiled bowl, cover loosely with greased plastic wrap and leave for 1 hour, or until doubled in size.

3 Punch down and knead for 1 minute. Divide the dough in half and shape each half into 10 flat discs, 6 cm (2½ inches) in diameter. Mix the fresh

herbs with the Cheddar and put 2 teaspoons on a disc. Press another disc on top. Repeat with the remaining discs and herb mixture.

4 Grease a 21 x 10.5 x 6.5 cm (8½ x 4¼ x 2½ inch) loaf tin. Stand the filled discs upright in the prepared tin, squashing them together. Cover the tin with a damp tea towel and set aside in a warm place for 30 minutes, or until well risen. Preheat the oven to hot 210°C (415°F/Gas 6–7).

5 Glaze with a little milk and bake for 30 minutes, or until brown and crusty.

NUTRITION PER SERVE (8)
Protein 10 g; Fat 4 g; Carbohydrate 60 g; Dietary Fibre 3 g; Cholesterol 8 mg; 1255 kJ (300 cal)

Working on a lightly floured surface, flatten the dough into flat discs.

Spoon the filling onto one disc and top with another, pressing down firmly.

Stand the discs upright in the loaf tin, squashing them together.

CARAMELISED ONION BRAIDS

Preparation time: 1 hour
+ 1 hour 35 minutes rising
Total cooking time: 1 hour 35 minutes
Serves 8–10

2¹/₂ cups (310 g/10 oz) plain
    flour
1 cup (130 g/4¹/₄ oz) buckwheat
    flour
1 teaspoon salt
15 g (¹/₂ oz) fresh yeast or
    7 g (¹/₄ oz) dried yeast
1¹/₄ cups (315 ml/10 fl oz) warm
    milk
30 g (1 oz) butter
1 tablespoon oil
1 kg (2 lb) onions, thinly sliced
    into rings
1 egg, lightly beaten
2 teaspoons fennel seeds

1 Sift the flours and salt into a large bowl and make a well in the centre. Dissolve the yeast in ¹/₂ cup (125 ml/4 fl oz) of the warm milk in a small bowl. Then add the remaining warm milk. Pour into the well and mix to a dough. Turn out onto a floured surface and knead for 8 minutes, or until smooth. Place in a large oiled bowl, cover loosely with greased plastic wrap and leave in a warm place for 45 minutes–1 hour, or until doubled in size.

2 Melt the butter and oil in a frying pan, add the onion and cook over medium-low heat for 40–50 minutes, or until the onion is golden.

3 Punch down the dough, turn out onto a lightly floured surface and knead for 10 minutes, or until smooth and elastic.

4 Lightly grease 2 baking trays. Divide the dough in half. Working with 1 piece at a time, divide it into 3 pieces. Roll each piece out to a 30 x 10 cm (12 x 4 inch) rectangle. Divide the onion mixture into 6 portions and spread a portion along the middle of each rectangle, leaving a 2 cm (³/₄ inch) border. Brush the edge with some of the beaten egg and roll over lengthways to enclose the filling.

5 Plait the 3 pieces together and place seam-side-down on a baking tray. Pinch the ends together. Repeat with the remaining dough and caramelised onion. Cover with a damp tea towel and leave in a warm place for 45 minutes, or until well risen.

6 Preheat the oven to moderate 180°C (350°F/Gas 4). Brush the top with the beaten egg and sprinkle with the fennel seeds. Bake for 35–45 minutes, or until well browned. Transfer to a wire rack to cool.

NUTRITION PER SERVE (10)
Protein 8 g; Fat 7 g; Carbohydrate 40 g; Dietary Fibre 3 g; Cholesterol 30 mg; 1030 kJ (250 cal)

On a lightly floured surface, roll each portion out into a rough rectangle.

Brush the edge with the beaten egg and roll over to enclose the filling.

Plait the 3 pieces together and place seam-side-down on a baking tray.

OLIVE SPIRALS

Preparation time: 25 minutes
  + 1 hour 30 minutes rising
Total cooking time: 35 minutes
Makes 12 spirals

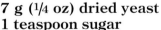

7 g (¼ oz) dried yeast
1 teaspoon sugar
4 cups (600 g/1¼ lb) plain flour
1 teaspoon salt
2 tablespoons olive oil
2 cups (250 g/8 oz) pitted black
  olives
½ cup (50 g/1¾ oz) finely
  grated Parmesan
3 cloves garlic, chopped

1 Mix the yeast, sugar and ½ cup (125 ml/4 fl oz) warm water in a bowl. Cover and set aside in a warm place for 10 minutes, or until frothy.
2 Sift the flour and salt into a bowl and make a well in the centre. Add the frothy yeast, oil and 1 cup (250 ml/8 fl oz) of warm water. Mix to a soft dough and gather into a ball. Turn out onto a floured surface and knead for 10 minutes, or until smooth. Cover loosely with greased plastic wrap and set aside for 1 hour, or until well risen.
3 Process the olives, Parmesan and garlic in a food processor until chopped. With the motor running, add 1 tablespoon of oil and process to a paste.

4 Punch down the dough and knead for 1 minute. Roll out to a rectangle 42 x 35 cm (18 x 14 inches). Spread with the olive paste, leaving a plain strip along one of the long sides. Roll up lengthways, ending with the plain long side.
5 Cut into 12 slices and place close together on a greased baking tray. Cover with a damp tea towel and set aside for 30 minutes, or until well risen. Preheat the oven to moderately hot 200°C (400°F/Gas 6). Bake for 35 minutes, or until golden brown.

NUTRITION PER SPIRAL
Protein 8 g; Fat 8 g; Carbohydrate 40 g; Dietary Fibre 3 g; Cholesterol 4 mg; 1050 kJ (250 cal)

Spread with olive paste and roll up lengthways.

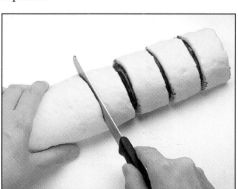

Using a serrated knife, cut the logs into 12 equal slices.

Place the spirals close together on the baking tray.

SOUR CREAM POLENTA BREAD

Preparation time: 15 minutes
Total cooking time: 50 minutes
Serves 6–8

1½ cups (225 g/7 oz) fine
   polenta
½ cup (60 g/2 oz) plain flour
2 tablespoons soft brown sugar
1 teaspoon baking powder
½ teaspoon bicarbonate
   of soda
½ teaspoon salt
1 egg
⅓ cup (80 ml/2¾ fl oz) milk

1¼ cups (310 g/10 oz) sour
   cream
2 tablespoons vegetable oil
½ teaspoon poppy seeds

1 Preheat the oven to moderately hot 200°C (400°F/Gas 6) and grease one 11 x 18 cm (4½ x 7 inch) loaf tin.
2 Combine the polenta, flour, sugar, baking powder, bicarbonate of soda and salt in a large bowl.
3 Whisk together the egg, milk, sour cream and oil and add them to the dry ingredients, mixing just long enough for them to be evenly combined. Pour the mixture into the tin and sprinkle with the poppy seeds.
4 Bake for 30 minutes, reduce the

temperature to moderate 180°C (350°F/Gas 4) and continue baking for a further 15–20 minutes, or until the loaf is golden.

NUTRITION PER SERVE (8)
Protein 5 g; Fat 20 g; Carbohydrate 30 g; Dietary Fibre 1 g; Cholesterol 70 mg; 1400 kJ (335 cal)

COOK'S FILE

Serving suggestion: Served warm spread with plenty of butter.
Note: There are different grades of polenta; some are finer than others. Compare different brands before purchasing. The fine-textured polenta is best for this recipe as it produces a less coarse bread.

Combine the dry ingredients in a large bowl and mix with a wooden spoon.

Add the combined egg, milk, sour cream and oil and mix until just combined.

Sprinkle the poppy seeds over the top before baking.

INDEX

INTERNATIONAL GLOSSARY OF INGREDIENTS

capsicum	red or green pepper	English spinach	spinach
eggplant	aubergine	silverbeet	Swiss chard
zucchini	courgette	sambal oelek	chilli paste
tomato paste (Aus.)	tomato purée, double concentrate (UK)	snow pea	mangetout
		spring onion	shallot/green onion
tomato purée (Aus.)	sieved crushed tomatoes/ passata (UK)	coriander	cilantro
		orange sweet potato	kumera
thick cream	double cream	prawns	shrimp
cream	single cream	plain flour	all-purpose flour
polenta	fine cornmeal	caster sugar	superfine sugar

First published 2000 by Merehurst Ltd, Ferry House, 51–57 Lacy Road, Putney, London SW15 1PR
This edition published 2000 for Index Books Ltd, Henson Way, Kettering, Northamptonshire, NN16 8PX United Kingdom

Project Editor: Jane Price
Project Designer: Michele Lichtenberger
Photographers: Jon Bader, Joe Filshie, Luis Martin, Reg Morrison (step photography)
Food Stylists: Carolyn Fienberg, Mary Harris
Food Preparation: Christine Sheppard, Jo Forrest
Publishing Manager: Fia Fornari
Production Manager: Lucy Byrne
CEO & Publisher: Anne Wilson
International Sales Director: Mark Newman
UK Marketing & Sales Manager: Kathryn Harvey

The nutritional information provided for each recipe does not include any accompaniments, such as rice, unless they are listed in the ingredients. The values are approximations and can be affected by biological and seasonal variations in food, the unknown composition of some manufactured foods and uncertainty in the dietary database. Nutrient data given are derived primarily from the NUTTAB95 database produced by the Australian New Zealand Food Authority.

ISBN 1-85391-817 2 A catalogue record of this book is available from the British Library.
Printed by Toppan Printing Hong Kong Co Ltd. PRINTED IN CHINA.

COVER RECIPES: Beef bourgignon, page 156; Chilli con carne, page 160; Cream of tomato soup, page 66; Roast pumpkin soup, page 69; Hearty pork and red lentils, page 144; Potato and zucchini mash with parmesan, page 214; Seafood, fennel and potato stew, page 187; Vietnamese chicken and noodle casserole, page 152.